Indigenous Knowledges and the Sustainable Development Agenda

This book discusses the vital importance of including indigenous knowledges in the sustainable development agenda. In the wake of colonialism and imperialism, dialogue between indigenous knowledges and Western epistemology has broken down time and again. However, in recent decades the broader indigenous struggle for rights and recognition has led to a better understanding of indigenous knowledges, and in 2015 the Sustainable Development Goals (SDGs) outlined the importance of indigenous engagement in contributing to the implementation of the agenda.

Drawing on experiences and field work from Africa, Asia, Latin America and Europe, *Indigenous Knowledges and the Sustainable Development Agenda* brings together authors who explore social, educational, institutional and ecological sustainability in relation to indigenous knowledges. In doing so, this book provides a comprehensive understanding of the concept of "sustainability", at both national and international levels, from a range of diverse perspectives.

As the decolonizing debate gathers pace within mainstream academic discourse, this book offers an important contribution to scholars across development studies, environmental studies, education, and political ecology.

Anders Breidlid is Professor of International Education and Development, Oslo Metropolitan University, Norway.

Roy Krøvel is Professor of Journalism, Oslo Metropolitan University, Norway.

Routledge Studies in Indigenous Peoples and Policy

There are an estimated 370 million Indigenous Peoples in over 70 countries worldwide, often facing common issues stemming from colonialism and its ongoing effects. Routledge Studies in Indigenous Peoples and Policy bring together books which explore these concerns, including poverty; health inequalities; loss of land, language and culture; environmental degradation and climate change; intergenerational trauma; and the struggle to have their rights, cultures, and communities protected.

Indigenous Peoples across the world are asserting their right to fully participate in policy making that affects their people, their communities, and the natural world, and to have control over their own communities and lands. This book series explores policy issues, reports on policy research, and champions the best examples of methodological approaches. It will explore policy issues from the perspectives of Indigenous Peoples in order to develop evidence-based policy and create policy-making processes that represent Indigenous Peoples and support positive social change.

Human Capital Development and Indigenous Peoples
Nicholas Biddle

Indigenous Knowledges and the Sustainable Development Agenda
Edited by Anders Breidlid and Roy Krøvel

Indigenous Knowledges and the Sustainable Development Agenda

**Edited by
Anders Breidlid and
Roy Krøvel**

LONDON AND NEW YORK

First published 2020
by Routledge
2 Park Square, Milton Park, Abingdon, Oxon OX14 4RN

and by Routledge
52 Vanderbilt Avenue, New York, NY 10017

Routledge is an imprint of the Taylor & Francis Group, an informa business

British Library Cataloguing-in-Publication Data
A catalogue record for this book is available from the British Library

Library of Congress Cataloging-in-Publication Data
Names: Breidlid, Anders, 1947– editor. | Krøvel, Roy, editor.
Title: Indigenous knowledges and the sustainable development agenda / edited by Anders Breidlid and Roy Krøvel.
Description: 1 Edition. | New York : Routledge, 2020. |
Series: Routledge studies in indigenous peoples and policy |
Includes bibliographical references and index.
Identifiers: LCCN 2019058836 (print) | LCCN 2019058837 (ebook)
Subjects: LCSH: Sustainable Development Goals. | Sustainable development. | Ethnoscience. | Ethnophilosophy.
Classification: LCC HC79.E5 I51443 2020 (print) |
LCC HC79.E5 (ebook) | DDC 338.9/27—dc23
LC record available at https://lccn.loc.gov/2019058836
LC ebook record available at https://lccn.loc.gov/2019058837

ISBN: 978-0-367-42596-8 (hbk)
ISBN: 978-0-367-85378-5 (ebk)

Typeset in Times New Roman
by codeMantra

Contents

Figures

Tables

Contributors

Hanne Kirstine Adriansen is an associate professor of educational anthropology at Aarhus University, where her research concerns the geography of knowledge and education. She is particularly interested in how universality and particularity are assigned to different types of knowledge by different actors and thus how global knowledge hierarchies are created and contested. Originally trained as a human geographer, she has extensive fieldwork experience from West and North Africa where she has worked in close collaboration with universities and other research institutions. She has also participated in a number of research capacity building projects in Africa and Asia. This led to publications about decolonization of international academic collaboration and the edited book (together with Lene Møller Madsen & Stig Jensen) Higher Education and Capacity building in Africa (published by Routledge in 2016).

Shrishtee Bajpai is a researcher-activist based in Pune and is member of an environmental action group-Kalpavriksh. Her current research is focused on exploring alternatives to mainstream development models, documenting worldviews of communities and networking on alternatives. She helps in coordinating a process called the Vikalp Sangam (Alternatives Confluence) that brings together practitioners, thinkers, researchers, and others working on alternatives to currently dominant forms of economic development and political governance. She is a core team member of a global process – Global Tapestry of Alternatives aimed at creating exchanges, synergies, cross-learning, and collaboration amongst the various radical alternative and social/ecological justice movements around the world. She is also involved in organizing Rights of Rivers dialogue in India next year and involved in research and advocacy for recognizing rights of rivers in India.

Anders Breidlid is a professor of International Education and Development at Oslo Metropolitan University and Professor ll (Adjunct professor) at Hawassa University, Ethiopia. He has a PhD from the School of Oriental and African Studies (SOAS), University of London. His main professional interests include education in crisis and conflict situation, girl's education and gender equality, education quality, human rights, HIV/ AIDS, education systems, culture and education, indigenous knowledges and sustainable development, literacy and nation building. He has published articles and books on education and development, as well as on African history and on fiction.

Eva Maria Fjellheim is a PhD candidate at the Centre for Sámi Studies at the UiT the Arctic University. She is currently affiliated to the research project "TriArc – The Arctic Governance Triangle: Government, Indigenous Peoples and industry in change."

Randi Kaarhus is currently a professor of Global Development Studies at Noragric, and also Head of Research at the Faculty of Landscape and Society, at NMBU – the Norwegian University of Life Sciences. With a PhD in social anthropology from the University of Oslo, she has carried out research on policies, resource management, and community processes in Norway, but also in the Andean region of Latin America and in south-eastern Africa, where the focus of research has been local people's knowledges and livelihoods in relation to environment and agricultural policies, gender and land rights, food production and food culture.

Torsten Krause is an associate senior lecturer in Sustainability Science at Lund University. He has ten years of research experience in the Amazon region on issues around forest governance and the impact of conservation projects on indigenous communities. He is particularly interested in indigenous knowledges around hunting of forest fauna in the Colombian Amazon.

Roy Krøvel is a professor of journalism at Oslo Metropolitan University and visiting professor at the indigenous Sámi University College. He also heads the research group Media, War, and Conflict at Oslo Metropolitan University. Krøvel is a civil engineer and holds a PhD in History. For more than 20 years, Krøvel has been involved in academic cooperation with indigenous and communitarian universities in Latin America.

Uldarico Matapí Yucuna is the only shaman left to the Matapí ethnic group in the Colombian Amazon region. Since the 1980s, he has worked to document and preserve the indigenous knowledges of the Matapí together with different organizations, but foremost Tropenbos International. He has published numerous reports and books about indigenous cosmology and knowledge.

Neema Pathak Broome has studied environmental science and completed a postgraduate diploma in wildlife management. She is a member of Kalpavriksh, coordinating the Conservation and Livelihoods programme. She is part of the team monitoring implementation of conservation laws and policies in particular the Wildlife Protection Act and the Scheduled Areas and Other Traditional Forest Dwellers (Recognition of Forest Rights) Act 2006. Her main area of interest is conservation governance, particularly Indigenous Peoples and Local Communities Conserved Territories and Areas (ICCAs). She has been involved with documentation, research, analysis, and advocacy related to inclusive conservation governance and ICCAs in India and South Asia. She has been part of team coordinating the National Community Forest Rights Learning and Advocacy Process since 2011. She also coordinates a local process of participatory conservation governance in Bhimashankar Wildlife Sanctuary in Maharashtra.

Maria Paula Quiceno Mesa is a biologist from Colombia and an expert in research and participatory monitoring systems with local indigenous, peasant, and Afro-descendant communities. For 14 years, she has researched the use, management, and conservation of natural resources and biodiversity with a socio-ecosystem approach. Currently, she investigates Colombia's post-conflict justice processes with victims and support the documentation and monitoring of human rights violations.

Camilla Risvoll is a researcher at Nordland Research Institute with a PhD in Sociology. Her experience is in interdisciplinary research on impacts from climate change in combination with cumulative effects and how multiple changes affect the adaptive capacity of reindeer husbandry communities in the arctic. Risvoll has particular emphasis on participatory processes and knowledge co-production, risk perceptions, participatory mapping methodology with reindeer herders, land-use issues, and governance.

Ginés A Sánchez Arias holds a PhD in Geography and Anthropology and works in Panama for VIS Group, Inc. as an analyst on corporate financial integration projects, and as a consultant for the Ngäbe Reading and Writing Organization, an indigenous NGO. He received a bachelor's degree in economics and international politics from The Colorado College in 2012. During this period, Sánchez studied Mandarin and Chinese literature, comparative politics, macroeconomics, and segregation policies, with special attention to unequal power relations in colonial settings. After an extensive expedition through China and Tibet in 2010, where the military presence openly shows the colonial process, he set out to investigate the current state of the colonial legacy in his country, among the Indigenous Peoples of Panama. In 2013, Sánchez visited the Ngäbe-Buglé region where he identifies a series of farmhouses (communities) in a process of cultural revitalization that was also openly decolonial. Together with their new Ngäbe hosts, Sánchez manages to study the spelling and pedagogy of this Chibcha language. Since then, Sánchez explores new methods to involve the public about the benefits of a genuine friendship with otherness (as a concept and in reality). His work seeks the application of geography and anthropology that, combined with visual arts, can provide an inter-pragmatic understanding to a general audience.

Vandana is a doctoral student in the Public Policy and Management Group of Indian Institute of Management Calcutta. Sharma has a Masters in Social Work and extensive experience in working with the tribal communities in India as a development practitioner and also as a policy researcher. She is currently working on her PhD thesis which uses the Political Ecology approach to examine changes in notions of food, forest, and traditional systems of agriculture in a tribal community in India. Her research interests lie in the field of political ecology, sustainable development, agriculture and nutrition linkages, and Degrowth in the context of global south.

Mukesh Shende has done his masters in Social Work from TISS, Mumbai. He is currently working as Programme Director for Livelihood at Amhi Amchaya Arogayasathi. He is monitoring projects on "Promotion of Sustainable Tribal Livelihood programme" supported by SWISSAID India and "Employability and Skill Enhancement of the Persons with Disabilities" supported by Paul Hamlyn Foundation, UK. Other key responsibilities at organizational level are report writing, documentation, advocacy and network building of the organization, proposal writing for fund raising, development of the tools for the presentations, reports, compilation of data, etc.

Lisa Waller is a professor of Digital Communication in the School of Media and Communication, RMIT University, Australia. Her research investigates how the news media shapes society, from Indigenous Affairs, to its roles in rural and regional communities and the justice system.

Andreas Ytterstad is an associate professor at the Department of Journalism and Media Studies at Oslo Metropolitan University. He has traveled regularly to Nicaragua, Ecuador, and Colombia for more than a decade, to teach at indigenous universities. He is Chair of Concerned Scientists Norway and helped found the Bridge to the Future Alliance in 2014, which spawned a 4-part TV series on the public broadcaster NRK in 2018. Both in his theoretical and practical work, he has been inspired by Antonio Gramscis writings, particularly the concept of good sense. In 2019, he was a visiting scholar at the Centre for Environmental Journalism (CEJ) in Boulder, Colorado, and he is currently part of the research project Work, Labor and Greening the Economy (WAGE) financed by the Norwegian Research Council, where he investigates the hegemony of oil in media debates.

Introduction

Anders Breidlid and Roy Krøvel

This is a book on indigenous knowledges and sustainable development. The reasons for such a book are multiple. Many chapters address, albeit critically, the rationale of the Sustainable Development Goals (SDGs) and particularly the epistemological and ideological foundation on which the SDG is based.

The lack of critique of the Western epistemological paradigm in the SDGs is exposed in most of the SDGs, for example, in goal number 4 (quality education) as well as goal number 13 (climate action). At the same time, Indigenous Peoples are only referred to a few times, whereas indigenous knowledges do not figure in the SDGs at all. This is a serious flaw since both the learning crisis in the global South and climate change are to a large extent, if not exclusively, due to the superiority claims of Western knowledge defined as the global architecture of education (Jones, 2007) and the extractivist ideology of Western epistemology which is a fundamental reason for the current climate crisis. The grabbing of indigenous land, the destruction of the rain forests globally and the unacceptable consumption levels in the global North are not discussed in any meaningful way the SDGs, nor is the importance of alternative knowledge systems and epistemologies, i.e. indigenous knowledges, referred to once.

It is the claim of this book that there is a need to expand the discussion of the SDGs beyond the Western paradigm, particularly because the previous UN goals, i.e. Millennium Development Goals (MDGs), to a large extent failed, and in our opinion, the SDGs will not be able to achieve their goals by 2030 because the strategies are mostly similar to the MDGs with few adjustments, and without the inclusion of alternative approaches to the multiple crises that the world is facing.

The current book is – intentionally – primarily written by non-indigenous scholars because there is a need for Western scholars to write back to the epistemological center where we are located, distance ourselves from the superiority claims of the West and the Orientalizing discourse towards Indigenous Peoples and indigenous knowledge systems and thereby strengthening the ties with the indigenous people's fight for alternative and indigenized ways of sustainability. Most of the authors in this book are trained and work at Western universities where the focus on decolonizing academia has been more or less non-existent. Some authors, like the editors, have spent decades working with indigenous researchers in Africa or Latin America and seek to understand what the Global North can learn from indigenous knowledges.

The chapter co-authored by researchers coming from two epistemological traditions, i.e. both the Western and the indigenous (Krause et al.), and the chapter written by an indigenous scholar based at a Norwegian university (Fjellheim) give a more insider perspective on indigeneity, which is vital for a counterhegemonic strategy of knowledge-making. Despite the inclusion of these two chapters, however, the editors realize, on the one hand, that the fact that the majority of authors are non-indigenous and from the hegemonic epistemological tradition raises the question of inappropriate appropriation. On the other hand, however, the limitations of a decolonizing agenda by outsiders are also a strength because it means, as many indigenous leaders across the globe want, a joint fight against coloniality between Indigenous and non-Indigenous Peoples for a more sustainable planet.

Indigenous knowledges and Indigenous Peoples

This book includes a variety of definitions and understandings of "Indigenous Peoples" and "indigenous knowledges." We recognize the fact that the concepts frequently will have varying definitions and understandings depending on place and context and that the various definitions are contested. The UN system, for instance, has not adopted an official definition of "Indigenous Peoples" relying instead on what the UN calls "a modern understanding" based on (UNPHII. Who are Indigenous Peoples?):

- Self-identification as Indigenous Peoples at the individual level and accepted by the community as their member.
- Historical continuity with pre-colonial and/or pre-settler societies
- Strong link to territories and surrounding natural resources
- Distinct social, economic or political systems
- Distinct language, culture and beliefs
- Form non-dominant groups of society
- Resolve to maintain and reproduce their ancestral environments and systems as distinctive peoples and communities.

For Indigenous Peoples, being recognized as indigenous defines not only individual but also collective rights. Perhaps even more importantly, Indigenous Peoples demand the right to autonomy and self-governance.

However, there are also other definitions of "Indigenous Peoples": One definition refers to Indigenous Peoples as

> not only defined as people of indigenous minorities, like the Indians in the Americas, the Sámi in the circumpolar North, or minority

indigenous groups in Asia or Oceania, but also the majority population in Africa that originated on the continent before the colonization process of the 19th and 20th century.

(Breidlid, 2013, p. 30)

Moreover, as Tuck and Yang state, Indigenous Peoples "are those who have creation stories, not colonization stories, about how we/they came to be in a particular place – indeed how we/they came to *be a place*. Our/their relationships to land comprise our/their epistemologies, ontologies, and cosmologies" (Tuck and Yang, 2012, p. 6).

For most activists and scholars in Latin America, Australia and parts of Asia, indigenous knowledges would be intrinsically linked to "Indigenous Peoples" derived from a so-called UNPHII understanding of the term referred to above.

From this perspective, *indigenous knowledges* are linked to collective struggles for autonomy with distinct social, economic or political systems, and with distinct languages, cultures and beliefs. More often than not, these struggles have pitted and still are pitting Indigenous Peoples against powerful opponents such as states, governments and transnational corporations (as many of the chapters in this book clearly illustrate). These struggles are thus against colonial and postcolonial forces which manifest themselves, as Sefa Dei underlines, "in the denial of Indigenous Peoples' sovereignty and self-autonomy, dispossession of the lands, the displacement of peoples, and the denial of people's basic humanity, as well as imperialistic projects that continue to design other peoples futures"(Sefa Dei, 2016, p. 2).

In an African context, however, indigenous knowledges are, in line with the more comprehensive definition of Indigenous Peoples, often extended to mean knowledges not only related to indigenous minority groups but to the majority of people in sub-Saharan Africa as well. This has, for example, important implications for the education system where there is an increasing demand for indigenous knowledges and indigenous languages in the classroom to mitigate the current learning crisis on the continent (see Chapter 1).

One common denominator of indigenous knowledges, albeit multifaceted (therefore plural form), is that they are holistic by recognizing the interconnectedness of the spiritual and the secular spheres (Goduka, 2000). As Greenwood states:

The foundations of Indigeneity, then, are comprised, in part, of values that privilege interrelationships among the spiritual, the natural and the self; reflect a sacred orientation to place and space; encompass a fluidity of knowledge exchanged between past, present and future, thereby allowing for constant and dynamic knowledge growth and change; and honour language and orality as an important means of knowledge transmission.

(Greenwood, 2005, p. 554)

Or, as Fatnowna and Pickett argue, "spirituality in an Aboriginal sense is encompassing and holistic in nature. It is the starting point that requires no demonstration of proof; it exists and all truths begin and end there" (2002, p. 214).

In the Western world, the Cartesian divide undermined this holism in the advent of modernity and the rise of modern science. Indigenous knowledges are often practical in nature, both affirming cultural heritage and ensuring peoples' flourishing and survival. There are both commonalities and contradictions between indigenous and Western so-called scientific knowledges, but one basic difference is assumptions about what valid knowledges are and how valid knowledges are generated.

Sustainability

It is the conviction of the authors of this book that indigenous knowledges have to be included in order to reach the SDGs. While also sustainability is a contested concept, used in various contexts with various and often contradictory meanings, sustainability in this book means to balance the contemporary needs without compromising the ability of future generations to meet their needs. Such a balance can only be struck if indigenous knowledges and epistemologies are actively being included in decision-making processes in terms of economic, ecological and social and educational aspects/fields. It means embracing, although critically, indigenous worldviews, languages and cultural practices in the fight for a sustainable planet and where a decolonizing strategy against the current hegemonic epistemology which systematically is making the planet unsustainable is a must. The daily erasure of indigeneity due to colonial and postcolonial policies in the global South has to be countered by decolonizing narratives and struggles, necessitating a joint endeavor comprising both Indigenous and non-Indigenous Peoples. The book's indigenous and non-indigenous contributors call for privileging indigenous epistemologies and knowledges in a situation where the hegemonic Western epistemology in many ways is bankrupt and where the power dynamics between Western and indigenous knowledge systems is so skewed that indigenous knowledges are more or less pushed into oblivion. Decolonization is not complete without epistemological justice. It is therefore a need to rebalance this skewed relationship in favor of the knowledge systems of the global South if the UN SDGs are to move beyond the utopian dream upon which these goals are currently founded.

The current interest in indigenous knowledge production and research

The interest in indigenous research methodologies has increased significantly over the last two decades, also among non-indigenous scholars.

This book speaks to a growing body of literature on indigenous knowledges and indigenous research methodology.

Recent indigenous scholarship focuses to a large extent on relationality, rebuilding connections and relationships, reciprocity as well as ethics as methodology. Shawn Wilson documents the "shared aspects of an Indigenous ontology and epistemology" in Australia and Canada and finds it to be "relationality, or that relationships form reality" (Wilson, 2008, p. 137). In line with our definition of indigenous knowledges in this book, Wilson notes that "many things in our modern world try to force us to be separated, isolated individuals" (Wilson, 2008, p. 137), whereas indigenous knowledges are holistic of nature. Relationality focuses on the multiple influences that shape research and knowledge production, and underscores in addition to reciprocity, the subjectivity of knowledge production that cannot be divorced from the context where the research is generated. Moreover, as noted above, this relationality is spiritual in nature thus acknowledging spirituality as real and integral to knowledge-making. In this way, indigenous knowledge production distances itself from the so-called objective truth claims of Western, positivist epistemology and asserts the primacy of relationships in the constitution of subjectivity and even knowledge production.

Similarly, Jeannine Carriere, an Indigenous researcher, argues that "the self as it comes to know" should be captured in the research itself (quoted in Kovach, 2009, p. 18). As an ideal, it is far removed from the ideal of a "detached" and "objective" researcher. Nevertheless, as Kovach has observed, there are a number of similarities between indigenous methodologies and existing qualitative approaches, especially between "story as an Indigenous research method" and reflexivity within existing qualitative research (Kovach, 2009, p. 18). According to Kovach, ethics is a methodology, and reciprocity is "an ethical starting point" (Kovach, 2009, p. 19). But there will always be tensions between conducting ethical research according to collectivist traditions and the norms and values of individualist spaces of academia. Building on these ideals concerning research ethics, the authors represented in this book have taken care to ensure that the knowledge holders do not view the use of the ideas and thinking as inappropriate. When appropriate, indigenous knowledge holders have been included in the research process and are recognized as co-authors. In other chapters, care has been taken to obtain permission to use information referred to in the texts.

Much of the scholarship published on indigenous research so far comes from the field of education, perhaps, as Eve Tuck points out, because education is a field that is particularly concerned with relationality (Smith et al., 2019, p. 9).

Tuck and Yang point to possible similarities between indigenous research and social justice education and educational research, and in particular with "revolutionary critical pedagogy" and "decolonial participatory action research." While the concept of relationality to a large extent defines indigenous research in education Cartesianism and Western epistemology is still hegemonic in the education systems in the global South (as well as in North) resulting in low literacy rates, poor learning outcomes and unsustainable states, particularly in sub-Saharan Africa (as documented in Chapter 1). This can to a large extent be ascribed to the lack of epistemological and cultural interrelationship, i.e. lack of epistemic relationality between home and school necessitating a paradigmatic shift in education in many parts of the global South to make education and schooling more sustainable (see e.g. Tungarazaa, Sutherland and Stack (2013)). In order to achieve the SDGs, and particularly SDG 4, such a fundamental epistemological shift is imperative, but it is difficult to obtain due to power structures and decision makers both internationally and nationally that are aligned with a Western epistemological discourse (see chapters by Breidlid and Waller).

In Tuhiwai Smiths ground-breaking research man, community, nature and the spiritual play pivotal roles in the understanding of research, and most of the chapters in the book : (i.e. chapters by Adriansen, Fjellheim, Krause, Quiceno and Matapí, Krøvel, as well as Sharma, Broome, Bajpai and Shende), research on the relationship and relationality between nature and Indigenous Peoples is highlighted, but also the fierce fight against colonial and postcolonial imposition and destruction of indigenous land and nature which also has huge implications for the fight against climate change. The plight of Indigenous Peoples and the role they may play in combating climate change are too seldom considered in public discourses on climate change. In his chapter, Ytterstad seeks to open a space for a dialogue between indigenous knowledges and the Gramscian concept of good sense vis-à-vis global warming on the other. He underlines the importance of combining aspects of indigenous good sense with the good sense of other groups in order to develop efficient collective climate action projects and to achieve the SDGs on climate change.

Importantly, the book also raises issues of current and expanding colonial practices and developments in the global South, as well as towards Indigenous Peoples in the Global North (see, for example, Risvoll's and Kaarhus' chapter on clear zoning in Norway and Fjellheim's chapter on south Sámi history, indigeneity and territorial rights).

The book draws on studies carried out in both Europe (Norway), Africa (Senegal), Asia (India), Australia and Latin America (Colombia and Panama) as well as more continental and global macro studies. The two first chapters deal with education and indigenous knowledges in Africa and Australia, two chapters are on malnutrition and forest rights from India, whereas the remaining chapters are primarily situated in the field of political ecology.

Anders Breidlid argues in the first chapter that a literate population is paramount for sustainable development and he therefore proposes that a discussion on sustainability is extended to include the important link between the literacy situation of a state and its functioning and sustainability, a link which is completely under-communicated and under-researched in international literacy studies. Many states in sub-Saharan Africa are unsustainable in the sense that they cannot provide the basic needs for their population. Moreover, the literacy situation in sub-Saharan Africa is dismal, if not catastrophic. Breidlid claims that this is to a large extent due to the imposition of a Western epistemology in school where the pupils' own indigenous languages, cultural and epistemological background are neglected. This means that pupils are alienated in school and do not acquire functional literacy skills. Breidlid critiques the SDG for Education (SDG 4) because it addresses learning outcomes in traditional, non-innovative ways and do not take into account the epistemology of Indigenous Peoples on the continent. This indicates that the SDGs, and particularly SDG 4, will not be reached by 2030.

The chapter concludes by suggesting a radical reorientation of literacy teaching in order to overcome the functional literacy deficit in sub-Saharan African and to come closer to achieving the SDGs by indigenizing, localizing and decolonizing the education systems in sub-Saharan African states and thus contributing to making the states more sustainable.

In the second chapter, Lisa Waller explores how a range of complex methodological and ethical challenges can be addressed by working with indigenous epistemologies based in land and introduces conceptual frameworks from First Nations in the north of Australia. Engoori is a set of diplomatic protocols for resolving conflict that belong to the Mithaka people of southwest Queensland that have been adopted and extended to assist schools and communities to surface and challenge the social legacies of colonization. This chapter explores cases where these approaches have informed fresh understandings of the role of Indigenous media practices in shifting discourses of deficit about indigenous identity in education in Australia.

In Chapter 3, Neema Pathak Broome, Shrishtee Bajpai and Mukesh Shende explore forest rights act, local collectivization and transformation in Korchi, Indal, India. The world over Indigenous Peoples and other traditional communities and their habitats are facing destruction due to the demand for industrial growth and development. The peoples and the communities nevertheless are not only resisting the ongoing onslaught of 'accumulation by dispossession', but are also voicing the urgency of looking for fundamental alternatives to the current global order. The authors explore how the adivasis and other traditional forest dwellers of Korchi in Gadchiroli district, Maharashtra, India have protected their water, forests and land using their traditional knowledges generation after generation. The authors discuss how the village assemblies in Korchi are actively engaged in reimagining and reconstructing local governance institutions. The women's collective is also asserting their voice in these emerging decision-making spaces. This chapter reports on a participatory study examining the emergence of this multi-dimensional transformative process carried out in 2017–2018. The process of establishing direct forms of democracy, management and conservation of forest, localizing control over their livelihoods, raising gender and caste equity concerns, and reviving cultural identity are some of the elements in this story of transformation. An analysis of the process contributes to a more general understanding of transformations that this study is part of. The study also attempts to articulate visions of development or well-being inherent in these processes of transformations.

In Chapter 4, Vandana discusses how tribal communities in India living around forests are confronted with a transition in the food production system leading to changing consumption as well. The State-run Public Distribution System has recently come under criticism for providing cheap wheat and rice which has resulted in the wiping out of traditional food grains like millets. At the same time, revival of millets has gained policy attention as several experts propose it to make the current agriculture system more sustainable and sensitive to the problem of malnutrition. This chapter discusses the changes in agriculture production, consumption preferences and ideas of health in tribal communities in Jharkhand. It argues that these changes in the food system – both production and consumption – at the material and discursive level further reproduces the existing asymmetries of power and hegemonic knowledge systems. With a focus on the inherent politics of food production and consumption changes, this chapter suggests that there is an urgent need to rethink the existing policy mechanisms.

In the chapter in the ecology section, Ginés A. Sánchez Arias deals with the political ecology of the Tabasara River Basin in Panama.

In this chapter, Sanchez discusses research he has conducted in the Comarca Ngäbe-Buglé, an indigenous territory in Panama, exploring how a for-profit hydroelectric dam backed by the Panamanian Government threatened to destroy a school, a river and a 50-year long process of cultural revival. The situation became truly alarming when an addendum to the construction plans would allow an expansion of the dam's generation capacity, which would mean a taller wall, and that the future flood level of the reservoir would increase to the point of inundating homes, crops, fruit gardens. Sanchez looks at three aspects that drive colonization today: (1) Global-Remote Capitalism, (2) Internet hashtag movement known as #TabasaráLibre, (3) Legibility of borders (Map making). In opening up mapping as both a didactic activity and legal action, participatory counter-mapping requires indigenous groups and researchers to appeal to the benevolence of bureaucrats, judges and government executives for legitimation. The chapter explores what do the Ngäbe do to resist and to adapt.

Torsten Krause, Maria Paula Quiceno Mesa and Uldarico Matapí Yucuna discuss the very topical issue of the tropical forests of the Amazon region in Colombia and that their biological diversity is being lost rapidly by the onslaught of extractive industries, large-scale agriculture and infrastructure development. These are the symptoms of an ongoing market integration that also undermines the integrity of indigenous territories and ethnicities, threatening the tremendous cultural diversity of the Amazon.

The loss of forest, the disintegration of local communities and the increase of the market economy erode indigenous ecological knowledges that are intricately tied to the territory and the forest itself, with all that is contained within it.

This chapter draws on collaborative research with an indigenous knowledge holder in the Colombian Amazon and presents insights into the wealth of indigenous ecological knowledges that still exist and that are of tremendous importance for understanding the different ways of seeing and relating to the social-ecological systems still present in the Amazon region. The authors argue for more inclusive approaches to forest governance that include indigenous ecological knowledges, particularly relating to forest fauna. Moreover, indigenous knowledges on hunting must be included in future forest governance in order to ensure the continuous existence and practice of the wealth of these knowledges that have been accumulated by indigenous people over many generations.

In the next chapter, Roy Krøvel explores and compares the development of Nordic deep ecology and the philosophy of indigenous and communitarian universities in Latin America. According to the Deep Ecology platform, the well-being and flourishing of human and nonhuman life on Earth have value in themselves while richness and diversity of life forms are also values in themselves. The indigenous concept of "Buen Vivir" embraces the "inseparability and interdependence of humans and nature" and informs "critiques of the prevailing development model, confronting basic assumptions about progress, competition, consumerism, and materialism" (Escobar).

As world leaders and the UN try to construct global blueprints to achieve a better and more sustainable future for all (the SDGs), the indigenous and communitarian universities and the deep ecologists remind us of the pitfalls of "guided dialogues", "world-wide criteria of learning" and loss of diversity. Both agree that only communities can be creators of widening classless diversity.

Andreas Ytterstad writes about indigenous good sense and climate change. In the wake of intensified climate change, a broad array of critics, NGOs and social movements have summoned indigenous knowledges, oftentimes specified as traditional ecological knowledges (TEK) as a source of inspiration. Even as the actual existence of indigenous cultures is under siege, indigenous knowledges appear to enjoy something of a renaissance. The chapter opens up a dialogue between the substance of indigenous knowledges on the one hand, and the Gramscian concept of good sense vis-à-vis global warming on the other. The author sees climate justice as the singular most important example of *good sense in motion* and the emergent themes of "anti-extractivism" and "yes to more public goods" are considered vital for the building of a broader popular climate struggle. According to Ytterstad, all the dimensions of good sense need to be tapped and developed into the most efficient collective climate action project possible, if indigenous planetary consciousness is to matter and supersede the current hegemonic order.

In next chapter, Hanne Adriansen argues, in an ethnographic study of mobility amongst Fulani pastoralists in Senegal, that so-called academic knowledges are neither singular nor static. Changes in these knowledges and their hierarchies have implications for Indigenous Peoples and how their knowledges and land use are interpreted in a context of sustainable development. Today, their practices are seen as sustainable, but until the 1990s and the so-called new rangeland paradigm, the international donor community often accused pastoralists of causing land degradation. While this has changed and the academic community today recognizes pastoral mobility as a flexible strategy that balances the variability in natural resources, the pastoralists' epistemologies and own perceptions of mobility, nature and sustainability still need to be understood. Thus, the chapter intends to deconstruct colonial aspects of Western academic discourses while at the same time problematize how we can work with different knowledge systems for sustainable development in relation to the SDGs.

In the next chapter, Camilla Risvoll and Randi Kaarhus describe the revision of the Carnivore Management Plan for the Nordland region in northern Norway. The national government expected this revision to harmonize conflicting interests, expressed in a 'double objective' of safeguarding sustainable carnivore populations and maintaining local pastoralist livelihoods. 'Clear zoning' has been established as a basic management instrument to achieve national 'population goals' for carnivores. In the Nordland Regional Carnivore Committee, which includes political parties' and Sámi Parliament representatives, a majority opted for a revision that challenged this zoning principle. The authors describe three successive acts in this revision process, analyzed as a 'discursive field' where local actors, especially pastoralists' representatives, seek to articulate relevant views on the nature of the problem and the rules defining what counts as evidence and valid knowledge in carnivore management.

Through literature review and storytelling informed by indigenous methodologies, Fjellheim in the final chapter critically addresses colonial narratives about her family's origin, existence and rights to practice reindeer husbandry in the Røros area of Norway. The chapter thus contributes with decolonial perspectives on south Sámi history, indigeneity and territorial rights.

Fjellheim argues that the academic depictions of the South Sámi during the late 1800s and 1900s as racially inferior immigrants have severe implications for the legal status of Sámi reindeer husbandry and discourses around Indigenous Peoples' rights. Yet, the counter stories of south Sámi scholars and knowledge holders continue to challenge colonial legacies in academia, public debates and in the justice system. Through these stories, the Sámi continue to resist.

References

Breidlid, A. (2013). *Education, Indigenous Knowledges and Development in the Global South. Contesting Knowledges for a Sustainable Future.* London: Routledge.

Fatnowna, S., and Pickett, H. (2002). 'Indigenous Contemporary Knowledge Development through Research'. In *Indigenous Knowledge and the Integration of Knowledge Systems: Towards a Philosophy of Articulation*, edited by Catherine Hoppers, 209–236. Cape Town: New Africa Education.

Goduka, I. N. (2000). 'African/Indigenous Philosophies: Legitmizing Spiritually Centred Wisdoms within the Academy'. In *African Voices in Education*, edited by P. Higgs, N. C. G. Vakalisa, T. V. Mda, & N. T. Assie-Lumumba, 63–83. Lansdowne: Juta Academic.

Greenwood, M. (2005). Children as Citizens of First Nations: Linking Indigenous Health to Early Childhood Development. *Pediatric Child Health*, 10(9), 553–555.

Jones, P. W. (2007). Education and world order. *Comparative Education*, 43(3), 325–337.

Kovach, M. (2009). *Indigenous Methodologies. Characteristics, Conversations, and Contexts.* Buffalo: University of Toronto Press.

Sefa Dei, G. J. (2016). 'Anti-Colonial Education'. In *Encyclopedia of Educational Philosophy and Theory*, edited by M. A Peters, 1–6. Singapore: Spring.

Smith, L. T., Tuck, E., Yang, K. W. (eds.) (2019). *Indigenous and Decolonizing Studies in Education. Mapping the Long View.* New York and London: Routledge.

Tuck, E., and Yang, W. (2012). Decolonization Is Not a Metaphor. *Decolonization: Indigeneity, Education & Society*, 1(1), 1–40.

Tungarazaa, F., Sutherland, M., and Stack, N. (2013). Universal Education or Open Education Opportunities for All? *Compare: A Journal of Comparative and International Education*, [Online]43(6), 822–824.

Wilson, S. (2008). *Research Is Ceremony. Indigenous Research Methods.* Halifax & Winnipeg. Fernwood Publishing.

1 Beyond the Western paradigm

Indigenization of education systems, the Sustainable Development Goals and state building in sub-Saharan Africa

Anders Breidlid

Introduction

This chapter explores a little discussed but significant aspect of why many states in sub-Saharan Africa are unsuccessful, fragile and unsustainable, namely, the issue of literacy and the significance of cultural and social capital in sustainable state formation. The discussion is related to the Sustainable Development Goals (SDGs, UN, 2015b) and to what extent literacy and increased social and cultural capital in the population are key to achieving the overall SDGs. While the chapter confirms the importance of functional literacy in sustainable state formation, it suggests strongly that the current interventions in increasing the literacy in the global South, and in sub-Saharan Africa in particular, are grossly inadequate due to the lack of a substantial increase in functional literacy figures over the last decades despite massive literacy campaigns.[1] It is therefore the claim of this chapter that there is a strong need to include alternative knowledge systems, i.e. indigenous knowledges and epistemologies in literacy education if goal 4 of the SDGs is to be achieved, and if states in sub-Saharan Africa are to become more sustainable. Indigenous knowledges and epistemologies pre-existed colonial conquest, and are thus unique knowledges in many ways different from Western epistemology and knowledge making.

Indigenous knowledges encompass, as Dei et al. argue,

> the cultural traditions, values and belief systems concerned with the everyday realities of living in a particular place. They are imparted to the younger generation by community elders or are gained through direct experience of nature and its relationship with the social world.
>
> (Dei et al., 2000, 2)

Moreover, indigenous knowledges are fundamentally relational where the unity of man, nature and the spiritual make up the construction of knowledges. While indigenous knowledges thus are radically different from Western positivist knowledge they must nevertheless be seen in relation to Western epistemology and knowledge production since indigenous knowledges changed status during colonialism and were inferiorized due to the imposition of Western knowledge which claimed hegemony and superiority.

Indigenous Peoples are not, as I define it, only people of indigenous minorities, like the Indians in the Americas, or minority indigenous groups in Asia or Oceania, but also the majority population in Africa that originated on the continent before the colonization process of the 19th and 20th century (for more comprehensive definitions of indigenous and Indigenous Peoples, see introduction in this book).

The issue of the sustainability of states is complicated since defining sustainability in times of climate change is – to put it mildly – problematic.[2] The conventional definition of a sustainable state is currently untenable: failure to achieve economic development and a gross national product comparable to many countries in the global North (Nair, 2018). It has been suggested that if everyone on the planet consumed as much as the average US citizen, four Earths would be needed to sustain them (McDonald, 2015). In a sustainability perspective, the US and most states in the global North are clearly unsustainable (see also Ytterstad's chapter in this book on climate change). However, in the context of this chapter, the term unsustainable relates to states in sub-Saharan Africa where many citizens are suffering from famine, poverty, unemployment, war, migration, corruption and weak and non-representative institutions. According to Matasa (2008), "Africa is known as one of the richest parts of the world when it comes to natural resources, yet it is also the poorest region — despite the natural wealth and the aid flow." Since many African countries do not manage to satisfy basic human needs among their citizens despite huge natural resources, I define such countries as unsustainable even though their ecological footprints on the earth are not linked to over-consumption. One important reason for being the poorest continent is "the ecological debt caused by natural resource exploitation" (Matasa, 2008) which often leads to environmental problems such as air and water pollution. This resource exploitation by the countries in the global North impacts negatively on the people in many African countries, like copper mining in Zambia and cobalt extraction in DRC, activities conducted by the North to stimulate consumption in the North or to contribute to a more environment friendly livelihood in the North at the expense of sub-Saharan Africa. One reason why this exploitation and in many ways recolonization of Africa is possible is, *inter alia, a* non-representative governments and the lack of control mechanisms put in place, and that there is very little transparency about who profits from this exploitation in the home country.

In order to control resource exploitation the states must, as Stigliz (2012) argues

> do more to ensure that their citizens get the full value of the resources. There is an unavoidable conflict of interest between (usually foreign) natural-resource companies and host countries: the former want to minimise what they pay, while the latter need to maximise it.

When historians, economists, sociologists and other scholars address the issue of why some states are more successful than others in terms of conventional economic development and sustainability, we are given multiple answers, often mutually incompatible.

While there is more or less scholarly consensus that colonialism was a major, if not the only factor in having created the gap between the global North and South, there is disagreement why this gap is not closing and why some states seem to remain unsustainable. In the discussion below, I first refer to three different major reasons advocated by historians and political scientists. It is worth noting, however, that none of explanations below refer to the issue of social capital and literacy (except marginally by Diamond, 2005) as a major reason for an unsuccessful, unsustainable or failed state.

Institutional reasons

Some scholars identify weak institutions as a main reason why states are fragile or more or less failures. For instance, Acemoglu and Robinson claim in their book *Why Nations Fail* (2013) that the reason for the huge gap between the rich and the poor is institutional, i.e. that states differ institutionally between states with inclusive political institutions on the one hand and states with extractive institutions on the other. Unfortunately, they hardly discuss what is meant by failed or weak states apart from the classical wisdom of differences in gross national product. The authors define inclusive political institutions as "those that allow and encourage participants by the great mass of people and enable individuals to make choices they wish" (Acemoglu and Robinson, 2013, p. 74) while extractive political institutions are institutions which "concentrate power in the hands of a narrow elite and place few constraints on the exercise of this power" (Acemoglu and Robinson, 2013, p. 89). Admittedly a clear line of demarcation between inclusive and extractive institutions is not easily drawn and their definition of inclusive states as states of mass participation in the political process is of course somewhat simplistic. Is taking part in elections every four years a sign of inclusivity? Whatever their definitional vagueness Acemoglu and Robinson offer some interesting insights into the debate even though their claim that their theory gives THE explanation or even solution to the problem is of course an exaggeration.

Undoubtedly, the specific characteristics of institutions in the countries around the globe are relevant when we seek answers to the probably most pressing question in today's world besides climate change. Institutions that are inclusive and allow democratic processes in their political system (to a larger and lesser extent) seem to fare better in the long run than extractive institutions.[3] Institutions in many states in sub-Saharan Africa are basically extractive of nature where a small minority (elite) controls the institutions of the country (even though elections take place), and where the high functional illiteracy rates mean that the majority of the population in these states are basically excluded from participating in political and economic activities. In many states in sub-Saharan Africa, the extractive institutions do not seem very eager to introduce mass education. One likely reason is that high illiteracy serves the interests of the elite, and that more money spent on the military is more conducive to keep the governments in power (UNESCO, 2011).

Geographical reasons

Other scholars try to explain the successful/unsustainable state discussion or enigma in terms of geographical differences. In *Why the West Rules-for Now* (2011), Ian Morris claims that "biology and sociology explains the global similarities while geography explains the regional differences. And in that sense, it is geography that explains why the West rules" (Morris, 2011, p. 30). Morris goes on to argue that that

> when the Atlantic rose to prominence in the seventeenth century CE, those people best placed to exploit it – at first chiefly the British, then their former colonists in America – created new kinds of empires and economies and unlocked the energy trapped in fossil fuels. And that, I will argue, is why the West rules.
>
> (Morris, 2011, p. 30)

This does not mean that culture, religion and politics are not important. As Morris argues:

> It is one thing, several have said to me, to reject the old idea that a few great men determined that the history would unfold differently in East and West; it is another altogether to say that culture, values, and beliefs were unimportant and to seek the reason why the West rules entirely in brute material forces.
>
> (Morris, 2011, p. 29)

However, the differences in politics, culture and values are, according to Morris, primarily due to geographical factors.

Environmental reasons

A view somewhat similar to the geographical argument is furthered by Jared Diamond in his book *Collapse. How Societies Choose to Fail or Survive* (2005) where he attests the failure of societies to the unsuccessful adaptation to a changing environment. While Diamond admits that environmental differences can partly explain the difference between success and failure, he goes on to argue that "the proper choice of an economy to fit the environment is important....some societies evolve practices to avoid overexploitation, and other societies fail at that challenge" (Diamond, 2005, p. 308). Clearly, decision-making processes are crucial in making the proper choices, and Diamond suggests a road map of factors contributing to failures of group decision-making. The first factor according to Diamond is that wrong decisions may be due to a failure

> to anticipate a problem before the problem actually arrives. Second, when the problem does arrive, the group may fail to perceive it. Then, after they perceive it, they may fail even to try to solve it. Finally they may try to solve it but may not succeed.
>
> (Diamond, 2005, p. 421)

Moreover, Diamond argues that even prior experience of a problem is not a guarantee for right decisions. The crucial question is of course why some succeed in making the right decisions while others do not. Or is it possible to find examples of countries which currently make the right decisions? 14 years after the publication of Diamond's book, there is a sense that defining unsustainability in terms of adopting to the environment is crucial, but would as noted include most countries in the global North as well given the current unsustainable environmental situation globally. Interestingly, Diamond offers at least a partial explanation about the failure to make the right decisions by claiming that such a failure is especially a problem for illiterate societies. However, Diamond never elaborates on why illiterate societies face problems in this respect.

Illiteracy and unsustainable states

The explanations from the three authors above offer interesting insights (and I could have included additional explanations from other scholars as well), but the almost total lack of including literacy in the discussion of sustainability is striking, if not surprising since the issue of education/literacy and sustainability is under-communicated both by educational scientists and social scientists in general. Among educational scientists and even educational sociologists, there is a tendency to neglect macro issues; i.e. the impact of education on sustainable development.

The field of sociology of education was initiated almost a century ago (in 1922) by Emile Durkheim with his seminal work *Education and Sociology*. Sociology of education also emerged as an important field in England in the 1950s as well as the development of "comparative education sciences or the economics of education" (see Bray et al., 2007; Stevens et al., 2008; Rouse and Barrow, 2009 for respective overviews referred to in Busemeyer and Trampusch, 2011).

While Durkheim refers to modern societies (Europe in the 1920s) his theories are also relevant in the global South, and not the least for countries in sub-Saharan Africa to-day. Durkheim emphasizes the importance of education to provide necessary knowledge and skills in the workplace and particularly as an important factor in socialization, i.e. preparing children for collective life and socialization with others, i.e. to socialize and humanize people "by providing the normative and cognitive frameworks they lack" (Blackedge and Hunt, 1985, p. 10). To Durkheim, education is thus systematic socialization to transmit society's culture and social order and thus extremely important in state building.

Even though Durkheim underlined the importance of education in state building, I agree with Busemeyer and Trampusch that

> comparative education sciences still are more interested in the effects of education policies on social indicators and societal outcomes ... rather than the political and institutional factors that explain their enactment.
> (Busemeyer and Trampusch, 2011, p. 418)[4]

While education scholars have a tendency to focus on education issues separated from the macro issues of sustainable development, state formation and poverty alleviation scholars in the other social sciences like political science, comparative political science and sociology have been little concerned with education as a major factor in political processes and sustainable development, rather privileging other areas like, for example, welfare state research.

Similarly, Burton Clark complains that scholars of the social sciences remained interested in education 'too briefly' and soon wandered back to their respective home turf, allowing:

> organizational theorists to gaze awhile upon the odd ways of universities and then return to the business firm; political scientists to assemble some essays on government and higher education and then go back to traditional political institutions; economists to measure some inputs and outputs and speculate on benefits and costs and then find other topics for their tools; sociologists to absorb education in the study of stratification and forget about the rest
> (Clark, 1983, p .1)

However, there is a sense that social scientists have recently started to take issues on education somewhat more seriously. For the purposes in this chapter, the works of political scientists like Ansell (2008, 2010) and Lindert (2004) are interesting since they have emphasized the significant relationship between education and democracy. While Ansell finds a correlation between democracy and educational expansion, Lindert discusses the importance of education in the context of the welfare state. Still it seems that social scientists, whether they are educationists, sociologists and political scientists focusing on education, do not discuss the macro questions of sustainable development on country level in relation to education policies, human capital and mass literacy comprehensively.

Literacy, democracy and sustainable development: the case of Scandinavia

The lack of scholarly concern for the admittedly complex relationship between education, literacy and sustainable development of countries in the global South is conspicuous and also lamentable since history shows that literacy competence and the focus on human capital can play a very important role in state formation processes. The historical example discussed below raises the question if it is at all appropriate for a non-indigenous, Western writer to use examples from the global North, and even from my own geographical region, to address issues in the global South. While suspicions of neocolonial imposition should not be rejected outright, there is a sense, even for postcolonial scholars like myself, that exchange of ideas between the global North and the global South might sometimes be fruitful and even indispensable. It does not mean that experiences from the global North can or should be copied *in toto*, but there are at least lessons or experiences that might seem worth considering in the discussion of unsustainable countries.[5]

The focus on education for the masses started early in Scandinavia. Already in 1739, Norway's first primary education law was introduced in the wake of the Protestant Reformation and where the parents had the principal responsibility for the education of their children. The church believed that it was important for people to be able to read the Bible and learn about Christianity.

In 1814, Denmark's Education Act was introduced. This was Europe's first compulsory education law. The other Scandinavian countries followed suit: Norway introduced "folkeskole" in 1827, a primary school which became mandatory for *seven* years in 1889. A similar law was introduced in Sweden in 1842, and in Finland in 1866 (see Einhorn and Logue, 2003).

The crucial importance of education and literacy in the fight for democracy in Scandinavia cannot be overestimated. In the 19th century, the folk high school movement was introduced and founded by N.F.S. Grundvig. The folk high school movement contributed a lot to the enlightenment of the masses by focusing on giving people from the working and lower classes literacy and organizational skills. Pedagogically Grundvig's ideas were foregrounding, for example, Freire's ideas more than 100 years later by focusing on the democratic interaction and communication between teacher and pupil. Even though the teacher is more knowledgeable in the various subjects, the pupils and teachers are equal, according to Grundvig, when it comes to knowledge about what is important for man.

Increased enlightenment and conscientization level among the ordinary people, i.e. worker and farmers, via literacy meant that they acquired necessary knowledge to organize themselves to combat exploitation and harassment from the upper and privileged classes.[6]

As Einhorn and Logue write:

> Poor laws became less oppressive, but, most dramatically, the spread of compulsory primary education began the transformation of the rural peasantry into literate and active citizens. The great nineteenth-century political, social, and economic changes in Scandinavia were accompanied by the spread of literacy and access to a variety of cultural and educational resources.
>
> (Einhorn and Logue, 2003, p. 148)

The introduction of literacy was therefore important in the fight for democracy and the drive for public participation in the public domain. Even though Norway became an independent state as late as in 1905, the union between Sweden and Norway (from 1814 to 1905) was a loose union of the separate kingdoms of Sweden and Norway and where the two countries had separate institutions in the most important areas such as constitutions, laws, state churches, schools and armies. In 1905, Norway had a functionally literate population, and the emergence of the Scandinavian welfare state a few decades later was based on mass literacy.

The close link between socio-economic development (i.e. the Scandinavian welfare state) and functional literacy for all thus paved the way for Scandinavian social democracy.[7]

The campaign for a literate population in the three countries was basically based on local knowledges and local languages as media of instruction. In Norway, however, the situation in the 19th century was somewhat complex where the learners had to learn to read in Danish. The situation can to some extent be compared to the situation in the UK today where working-class children encounter a different code (elaborate code) in school (see Bernstein, 1971) compared to that of home (restricted code) and where the pupils have to overcome epistemological challenges in the reading and learning process. Not much research has been done on code switching in the Norwegian education system in the 19th century, but it was obviously a learning obstacle until Norwegian was standardized as the languages in school (both Norwegian and new Norwegian). Still the linguistic and epistemic challenges of Danish in the Norwegian education system cannot be compared with the challenges faced by African children even today.

A dark history in Scandinavian education is, however, the treatment of the Sámi, the indigenous groups in Scandinavia. A severe assimilation policy from the 18th century up till the 1980s forced the Sámi to give up their own language and culture in the education system, and where the Sámi languages were forbidden in school. It was a situation similar to what Africans experience even to-day where the indigenous languages are not taught or even tolerated in schools. Not until 1967 was the teaching of Sámi as the medium of instruction established as a right in Norway (see chapter by Fjellheim in this book). In 1992, Norway and Finland passed the Sámi Language Acts which made the Sámi language official together with the hegemonic languages in the indigenous communities of both countries. It means that the Sámi has the right to use their indigenous languages in schools, and in courts. Moreover, besides including the indigenous languages in the teaching there is now more attention paid to the importance of incorporating relevant, indigenous content and values in the curriculum. The situation of the Sámi languages is remarkably better compared to many indigenous languages in Canada and the United States. The brief, but very destructive colonial period on the North American continent meant assimilationist education policies which undermined indigenous languages as well as the decimation of the indigenous population. Currently, scholars have started the process of reviving indigenous languages as well as the epistemological knowledges of the Native Americans and First Nations, and have started including indigenous world views and values in the education systems (see Kuokkanen, 2006). Clearly, the colonialist policies and practices in Scandinavia and even more in North America have slowed the process of making the indigenous communities sustainable on their own terms.

Education in the global South with a particular focus on Africa

If the experiences from Scandinavia are anything to go by the potential correlation between high literacy rates, democracy and state building in many countries in the global South, and particularly sub-Saharan Africa, might be worth pursuing.

It is a well-established fact that many schools in sub-Saharan Africa are of low quality with poor, uneducated teachers, lack of adequate textbooks and school material, a Western, alienating curriculum and often a foreign language as medium of instruction. The question is to what extent the poor state of education in many states in sub-Saharan Africa impacts on state formation and sustainable development.

The literacy situation in sub-Saharan Africa is critically low, both in terms of conventional and functional literacy. Only 62% of the adult population are literate in the conventional or basic meaning of the term. Such a figure implies that 153 million Africans are illiterate, and two thirds of them are women (UNESCO, 2017).

Zambia and Uganda were ranked 14th and 16th out of 20 African countries on a per capita basis in 2015 (1200 US$ and 900 US $ respectively) (New World Wealth, 2015). The situation of poverty in the two countries seems to be reflected in poor literacy rates. In Zambia, for example, the conventional literacy level has remained relatively stable of around 60% since 2000 (63.4%). According to recent statistics from Zambia, 70.9% of males while only 56% of females are literate. The situation in Uganda is in many ways similar to that of Zambia with an official average basic adult (15+) literacy rate of 73.9 (80,9 for males, 66,9 for females; (UNESCO, UIS, 2018). However, the situation is dramatic when one, for example, studies figures on illiteracy among primary school teachers in Uganda. According to *Daily Monitor* (2016),

> Eight out of every 10 primary school teachers who qualified last year can neither read nor solve basic primary-level mathematics questions, according to a new government evaluation, re-confirming a systematic decay in quality of the country's education.

The basic literacy figures from South Africa are far higher than in the other sub-Saharan countries stating that 94, 37% of the +15 population across ethnicities has acquired basic or conventional literacy, presumably either in a colonial or indigenous language (UNESCO, UIS, n.d.).

It is worth noting, however, how UNESCO defines literacy used in the statistical material:

> Current literacy data are generally collected through population censuses or household surveys in which the respondent or head of the household declares whether they can read and write with understanding a short, simple statement about one's everyday life in any written language. Some surveys require respondents to take a quick test in which they are asked to read a simple passage or write a sentence, yet clearly literacy is a far more complex issue that requires more information.
>
> (UNESCO, UIS, 2019)

One crucial question is therefore whether basic or conventional literacy really is useful in the local community, in the work place, in a functioning democracy. Is such a literacy level important or relevant for personal and national development? The probably most efficient method of knowledge transfer today is through reading and understanding published information, either on paper or online. If a person's literacy level is limited to understanding simple statements from everyday life, it can be assumed that the person is more or less excluded from the wider community and from decision-making processes in society, and the wider society cannot make use of his/her capabilities. Moreover, there is a sense that not even UNESCO's literacy statistics that show basic and conventional literacy rates may measure the actual literacy levels. As UNESCO suggested already in 2006 that literacy may be much lower than reflected in data presented here, which are based on conventional methods of measurement that do not actually test a person's literacy skills (UNESCO, 2006, 1).

Functional and critical literacy

Given the uncertain and most likely inflated basic or conventional literacy rates referred to above, there is of course reason for national governments and the aid community to not only increase their efforts to combat illiteracy in sub-Saharan Africa, but to adjust their ambitions with the proclaimed goal of making the majority population in sub-Saharan Africa not only basically literate, but what is often termed functionally literate.

Functional literacy is an extended form of literacy and was first defined at the World Congress of Ministers of Education on the Eradication of Illiteracy, Teheran September 1965:

> Rather than an end in itself, literacy should be regarded as a way of preparing man [sic] for a social, civic and economic role that goes beyond the limits of rudimentary literacy training consisting merely in [sic] the teaching of reading and writing.
>
> (UNESCO, 2005)

During the 1960s and 1970s, 'functional literacy' was often linked to socio-economic development, but teaching and learning literacy was nevertheless to a large extent not contextualized, i.e. related to the learners' own experiences and values.

Pablo Freire's critical ideas of conscientization (Freire, 1970) deviated from the perception of literacy learning as a neutral and decontextualized process and introduced the importance of context and the learners' experiences in acquiring literacy. Freire's *critical literacy* implied the exploration of the social and political reality in the learning process in order for the learners in a global South setting to understand, challenge and fight the forces of oppression. Critical (functional) literacy was thus perceived to be a political force which many governments in the global South feared.

The importance of clarifying what literacy statistics actually implies

The importance of clarifying what kind of definition of literacy is actually used in various contexts becomes abundantly clear when one examines the situation in South Africa as well as in other African countries. The South African literacy rate of 94% referred to above is interesting in the light of what Paul Hoffman, the Director for the Centre For Constitutional Right in South Africa, had to say about functional literacy in South Africa in 2008:

> At present the South African public school system is delivering functionally literate Black (African) matriculants at a rate of 1 in 29 of those who enter our educational system ... The situation portrayed by these figures is a national disgrace. Unpacked and made digestible they mean that only 1 in 29 (i.e. 3.5%) Black children entering the school system emerge with matric certificates in a state which enables them to enter the realms of trainability, skills acquisition, higher education and employability in an economy in which skills are in short supply. Menial workers are no longer needed in any great numbers due to

globalization, mechanization and a labour dispensation that discourages their employment. Our school drop out rate is 77% over the twelve years of schooling. According to UNESCO figures, the international norm is 21%.

(Hoffman, 2008)

A report released in December 2017 by the Progress in International Reading Literacy Study (Pirls) confirms the serious literacy situation in one of the most advanced countries in sub-Saharan Africa. According to the Pirls report (2016), 78% of grade 4 pupils in South Africa are illiterate, probably meaning that 22% are basically literate. Moreover, there has been no significant progress in improving children's reading skills since the last survey five years earlier (Howie et al., 2017).

There is reason to believe that the (basic) literacy statistics in other countries in sub-Saharan Africa are any better, with a literacy level far from UNESCO's extended definition of literacy.

Education, literacy and the SDGs

The dismal literacy and education situation with the low human capital base on the sub-Saharan African continent is potentially one of the most important reasons for the unsustainability of these countries.

The Sustainable Development Goals

In 2015, 193 countries adopted the 2030 Agenda for Sustainable Development and its 17 SDGs. The SDGs replaced the Millennium Development Goals (UN, 2015a) and the key question here is whether the educational SDGs have adopted other ways and interventions, or if it is more of the same.

The SDGs consist of 17 goals and 169 targets that will apply to all countries, with a deadline of 2030 to be met. The final resolution "Transforming Our World: the 2030 Agenda for Sustainable Development" (A/RES/70/1) recognizes that education is essential for the success of all 17 of its goals. SDG 4 focuses in particular on education and aims to "ensure inclusive and equitable quality education and promote lifelong learning opportunities for all" (UN, 2015b).

SDG 4 underlines that major progress has been made for education access, specifically at the primary school level, for both boys and girls, but that access does not always mean quality of education, or completion of primary school. Currently, 103 million youth worldwide still lack basic literacy skills, and more than 60% of them are women. The SDG goal is therefore to "ensure that all girls and boys complete free, equitable and quality primary and secondary education leading to relevant and effective learning outcomes" by 2030 (UN SDG 4, pp. 1, 2). The SDGs go in theory beyond past attempts to ensure access to basic education, as set out in the Education For All goals and the education-related Millennium Development Goal (MDG) 2 (2000–2015) since learning outcomes are particularly emphasized.

The question that begs itself, however, is who has been in the driving seat to make these targets possible, and whether the transparency of the process make the goals more achievable than the MDGs goals.

Since the MDGs were partly unsuccessful, there is reason to question to what extent the new SDGs can be achieved by 2030. Admittedly, prediction is very difficult, especially if it is about the future, but the risk of failure is obviously there since there were few soul-searching activities that examined the past failures as the stocktaking before the new sustainable goals were launched in 2015 shows (UNESCO, 2015). What went wrong with the MDGs on education apart from the problem of untrained teachers, lack of school material and generally speaking poor government interventions? What were the underlying reasons for why the international interventions failed in securing functional literacy among the pupils in the global South? Is there any reason to believe that the SDGs will be more successful than the MDGs?

There is little, if anything in the SDGs that suggests a fundamental reorientation of the major interventions already taken. When, for *example, the conventional literacy level* in many African countries has not, as noted, changed substantially over the last 15–20 years, there is reason to ask what can be done to change this status quo. It is clearly not sufficient to proclaim that the focus in the next 15 years will be on quality rather quantity and that such a focus will inevitably increase the literacy level. Literacy is a complex term that needs to be understood by the various interventionists in this education game. As with the MDG goals, there is a sense that the goals for education for sustainability in the SDGs are defined in terms of a traditional, Western paradigm both ideologically and epistemologically. The fact that the SDGs do not refer to indigenous knowledges[8] in the education chapter (nor in the SDGs overall document) indicates clearly that epistemological issues are not on the SDGs agenda and signals that the likelihood for improved functional literacy rates are minimal. What the SDGs are signaling is more of the same medicine, i.e. the promotion of a Western educational discourse that leaves too many children behind.

The lack of references to indigenous knowledges in the SDGs reflect the situation among the important institutions behind the SDGs. The problem is that there is little discussion among the International Non-Governmental Organizations (INGOs) and the national governments about potential changes in learning strategies and knowledge transmission given the status quo in learning outcomes. Admittedly, mother tongue instruction is now increasingly being accepted as a must for effective learning in the lower grades, but the epistemological, ideological and ontological issues are completely omitted from the agenda. This omission is serious since research on primary and secondary discourses and on restricted and elaborate codes underlines the significance of these issues in a learning setting.

Primary and secondary discourses. The importance of indigenous knowledges

In order to comprehend the conditions for literacy teaching and learning in sub-Saharan Africa/global South, it is necessary to examine what goes on in the African classroom since literacy in the Western sense is most frequently supposed to be learnt in school. What kind of teaching takes place? Under what circumstances?

One important aspect that needs to be examined in this context is the discourse production in school that influences learning.

It is well known that each individual is part of different discourses/identities (Gee, 1999), and the important point in this context, as also Bernstein (1971) has underlined, is that some discourses fit better into the school's value system than others. This applies both to the global South and the global North. Gee links this discursive aspect directly to classroom studies with a focus on social and epistemological differences in school. If the pupils do not speak the language of the school and do not have the epistemological frame of references used in school, there are often problems related to language and learning. When the child acquires his/her mother tongue and home culture/epistemology, they acquire what Gee calls a **primary discourse**.[9] This is the discourse in which the child finds itself and unfolds and is of course a cognitive skill. The primary discourse is part of a discursive network which gives meaning. The primary discourse is according to Gee "a base within which we acquire or resist later discourses" (Gee, 2012, p. 143). In most African communities, the children speak a local or indigenous language and acquire indigenous knowledges which are not necessarily referred to in school.

In the school, the pupil encounters other discourses which Gee calls **secondary discourses**. Traditional learning methods in school, like reading of texts and solution of textual tasks, are based on secondary discourses which for some pupils are new and epistemologically alien. For pupils with educated parents, some of these secondary discourses might have already been introduced together with the primary discourse before entering the school, and these pupils are of course at an advantage compared to pupils with no such background. At school, also in the global North, the pupils experience that the primary discourse from their home environment is replaced by secondary discourses.

What needs to be communicated is that discourses are

> inherently 'ideological' ... They crucially involve a set of values and viewpoints about the relationships between people and the distribution of social goods (at the very least about who is an insider and who isn't, but often many others as well). One must speak and act, and at least appear to think and feel, in terms of these values and viewpoints while being in the Discourse, otherwise one doesn't count as being in it... Any

> Discourse concerns itself with certain objects and puts forward certain concepts, viewpoints and values at the expense of others. In doing so, it will marginalize viewpoints and values central to other Discourses. In fact, a Discourse can call for one to accept values in conflict with other Discourses of which one is also a member.
>
> (Gee, 2012, p. 144)

Gee acknowledges that discourses "are intimately related to the distribution of social power and hierarchical structure in society ... (and) can lead to the acquisition of social goods (money, power, status)" (Gee, 2012, p. 144). According to social reproduction theory, schools are not institutions of equal opportunity but mechanisms for perpetuating social inequalities (Bhattacharya, 2017). Social inequality results from the interplay of classrooms, schools and the wider societal context. To explore the role of secondary discourses in classroom teaching and learning is therefore of utmost importance, not the least in a sub-Saharan context.

While Gee is primarily concerned with secondary discourses in the global North and admits their ideological and epistemological nature, it is surprising that there is not much more critical analysis of secondary discourses in the education systems in the global South. When Gee defines literacy as mastering the secondary discourse in school (see H. Breidlid, 2014), it means that literacy in a functional sense is very much linked to the ability of crossing cultural and epistemological borders for many school children, i.e. from an indigenous epistemological background to a Western one.

The alien, non-indigenous nature of the secondary discourse: the global architecture of education

It is grossly under-communicated that educational institutions with their secondary discourses are extremely important institutions in extending the hegemonic role of Western epistemology (see Gramsci, 1971) since these Western secondary discourses affect all (or almost all members) of a given country. The epistemological transfer from home to school (from primary to secondary discourses) impacts school quality as it contributes to alienating indigenous students in the sub-Saharan region cognitively and epistemologically from their home environment by introducing them to a completely alien discourse and Western epistemology in school. In line with Jones (2007), I call this education secondary discourse(s) the global architecture of education (Breidlid, 2013), meaning a common Western, homogenous education discourse that is hegemonic. The dislocation of indigenous languages and epistemologies in school thus creates secondary discourses which require a profound identity transformation if you are to succeed in school. While the situation to some extent is similar to what Bernstein discussed about the working-class children in the UK with their restricted code (Bernstein, 1971), the code which the majority of indigenous school children in sub-Saharan

Africa bring to school is epistemologically completely different and contributes to huge learning problems if they are not able to undergo this epistemological identity transformation. The majority of indigenous students in Africa thus suffers because the knowledges (and often the languages) they bring from home are marginalized in the secondary discourses hegemonic in the classroom. As has been noted elsewhere, "If you as a pupil cannot quite understand what the teacher is saying, it will not help to try to figure out why she is saying it" (Botha and Breidlid, 2014). The fact that teaching is not contextualized and that indigenous languages and knowledges are not actively promoted by the governments is to a large extent due to these governments' elitist nature. It is worth noting that the alienating classroom situation in many sub-Saharan African countries is experienced by the *majority* population, and thus different from the situation of the Sámi *minority* described earlier in this chapter.

Literacy and unsustainable states: a tentative conclusion

The argument of this chapter is in line with Oghenekohwo and Frank-Oputu (2017) who state that "without massive investment and promotion of literacy education, development that is targeted at the 17-point SDGs will be bereft of citizen's empowerment, engagement, experiential values and evidential consequences in social change" (Oghenekohwo and Frank-Oputu, 2017, p. 126).

Oghenekohwo and Frank-Oputu's's argument of citizen's empowerment is similar to what Šlaus[*] and Garry Jacobs call the development of human capital which

> is the critical determinant of long-term sustainability and that efforts to accelerate the evolution of human consciousness and emergence of mentally self-conscious individuals will be the most effective approach for ensuring a sustainable future. Education is the primary lever.
>
> (Šlaus* and Garry Jacobs, 2011, p. 97)

Moreover, as Bouzekri (2015) stresses, the essential role of education and literacy as the most important production factor (is) ... "by helping individuals acquire knowledge which encourages participation in groups, opens doors to job opportunities, develops social interactions, makes individuals aware of their rights, improves health, and reduces poverty." In other words, you cannot build and contain a well-functioning state and institutions without educated people who are functionally literate. A literate population cannot so easily be manipulated, and nepotism and corruption can be better controlled by a population which is conscientized.

Education is critical for promoting sustainable development and enhancing the capacity to address their environmental and sustainability issues for effective public participation in decision-making.

While the need to invest heavily in literacy education to make countries in the global South more sustainable is indisputable, the argument in this chapter is that the current emphasis on literacy education by the SDGs, the INGOs and the national governments will not make the population in the various countries in the global south, and in sub-Saharan Africa in particular more functionally literate if the conventional interventions and learning strategies continue. Unfortunately, it has been noted that a change in pedagogical and epistemological strategies is not on the agenda of the SDGs and the various international and national stakeholders, making the goal of a functionally literate population as well as better functioning and transparent countries in sub-Saharan Africa by 2030 a utopian dream. An important intervention to achieve SDG number 4 is, as discussed in this chapter, a thorough *indigenization* and decolonizing of the education system in the global South, and in sub-Saharan Africa in particular, so that the well-documented increase in access over the last two decades is supplemented with quality education and where learning outcomes in terms of functional literacy are achieved by the majority of the learners. This is urgent because the functional literacy deficit is a crucial reason why governments are weak in sub-Saharan Africa with little democratic control, and where lack of transparency and control mechanisms defeat any attempt to make these countries more sustainable.

Notes

1 While sub-Saharan African countries have increased enrollment ratios substantially over the last decades (UNESCO, 2017), learning outcomes and functional literacy have not increased to the same extent (www.globalpartnership.org/blog/measuring-functional-literacy-and-numeracy-lifelong-learning).
2 While many states in the global South are unsustainable in line with the definition above, there is good reason to question the sustainability of nation states in the global North. Key words here are global warming, climate change, exploitation of the earth as well as exploitation of the South in multiple ways. The focus of this article is however on failed or unsuccessful states in the global South.

   The current territorial borders of the states in sub-Saharan Africa is a colonial construction. The pre-colonial entities in sub-Saharan Africa were complex and heterogeneous, but territorially different from the current states in Africa. It is however inconceivable that modern Africa will return to the precolonial situation.
3 Again there are definitional challenges. Do countries in the global North fare better in the long run given the current climate crisis? Since it is obvious that the institutions in the global North generally speaking are stronger than in the global South, the assumption is that they can address the climate challenges better. There are, however, many reservations here: while climate change seems to affect the poorer nations more, it is the nations in the global North that are primarily responsible for the consumption and emission levels that drive climate change.
4 The discussion on the role of political scientists and sociologists in education research is mainly indebted to Busemeyer and Trampusch's Review Article: Comparative Political Science and the Study of Education. *British Journal of Political Science*, 41, from 2011.

5 However, there is at least one important difference when comparing the Scandinavian experience and the situation in for example Africa south of Sahara. In the case of Scandinavia, we refer more to nation-building rather than state-building since the Scandinavian countries were/are relatively homogenous states (not forgetting the Sámi population).

Nation building often refers to the development of a state where citizens share the same social, cultural and often religious beliefs. In Africa, the various countries are more states than nations with boundaries often drawn haphazardly by the colonial powers. It means that there often is a huge variety of citizens within the countries, and that emphasis must be based more on equal rights and responsibilities rather than religious, ethnic and cultural identity.

6 The Education for All Global Monitoring Report (2006) states the following: "Prior to 1800, reading (though not always writing) skills were widespread in several northern European countries (e.g. Denmark, Finland, Iceland, Scotland, Sweden and Prussia), as well as in parts of England, France and Switzerland... By the 1860s, only a minority of adults in industrializing countries lacked rudimentary literacy skills. In eastern and southern Europe, however, the pace of change in literacy was slow and mainly extended to certain professions and elite populations" (UNESCO, 2005, p. 191).

7 For a summary of the development of Scandinavian education systems, see Sysiharju (1981). "Primary education and Secondary Schools."

8 The SDGs refer to Indigenous Peoples six times, three times in the political declaration; two in the targets under Goal 2 on Zero Hunger (target 2.3) and Goal 4 on education (target 4.5) – and one in the section on follow-up and review that calls for Indigenous Peoples' participation. The inclusion of Indigenous Peoples is clearly a result of Indigenous Peoples' strong engagement in the process towards the 2030 Agenda, but it is still somewhat puzzling that indigenous and local knowledges do not figure in the SDGS at all.

9 Basil Bernstein's (1971) exploration of working-class children's encounter with the middle-class English classroom is educative in this context. Bernstein tried to account for why working-class children in the UK perform relatively poorly on language-based subjects. The working-class children employ, according to Bernstein, a restricted language code learnt at home (primary discourse), whereas middle-class children use an elaborated language code also learnt at home. Since the classroom in the UK is middle class in a linguistic sense (using the elaborated language codes), the working-class children are exposed to an alien culture at school which impacts negatively on learning. It does not necessarily mean that the working-class children have a more limited vocabulary, but that they use language in a different way suitable in their working class contexts. The restricted language code is economical and rich, and conveys a lot of meaning with relatively few words. The problem is that this condensed way of communicating is not appreciated in the classroom.

References

Acemoglu, D. and Robinson, J. A. (2013). *Why Nations Fail: The Origins of Power, Prosperity and Poverty.* Profile Books Ltd., London.

Ansell, B. W. (2008). "Traders, Teachers, and Tyrants: Democracy, Globalization, and Public Investment in Education." *International Organization*, 62(2): 289–322.

Ansell, B. W. (2010). *From the Ballot to the Blackboard. The Redistributive Political Economy of Education.* Cambridge University Press, Cambridge.

Bernstein, B. (1971). *Class, Codes and Control, Vol. I. Theoretical Studies towards a Sociology of Language*. Routledge & Kegan Paul, London.

Bhattacharya, T. ed. (2017). *Social Reproduction Theory Remapping Class, Recentering Oppression*. Pluto Press, London.

Blackledge, D. and Hunt, B. (1985). *Sociological Interpretations of Education*. Routledge, London.

Botha, L. and Breidlid, A. (2014). Addressing the Root Causes of Our Poor Literacy Results. *Cape Argus*, Cape Town.

Bouzekri, D. (2015). "The Role of Education as Human Capital and a Determinant of Economic Growth." Morocco World News, New York.

Bray, M., Adamson, B. and Mason, M. (2007). *Comparative Education Research: Approaches and Methods*. Comparative Education Research Centre. University of Hong Kong, Hong Kong.

Breidlid, A. (2013). *Education, Indigenous Knowledges and Development in the Global South. Contesting Knowledges for a Sustainable Future*. ISBN: 978-0-415-89589-7. Routledge, London.

Breidlid, H. (2014). Tekstkompetanse og metabevissthet i RLE: Funn fra en kvalitativ studie i to flerkulturelle 10. klasser. Kleve, Bodil; Penne, Sylvi; Skaar, Håvard (eds.). *Literacy og fagdidaktikk i skole og lærerutdanning*. Kapittel 5. s. 106–148. Novus Forlag, Oslo.

Busemeyer, M. R. and Trampusch, C. (2011). Review Article: Comparative Political Science and the Study of Education. *British Journal of Political Science*, 41: 413–443.

Clark, Burton R. (1983). *The Higher Education System: Academic Organization in Cross-National Perspective*. University of California Press, Berkeley.

Daily Monitor, Uganda (September 26, 2016). Government Starts Probe into Teachers' Skills. Accessed at www.monitor.co.ug/News/Education/Government-starts-probe-teachers-skills/688336-3394684-pbgvln/index.html on July 3 2019.

Dei, G. J. S., Hall, B. L., Rosenberg, D. G., eds. (2000). *Indigenous Knowledges in Global Contexts: Multiple Readings of Our World*. Buffalo in association with University of Toronto Press, Toronto.

Diamond, J. (2005). *Collapse. How Societies Choose to Fail or Survive*. Viking Press, New York.

Durkheim, E. (1922). *Education and Sociology*. French original edition: *Education et Sociologie*, published posthumously, Alcan Press, Paris. Translated into English as *Education and Sociology* in 1956 (by Sherwood T. Fox). Free Press, New York.

Einhorn, E. S. and Logue, J. (2003). *Modern Welfare States: Scandinavian Politics and Policy in the Global Age*. Praeger, Westport.

Freire, P. (1970). *Pedagogy of the Oppressed*. Penguin Group, London.

Gee, J. P. (1999). *An Introduction to Discourse Analysis: Theory and Method*. Routledge, London and New York.

Gee, J. P. (2012). *Social Linguistics and Literacies: Ideology in Discourses*, 4th Edition. Routledge, London and New York.

Gramsci, A. (1971). *Selections from the Prison Notebooks*. International Publishers, New York.

Hoffman, P. (2008). *Reforming Basic Education in South Africa*. Centre for Constitutional Rights, F.W. de Klerk Foundation, Cape Town.

Howie, S., et al. (2017). *Progress in International Reading Literacy Study 2016 South African Children's Reading Literacy Achievement.* Pirls Literacy, University of Pretoria, Pretoria.

Iversen, T. and Stephens, J. D. (2008). "Partisan Politics, the Welfare State, and Three Worlds of Human Capital Formation." *Comparative Political Studies,* 41 (4–5): 600–637.

Jones, P. W. (2007). "Education and World Order." *Comparative Education,* 43(3): 325–337.

Kuokkanen, R. J. (2006). "Indigenous Peoples on Two Continents: Self-Determination Processes in Sámi and First Nations Societies." *European Review of Native American Studies,* 20(2): 25–30.

Lindert, P. (2004). *Growing Public: Social Spending and Economic Growth since the Eighteenth Century.* Cambridge University Press, Cambridge.

Matasa, C. (2008). "Africa: Why the Richest Continent Is also the Poorest." Accessed at https://climateandcapitalism.com/2008/09/05/africa-why-the-richest-continent-is-also-the-poorest/ on June 6 2019.

McDonald, C. (2015). How Many Earths Do We Need? Accessed at www.bbc.com/news/magazine-33133712 on April 5 2018.

Morris, I. (2011). *Why the West Rules- for Now.* Farrar, Straus and Giroux, New York.

Nair, C. (2018). *The Sustainable State: The Future of Government, Economy, and Society.* Berrett-Koheler, Oakland.

New World Wealth. (2015). https://businesstech.co.za/news/wealth/125197/the-richest-and-poorest-countries-in-africa/

Oghenekohwo, J. E. and Frank-Oputu, E. A. (2017). "Literacy Education and Sustainable Development in Developing Societies." *Journal of Education and Literacy Studies,* 5(2): 126–131.

Rouse, C. E., and Barrow, L. (2009). "School Vouchers and Students Achievements: Recent Evidence and Remaining Questions". *Annual Review of Economics,* 1: 17–42.

Šlaus, I. and Jacobs, G. (2011). Human capital and sustainability." *Sustainability,* 3(1): 97–154.

Stevens, M. L., Armstrong, E. A. and Arum, R. (2008). "Sieve, Incubator, Temple, Hub: Empirical and Theoretical Advances in the Sociology of Higher Education". *Annual Review of Sociology,* 34: 127–151.

Stigliz, J. (2012). "Africa's Natural Resources Can be a Blessing, Not an Economic Curse." Accessed at www.theguardian.com/business/economics-blog/2012/aug/06/africa-natural-resources-economic-curse on November 6 2019.

Sysiharju, A. L. (1981). "Primary Education and Secondary Schools." In *Nordic Democracy,* E. Allhardt et al. (eds.). Det Danske Selskab, Copenhagen, 419–443.

UNESCO (2005). Understanding Literacy: A Concept Paper. Accessed at https://unesdoc.unesco.org/ark:/48223/pf0000145986 on December 16 2019.

UNESCO (2006). Education for All. Global Monitoring Report. www.unesco.org/education/GMR2006/full/chapt8_eng.pdf. UNESCO, Paris.

UNESCO (2011). Education for All Global Monitoring Report: The Hidden Crisis: Armed conflict and education. UNESCO, Paris.

UNESCO (2015). The 2015 Global Monitoring Report – *Education for All 2000–2015: Achievements and Challenges.* UNESCO, Paris.

UNESCO (2017). *Literacy Rates Continue to Rise from One Generation to the Next.* Accessed at http://uis.unesco.org/sites/default/files/documents/fs45-literacy-rates-continue-rise-generation-to-next-en-2017_0.pdf on May 6 2019.

UNESCO UIS – UNESCO Institute for Statistics (2018). "Adult literacy rate population 15+ years." Accessed at https://en.wikipedia.org/wiki/List_of_countries_by_literacy_rate#cite_note-UNESCO-3 on December 6 2019.

UNESCO UIS – UNESCO Institute for Statistics. South Africa | n.d. Accessed at http://uis.unesco.org/en/country/za on October 3 2019.

UNESCO UIS – UNESCO Institute for Statistics. South Africa (2019). Accessed at http://uis.unesco.org/en/topic/literacy?page=1 on July 14 2019.

United Nations (2015a). The Millennium Development Goals Report. Accessed at www.un.org/millenniumgoals/2015_MDG_Report/pdf/MDG%202015%20rev%20%28July%201%29.pdf on January 5 2020.

United Nations (2015b). *Sustainable Development Goals.* Accessed at www.un.org/sustainabledevelopment/sustainable-development-goals/SDGs on June 5 2019.

2 Indigenous knowledges, education and media in Australia

Lisa Waller

Introduction: linking theory to the ground

Indigenous people(s) think and interpret the world and its everyday realities in ways that are different from non-Indigenous Peoples because of their relationship to land, their cultures, histories and values (Rigney, 1999). However, Indigenist researchers[1] have demonstrated that one of the legacies of scientific racialisation and its ideology has been to discount Indigenous knowledges and instead construct understanding about Indigenous people(s) through the 'common sense' colonial view (Rigney, 2006; Smith, 2004). In doing so, they have revealed the ways in which Eurocentric epistemologies reproduce and reaffirm the cultural assumptions of 'the world' and the 'real' by the dominant group (Denzin & Lincoln, 2008; Jones et al., 1998; Smith, 2004). Australian sociologist Raewyn Connell (2013) argues this intellectual hegemony 'makes other logics of knowledge seem exotic, objectionable or downright crazy' (2013: 9).

Land is enormously important in Indigenous thought and politics in Australia, but it is a topic that receives little attention in Eurocentric social theory (Connell, 2013) where globalisation is a dominant idea. This theory rests on the concept of time-space compression (Harvey, 1990), where modernity tears 'space' from 'place'. In sharp relief, Indigenous people(s) have knowledge systems that involve thinking from, and with, the land and the sea. Connell observes more generally of Indigenous cultures, 'land and sea are not just geographical co-ordinates but a concrete presence in social reality' (Connell, 2012: 212). She calls for researchers to link theory 'to the ground in which their boots are planted' (Connell, 2007: 206). This approach is described as 'dirty theory', which has been defined as theorising mixed up with specific situations: 'The goal of dirty theory is not to subsume, but to clarify; not to classify from outside, but to illuminate a situation in its concreteness' (Connell, 2007: 207). There are strong parallels here with what Michael Christie (2013) describes as the 'complex task' of taking seriously both Indigenous and Western academic knowledge practices. He describes non-Indigenous knowledge practices as: 'top down research [which] seeks for a general overarching theory'. He contrasts this with 'ground-up'

Indigenous knowledge systems, 'which develop and deploy theory in the service of action on local problems' (Christie, 2013: 4).

Connection with the environment and the universe, expressed as spirituality, has helped Indigenous people survive the brutality and intergenerational effects of Australia's colonisation (Atkinson, 2002; Delauney, 2013). Armed with this knowledge, Indigenous researchers and communities are increasingly turning away from the failure of Western 'solutions' to focus on Indigenous epistemologies and experience to address the social legacies of colonisation (Delauney, 2013). For example, researchers such as Judy Atkinson (2002) are working with this strength and drawing on Indigenous epistemologies to develop practical programmes for bringing about well-being in traumatised First Nations communities. Atkinson (2002) draws on the concept of *Dadirri* (Ungunmerr-Baumann, 2002),[2] which emphasises the importance of relationships – with self, with family and community, as well as the environment. For many Indigenous, feminist and materialist scholars, the essence of being comes about through relationships, and it is through these connections that deep listening and sustainable dialogues occur. Respectful relationships are the foundation for ethical research with Indigenous people, who have become highly critical of the research undertaken on their communities (see Smith, 2004 on this important topic). Dadirri provides a way for respectfully engaging, a way of listening and a form of interaction for research with Indigenous people. I have argued elsewhere that taking Dadirri as a starting point also expands the researcher's worldview and opens our ears to other Indigenous epistemologies and how we might engage with them in respectful and ethical ways (Waller, 2018).

This chapter documents and discusses my attempts as a non-Indigenous researcher to engage with Indigenous social theories in two studies about media and Indigenous education.[3] The first took a historical approach to understanding the relationships between news media and a campaign to save bilingual education programs in Australia's Northern Territory (McCallum & Waller, 2017a; Waller, 2012; Waller & McCallum, 2014). The second examined the news media's role in generating and perpetuating the deficit discourse attached to Indigenous identity in the field of Indigenous education (Waller et al., 2018). The key aim in both studies has been to undertake research that respects and serves the self-determined goals and interests of the Indigenous people who participated in the projects.

Study 1: Yolngu social theory and the media campaign to save bilingual education

Yolngu people from North-East Arnhem Land in Australia's Northern Territory often use water as a theoretical tool (Mundine, 1999). The estuarine area of a river is distinctive because it has different plant and animal species along its banks and in its waters, and this special ecology, notable for its constant renewal from fresh and salt water mixing and returning, is known as *ganma* (Marika, et al., 2009). Yolngu also use water as a metaphor to describe a different kind of mixing: bringing into concert non-Indigenous thought from overseas (salt water) and Indigenous wisdom from the land (fresh water) to create new life and new ways of thinking. Marika (1999) says while *ganma* is a social theory, it is first and foremost a place – Ganma Lagoon. It is a still body of water inside the mangroves near Yirrkala, where the salt water from the sea meets the fresh water from the land:

> The water circulates silently underneath, and there are lines of foam circulating across the surface. The swelling and retreating of the tides and the wet season floods can be seen in the two bodies of water. Water is often taken to represent knowledge in Yolngu philosophy.
>
> (Marika, 1999: 7)

Yirrkala is a settlement with a population of about 1,500 people. Yolngu people of the area are intimately connected to the Laynhapuy Homelands, which stretch 300–400 kilometres down the Northern Territory coast of the Gulf of Carpentaria. The concept of *ganma* is a key educational philosophy in Yirrkala and the homelands, which have run bilingual/bicultural education programs since 1974 and are collectively referred to as '*Yambirrpa* schools'. *Yambirrpa* means 'fish trap' and is another important metaphor for Yolngu educational philosophy.[4] Thirteen Yolngu clans share governance of two schools, and they have faced many challenges since the 1970s to maintain their distinctive curriculum, including government attempts to scrap, or significantly dilute the policy of bilingual education (Waller, 2012). The threat against bilingual programmes is directly linked to Sustainable Development Goal No. 4: 'Ensure inclusive and equitable quality education and promote lifelong learning opportunities for all' (United Nations, np). In response to this threat, Yolgnu have used media as a tool to defend their human rights to culturally appropriate education in their own language.

Yolgnu epistemologies, Indigenous education and political action

Aboriginal and Torres Strait Island social theories encompass the traditional owners' relationship to land, the significance of land and kinship to conceptualisations of collective discussion and decision making, as well as 'the complex dialectic of place and power' (Connell, 2007: 209). Some scholars have looked to these theories to understand Aboriginal processes of public discussion and political action. Notably, Tafler (2005), extending on O'Regan (1993), draws on Anangu social theory to ground his study of the workings of the public sphere on the Anangu[5] lands in Central Australia during the 'Rolling Thunder' community radio campaign. This study focuses on Anangu social practices and approaches the 'specific setting' on their lands in a respectful and ethical way as an integral part of the methodology (Tafler, 2005). In accordance with the principles of Indigenous research ethics (Australian Institute for Aboriginal and Torres Strait Islander Studies, 2010), they are factors Tafler has built into his research explicitly, thought about reflexively and declared openly as part of the research design and discussed as part of the results (Smith, 2004: 14). The analysis presented here is informed by this approach.

The non-Indigenous way of defining bilingual education is to explain it as an approach to schooling and curriculum organisation that uses two languages as the medium of instruction in a well-planned and formally organised programme (Hoogenraad, 2001). Devlin says it has another meaning for Yolngu: 'Bilingual, bicultural education is a tool for survival in a fast-changing, often confusing world' (Devlin, 2009: 2). Christie (2013) recalled why the bilingual curriculum instituted by Yolngu elders at Yirrkala Community School was called *garma*:

> In Yolngu languages, *garma* refers to an open ceremonial space where people from different ancestral and totemic lineages work together to produce a collaborative performance and celebration of history and ways forward, here and now.
>
> (Christie, 2013: 4)

The *garma* bilingual curriculum was deeply rooted in Yolngu epistemology. It involved identifying, respecting and maintaining differences, working collaboratively, coming to agreement, building agreed ways of knowing and going ahead together (Ngurruwutthun, 1991).

In December 1998, the Northern Territory Government made a media announcement that it was abolishing bilingual education programs (Hoogenraad, 2001). There was no parliamentary debate or community consultation, and the Government did not produce any data comparing bilingual and non-bilingual schools and their students' achievements (Hill, 2008; Nicholls, 2005). Indigenous communities and their supporters rallied in defence of bilingual education. This included Yolngu co-ordinating a sophisticated campaign with a strong media component under the slogan 'Don't cut off our tongues'. The arguments they put forward were based on four key elements: social identity, educational outcomes, language endangerment and human rights (Waller & McCallum, 2014). The campaign helped to generate a strong community backlash that culminated in the presentation of the largest petition ever received by the Northern Territory Government at that time (Simpson et al., 2009). In the same period, an independent inquiry into Indigenous education in the Northern Territory (Collins, 1999) recommended retaining bilingual education, and in response to these pressures, the government relented, and a watered down version of the bilingual programs was 're-badged' as 'Two-Way Learning' (Nicholls, 2005). This policy remained in place until October 2008, when the Government attempted to axe the programs again.

Decision-making circles and relationship to land

Indigenous people throughout the Northern Territory used Indigenous media to hear about, discuss and organise their campaign to retain bilingual education. However, at the epicentre of the campaign, traditional decision-making processes determined its direction. Yolngu use water, fire and ceremonial metaphors to describe and explain the operation of their governance processes, which are not public or democratic, as only certain people have the authority to speak about certain things:

> When our ancestors the *Djan'kawu* travelled through the land they made waterholes. These waterholes were perfect circles. Our *gurrutu*, kinship structures, are also circular ... traditional owner clan groups gather around the fire in a circle and have equal decision-making power to each other. The fire in the middle is the hearth, it represents a place where people talk, where the fire burns. This is the *wanga*, home, where you feel most comfortable. The coals, *lirrwi*, date you back to the land. This is the connection. The mind is on the land, not in the clouds. This is a system connected to the ground and curved around signifying level headedness. It represents collective, consensus thinking.
>
> (Marika et al., 2009: 409)

The intersecting circles described in the passage above are not abstract. They are a concrete presence in social space, intimately connected to Yolngu peoples' complex kinship structures and their land – to physical relationships and places – and their practices of caring for country (Marika, 1999). The 'Don't cut off our tongues' campaign provides evidence of the power and importance of these governance practices in informing activity in this specific Indigenous public sphere, which is shaped by land, culture and kinship (Marika et al., 2009). However, participants also identified a number of other circles that were active and connected. These included networks of Indigenous and non-Indigenous organisations and communities throughout the Northern Territory. These spheres are linked through land, kinship systems and personal relations, organisational networks, common interests and Indigenous media.[6]

The importance of collective, consensus thinking is evident in Yolngu governance structures, such as the school council, where decision-making powers are shared among clans and represented by a circle (Waller, 2017). Yolngu explain that:

> In our community, solutions come from the ground up – from the relationships, practices and shared or negotiated understandings that arise from working together. The real decision-making is done outside

of formal *Ngapaki*[7] structures, through Yolngu relationships and processes making sure that the right people make the decisions for the right
country.

(Marika et al., 2009: 406)

The Yirrkala School principal at the time of the 'Don't cut off our tongues'
campaign reflected on the importance of traditional governance processes
to its success. It was within the school council that slogans were devised;
political strategies were planned and a sophisticated media plan was put in
place. Yolngu decided to deal directly with Indigenous media outlets, and a
media consultant was hired by the school council to handle the mainstream
news media. She succeeded in attracting and managing national media interest that brought journalists to the 'remote' Laynhapuy Homelands and
the school at Yirrkala. Importantly, this strategy enabled Yolngu to articulate their policy position from their land to the national stage. Media coverage included several major television and radio documentaries, as well as
mainstream newspaper coverage and commentary.

Yolngu participants insisted that speaking from their land was crucial.
One senior teacher said journalists and politicians needed to visit her home-
land at Garrathalala, because showing them her land and culture was the
only way she could explain (and they could understand) the significance of
the bilingual program for the community: 'My strength, my strength is *here*',
she insisted during our research interview, pointing across the land and out
to sea.

The media consultant said her job was made easy because through their
traditional governance practices in the school and community councils,
Yolngu elders had discussed the issue at length, developed the positions
they wanted to take in the debate, decided who would speak on their behalf
and devised detailed strategies for challenging the Government. Another
participant recalled the detailed deliberations within the Nambarra School
Council: 'They developed a post-card ... and that was the slogan, if you're
going to do this, you're going to cut off our tongues, and they used that very
effectively'. She said that through their governance processes, 'the school
council were unified on the issue and very clear', so their position could be
stated simply, through media releases and in interviews with mainstream
journalists.

Marika et al. (2009) share two Yolngu metaphors – *Ngathu* the cycad nut
and *Yambirrpa* the fish trap – to explain the decision-making practices that
ensure unity and clarity. These can be understood to underpin their public
sphere activities:

> *Ngathu* identifies the need for right process, to make sure that the cy-
> anide is leached from the cycad nut so it can be prepared into sacred
> bread. If decision making, like the *ngathu*, has not gone through the
> right processes, the poison will remain. *Yambirrpa* is about working

together in partnership because if one of the rocks in the fish trap is removed, the fish will escape.

(Marika et al., 2009)

Discussing the importance of these Yolngu governance structures and forums to the public campaign for bilingual education, a leading Yolngu educator said the elders needed 'to create the space for us to express ourselves ... this became a collaborative project between community and clans' (in Marika, 1999: 9).

Indigenous media: transforming traditional forums

Indigenous Australians had their own communication systems for tens of thousands of years before colonisation and continue to use them in a wide range of contemporary ways (Molnar & Meadows, 2001; Tafler, 2005). One dimension of this is the development of Indigenous media – a worldwide phenomenon in which media is used as a tool in the struggle for cultural and political change – allowing the marginalised to 'speak as well as hear' (Alia, 2010). Indigenous media, especially community radio, provided a key forum for Yolgnu to share news and views about the bilingual policy debate and the 'Don't cut off our tongues' campaign. Participants underlined the central role of Indigenous media outlets as extensions of their traditional forums for people to deliberate together and advance their own policy discourses (Forde et al., 2009). Tafler (2005) argues that this represents a broadening and deepening of democratic practice. The Indigenous media system moves information horizontally, rather than it having to follow the traditional vertical flow down from the elders who speak for certain people and land. Participants said that Indigenous community radio in particular allowed people across Arnhem Land and throughout the Northern Territory to follow the issue as it unfolded and provided everyone with an opportunity to speak. Media technologies accelerate the speed of discussion, which helps to crystallise the issue.

The media consultant said Yolngu were confident in their ability to work with Indigenous community radio and TV on the 'Don't cut off our tongues' campaign because they interacted with them on a regular basis. They were enthusiastic about discussing the issue with Indigenous audiences: 'The people out there, they utilise Indigenous media a lot of the time off their own bat anyway. They knew them and they just worked them'.

Participants described the longstanding relationships between Indigenous media organisations and their sources from the Yolngu community as confident. and familiar. One recalled that when the national Indigenous television program *Living Black* visited her community, she not only participated in an interview but contributed to making the program about the 'Don't cut off our tongues' campaign by getting behind the television camera to record her own vision.

Voices from the land

Established Indigenous leaders can exert considerable influence in public and policy discussion through their use of both Indigenous media and the mainstream news media. Both provide platforms for advancing their agendas and taking on their opponents (McCallum et al., 2012). Yolngu leaders' legitimacy to speak is directly related to their relationship to land and kinship structures. Marika et al. (2009) say:

> On Yolngu land, people have their own leaders, people look after those places. We have to talk to the right people for the right place. We talk about communal decision making through the metaphor of berley, the berley you use when catching fish. The right people hear of that berley and come in their own time to talk. Time is flexible. Disagreements are discussed, often in family groups, there is not one person making the decisions.
>
> (Marika et al., 2009: 409)

It is important to note that the specific and complex cultural relationships that govern who can speak and when in Yolgnu society do not apply in other Aboriginal and Torres Strait Islander communities. There were more than 500 different 'clan' groups or 'nations' around the continent – many with distinctive cultures, beliefs and languages – before 1788 when the British arrived. The ongoing processes of settler colonialism have resulted in dispossession, destruction and disadvantage that play out differently in Indigenous communities across the country. Once consequence is that while some groups such as Yolgnu continue to practice ancient decision-making processes in their own languages, others may only speak English and have adapted some westernised forms of deliberation to suit their own contexts.

Study 2: Shifting deficit discourse in Indigenous education

Attacks on bilingual education programmes over many years have been based in arguments that students in 'remote' Aboriginal communities must learn in English only if they are to succeed at school. This policy and media narrative can be understood as a 'deficit discourse'. It contravenes Article 14 of the UN Declaration on the Rights of Indigenous People that recognises the right of First Nations people(s) to provide education in their own languages, in a manner appropriate to their cultural methods of teaching and learning. The Deficit Discourse and Indigenous Education[8] project has investigated the prevalence and impact of deficit discourses that frame and represent Aboriginal identity in a narrative of negativity, deficiency and disempowerment and explores ways to shift it. Deficit discourses in education are counterproductive, circular and persistent. In their research on the topic, Comber and Kamler (2004: 298) have observed that panics, crises and 'failures' of individuals, groups, schools and states are produced by the very same discourses that constitute and blame certain groups in society as lacking and responsible for their lack.

Recent work shows that deficit discourse surrounding Aboriginality is intricately entwined across different sites of representation, including the mainstream news media and Indigenous education policy (Fforde et al., 2013; Fogarty et al., 2017; Gorringe et al., 2011; McCallum & Waller, 2017a). Mithaka man, educator and researcher Scott Gorringe (2015) argues that 'when all the thinking, all the conversations and all the approaches are framed in a discourse that sees Aboriginality as a problem, very little positive movement is possible'. The Deficit Discourse project has responded to this by exploring ways to counteract the prevalence of deficit mentality in schools, communities, policy and mainstream media and understanding how such positive movements can improve the educational outcomes of Indigenous students. A major component was an action research intervention called Engoori® (Gorringe & Spillman, 2008), which was mobilised as part of the research at selected Australian schools.

The Engoori story belongs to *Koorithulla Tjimpa* (Black Hawk) of the Mithaka people of far south-west Queensland and was traditionally used in the *wurthumpa* ceremony as a method of diplomacy between conflicting ideologies and groups. In 2006, Gorringe and Spillman gained permission from Gorringe's old people to reinterpret the Mithaka ceremony,[9] and extend the concept and its related processes as a strength-based facilitation process for organisations, school leadership and in the classroom as a way of enabling and encouraging a shift away from a deficit mindset (Gorringe et al., 2011). It achieves this through recognition that people possess a range of strengths and by focusing on what keeps them strong. Engoori offers a guide to facilitating dialogues that can reaffirm strengths in communities; create safe spaces to change deficit conversations to ones of strength; as well as revealing and challenging the assumptions people bring to such conversations and co-creating powerful ways to address complex challenges (Gorringe, 2011). Prosser and colleagues (2015: 22) argue that through such a framework, Indigenous people can ensure all voices are heard; discuss historical perspectives and 'value add' to assets identified in the community. As such, Engoori provides both a methodological and analytical framework through which to examine contemporary Indigenous education discourses. An emerging finding of the research is 'that once people begin challenging the [deficit discourse] it changes the conversation about what is possible in Indigenous education and policy' (Fogarty & Wilson, 2016).

Engoori® as a methodological framework

At the start of the project in 2015, many of the seven-member research team knew little about the Engoori® process, or the social theory that underpins it. Scott Gorringe provided a workshop so everyone could experience and understand the principles and the practice, and how these could be used in the action research phase of the research to shift deficit thinking among teachers, students and school communities. Afterwards, through the cyclic steps of listening, reflecting, observing the feelings and actions of Indigenous people affected by the punitive Remote School Attendance Strategy (RSAS), and re-listening at deeper levels of understanding and knowledge building, the power of Engoori as a tool for research that can privilege Indigenous voices and shift perspectives became apparent. In a sub-project on news media representations of the RSAS (Waller et al., 2018), Engoori was extended as a methodological framework for examining how Indigenous people are using their own media forms to reveal and resist what we termed 'the truancy trap': a simplistic and powerful discourse of deficit that saturates mainstream media and government policy relating to 'remote'.[10] Indigenous school attendance and suppresses its historical, institutional, spatial and cultural contexts and complexities (Gorringe, 2011; Prout, 2009).

Australian Government policy initiatives over the past decade or more in Indigenous education aim to 'close the gap' between Indigenous and non-Indigenous educational outcomes. Authorised through the 2008 Council of Australian Governments (COAG) reform agenda, the policy framework is based on assumptions about the relationship between increased school attendance and increased student performance on standardised tests in English language (Australian Government, 2017; Ladwig & Luke, 2014). The policy is complicated by the controversial Federal Government 'Intervention', introduced in 2007 and later modified by subsequent administrations, that involves withholding welfare payments from those Indigenous parents whose children were reportedly missing school. The focus was intensified with the Remote School Attendance Strategy (known as RSAS) (Department of Prime Minister & Cabinet, 2017), which was introduced for two years from 2014. In 2015, the Federal Government announced it was extending the $28.4 million RSAS program for another three years to target schools with attendance rates below 70% from 1998 to 2014. At the time of writing, it operated in 77 schools across 74 'remote' Indigenous communities in five Australian states. RSAS funds a range of initiatives, including the employment of local people as school attendance supervisors, and is outsourced to the privately owned National Employment Services Association. The most recent Closing the Gap report indicated there had been no real change in school attendance, with Northern Territory rates falling by 1.6% (Australian Government, 2017).

A positive approach to media representation and media change

The Engoori research approach focused on Indigenous media as tools of resilience, resistance and education used by and for Aboriginal and Torres Strait Islander peoples to achieve their self-determined aims on school attendance and education more broadly. Engoori was activated to shift the researchers' thinking and develop a positive approach to media representation and media change. This was achieved by adopting a different starting point to where most scholarship about news media representation of Indigenous people and issues begins, which is with negative news framing, racist representation and a lack of Indigenous voice (McCallum & Waller, 2017b).

In the tradition of other Indigenous methodologies, especially Dadirri (Ungunmerr-Bauman, 2002; West et al., 2012) and 'Red Dirt Thinking' (Guenther et al., 2014; Lester et al., 2013), we connected Engoori with elements of critical theory, specifically Freire's (1990 [1970]) transformative education process. From the outset, Indigenist research has been closely entwined with the traditions of critical theory, which is guided by the goal of liberating people from domination, powerlessness and oppression (Rigney, 1999). For Freire (1970), and in Engoori→Gorringe et al., 2011), deep dialogue with structure, purpose and process provides the foundation of communication for positive change and takes place through an equal relationship among people. Engoori→ is a practice of deep conversation and co-creating transformative pathways. In the context of research, it is a method that enables working with Indigenous people and allowing their voices to be heard. Like Freire's transformational framework, Engoori provides a process for working through the challenges of how to create a space for what can be, and then co-creating it. As Freire explained: 'Thematic investigation becomes a common striving towards awareness of reality and self, thus making it a starting point for the educational process or for cultural action of a liberating character' (Freire, 1990 [1970]: 79).

Engoori provided the process for a thematic investigation of relevant historical, policy and Indigenous media texts related to 'remote' school attendance during the period when the issue was in the policy and media spotlight (2013–2017) (Waller et al., 2018). Three sets of data captured the diversity of contemporary Indigenous media from national Indigenous television and commercial print media, to community media and social media. Engoori guided all phases of the research, beginning with a question about how as Indigenous and non-Indigenous researchers working together we could contribute to affirming community strengths and relationships around 'remote' Indigenous school attendance. In order to provide background and context, we began with 'surfacing and challenging' the assumptions embedded through the trope of truancy, informing government policy and fuelling the deficit framing of 'remote' education in mainstream media. The data analysis provided evidence of Indigenous people using their own media to interrupt the dominant deficit discourse about school attendance (see Waller et al., 2018). As was the case in the 'Don't Cut Off Our Tongues' bilingual education campaign of the 1990s, Indigenous community media was used in relation to school attendance measures to assert the Aboriginal position on whose knowledges and whose reality counts in discussions of 'remote' education. The importance of children learning how to 'walk in both worlds', gaining English language and numeracy skills as well as opportunities to learn Indigenous knowledges and languages at school was a key message. The research found Indigenous media provided tools for affected communities to resist the 'truancy trap' in mainstream policy and media discourses and facilitated strength-based conversations about attendance and what constitutes 'success' in 'remote' schools and communities (Waller et al., 2018). There was no suggestion in Indigenous community media that attendance is not important to Indigenous people, or that Aboriginal and Torres Strait Islander children should not go to school. Indeed, our analysis demonstrated that promoting school attendance was high on the agenda across all the Indigenous media outlets in the sample during the study period.

Another important observation from the data was that Indigenous people work within the same broader discourses as non-Indigenous policymakers, media and public, but conduct the conversation in ways that are underpinned by cultural and local contexts, priorities and understandings. The community media data in this case provided rich evidence of people using their own broadcast and digital channels to innovate and reconstruct culturally appropriate messages for their local communities (Waller et al., 2018).

Examining Indigenous media discussion of 'remote' school attendance through the Engoori framework showed that when Aboriginal perspectives on education are paid proper attention, the range of issues and experiences is far more diverse than mainstream media and policy discourse suggests. An emerging finding from the wider research suggests the wealth of First Nations perspectives expressed via Indigenous media were not picked up or amplified by mainstream outlets (McCallum & Waller, 2017a). However, the narrow perspectives they decided to sponsor were in fact challenged, broadened and reframed in mediated discussion of education in Indigenous-led media. Engoori also shows us that 'strength-based' doesn't just mean 'positive'. It means confronting complex problems and creating a culturally safe space to sustain dialogues about how to reconstruct deficit conversations to strength-based ones.

Conclusions

In both cases discussed here, the research aim and project designs involved working with Indigenous knowledges 'in the service of action on local problems' (Christie, 2013: 4). Indigenous social theories including Dadirri, Ganma and Engoori are powerful tools for surfacing and problematising the deficit thinking inherent in the Western view of Indigenous people, but even more powerfully, to shift attention to Aboriginal and Torres Strait Islander peoples' strengths and provide safe forums for exploring the complex challenges that result from colonisation. For example, by exchanging a deficit lens for a strength-based one, it quickly becomes clear that on the subject of school attendance and education more broadly, Indigenous communities are saying and doing many innovative, positive and important things based in their physical and spiritual connections; reporting and discussing issues in their own media; and developing local policy responses grounded in their lore/law and their land.

For researchers who want to engage in ethical and responsible relationships with Indigenous communities and undertake projects that are based in their lands and serve their self-determined aims, Indigenous social theory opens up different knowledge practices and opportunities for dialogue. There has not been space here to discuss the Yolngu philosophy of education in detail (see Christie, 2000, 2009 on this important topic). However, it has much to offer scholarship and society, as Yolgnu bilingual/bicultural pedagogy is based in thinking and creating in new ways and new relationships involving both non-Indigenous and Indigenous knowledges and people (Marika, 1999). Yolngu scholars contend that non-Indigenous people often fail to recognise or understand their thinking, processes and activities because they are limited within non-Indigenous theories and traditions:

> Indigenous specific cultural and decision-making structures are ... imagined as being 'remote' from the 'mainstream'. For Indigenous Australians, however, it is connection to country, to our physical and spiritual homelands, that makes one feel 'in place' ... we argue that bureaucrats, policymakers, researchers and others wishing to work with Indigenous people need to learn to see outside their own cultural frameworks.
>
> (Marika et al., 2009)

Accepting this invitation to look beyond Eurocentric approaches and engage with Indigenous knowledges, practices and epistemologies connected to the land can open up a new range of frameworks for relationship with First Nations people(s) in research, policy and education practices. Unfortunately, Australian governments have been reluctant to see outside their own cultural frameworks until recently, and the outcomes reflect this. For example, in the Northern Territory under the Remote School Attendance Strategy (RSAS), the school attendance rate actually fell by around five percentage points between 2014 and 2018 (Australian Government, 2019). On the positive side, governments are learning from the outcomes of Indigenous approaches including Engoori and moving away from deficit discourse. For example, in 2019, the RSAS changed to have a stronger focus on engagement with communities and increasing local decision-making. The Australian Government said: 'The strategy will work to build stronger linkages with state and territory governments and schools, broadening its focus from "getting kids to school" to "keeping kids in school"' (Australian Government, 2019). The Northern Territory Indigenous Languages and Cultures Curriculum has also been revised through a process led by Indigenous educators from across the Northern Territory (Northern Territory Government, 2019). At the heart of the curriculum is cultural knowledge, organised across three strands: Country/Land, People and Kinship, and Natural Environment. The curriculum now caters for diversity across communities by providing four broad learner pathways: first language pathway, language revitalisation, revival and renewal pathway, second language learner pathway and language and cultural awareness pathway. Schools negotiate the choice of the focus language and the best language learning pathway with the school community. It is too early to say how these new policies will shape education outcomes, but they put Australia on a strength-based course for achieving the sustainable development goal of ensuring inclusive and equitable quality education for all (United Nations, np).

Notes

1 Rigney (2006) defines Indigenist research as informed by three fundamental and interrelated principles: involvement in resistance as the emancipatory imperative; political integrity; and giving privilege to Indigenous voices.
2 Dadirri is the language of the Ngangikurungkurr people of Daly River in Australia's Northern Territory. It is also a way of life that encompasses the role of spirituality in Aboriginal culture (West et al., 2012). The functions and principles of Dadirri were articulated in English by respected elder and artist from Daly River, Miriam Rose Ungunmerr-Baumann (2002).
3 Australian Research Council Discovery Project DP0987457 2009–2012: Australian News Media and Indigenous Policymaking 1988–2008 and Australian Research Council Discovery Indigenous Project IN150100007 2015–2018: Deficit Discourse and Indigenous Education: mapping the discursive environment, assessing impact, and changing the conversation.
4 *Yambirrpa* is used to describe how, within the Yolngu philosophy of education, the whole community works together to guide young people into Yolngu foundations for learning. Everyone helps to build the *yambirrpa* from rocks, which represent the elders, and the fish are the children. The children learn inside the *yambirrpa*. Yolngu say sometimes big storms come from the outside which break or fragment the *yambirrpa*. They work together as a community to mend it by putting more rocks in place (Marika et al., 2009).
5 Pitjantjatjara people from Australia's Central Desert refer to themselves as Anagnu, which means 'people' in Pitjantjatjara language.
6 At the time this included newspapers such as *Land Rights News* and the extensive network of remote community radio stations and television, especially commercial satellite licencee Imparja, a community satellite TV network (ICTV) and the terrestrial open narrowcasting service Larrakia TV in Darwin. See (author removed Waller, L., Dreher, T., & McCallum, K. 2015. The listening key: unlocking the democratic potential of Indigenous participatory media. *Media International Australia*, 154, for a detailed snapshot of the contemporary Australian Indigenous media sphere.
7 Ngapaki is a Yolngu term for non-Indigenous people, institutions and ideas.
8 The Deficit Discourse in Indigenous project (IN1501000007) was funded by the Australian Research Council 2015–2017.
9 Personal communication with David Spillman, 3 August 2017.
10 'Remote' appears in scare quotes throughout to problematise the Western centre/periphery assumption inherent in this term when applied to Indigenous communities.

References

Alia, V. (2010). *The new media nation: Indigenous Peoples and global communication*. New York, NY: Berghan Books.

Atkinson, J. (2002). *Trauma trails: Recreating song lines*. North Melbourne, Australia: Spinifex Press.

Australian Government (2017). *Closing the gap: Chapter 3 Education*. Retrieved from: http://closingthegap.pmc.gov.au/education.

Australian Government (2019). Closing the gap. Retrieved from: https://ctgreport.niaa.gov.au/education.html.

Australian Institute for Aboriginal and Torres Strait Islander Studies (2010). *Guidelines for ethical research in Indigenous Studies*. Canberra, ACT: AIATSIS.

Christie, M. (2000). Galtha: The application of Aboriginal philosophy to school learning. *New Horizons in Education*, 103: 3–19.

Christine, M. (2009). Engaging with Australian Indigenous knowledge systems: Charles Darwin University and the Yolgnu of North-East Arnhem Land. *Learning Communities: International Journal of Learning in Social Contexts* (Indigenous Community Engagement Edition), December: 23–35.

Christie, M. (2013). Generative and 'ground-up' research in Aboriginal Australia. *Learning Communities*, 13: 3–12.

Collins, B. (1999). *Learning lessons: An independent review of indigenous education in the Northern Territory*. Darwin, Australia: Northern Territory Department of Education.

Comber, B. and Kamler, B. (2004). Getting out of deficit: Pedagogies of reconnection. *Teaching Education*, 15(3): 293–310.

Connell, R. (2007). *Southern theory: The global dynamics of knowledge in social science*. Cambridge, UK: Polity.

Connell, R. (2012). A Fringe of leaves: Australian modernity and Southern perspectives. *Continuum*, 26(2): 207–214.

Connell, R. (2013). Using southern theory: Decolonising social thought in theory, research and application. *Planning Theory*, 12(4): 1–14.

Delauney, T. (2013). Fractured culture: Educare as a healing approach to indigenous trauma. *International Journal of Science and Society*, 4(1): 52–62.

Denzin, N.K. and Lincoln, Y.S. (2008). Introduction: Critical methodologies and indigenous inquiry. In *Handbook of critical and indigenous methodologies*, eds. N.K. Denzin, Y.S. Lincoln and L.T. Smith, pp. 1–20. Thousand Oaks, CA: Sage.

Department of the Prime Minister and Cabinet (2017). Remote school attendance strategy. Retrieved from: www.pmc.gov.au/indigenous-affairs/education/remote-school-attendance-strategy.

Devlin, B. (2009). *Bilingual education in the Northern Territory and the continuing debate over its effectiveness and value*. National Museum of Australia, Canberra, ACT: AIATSIS. Retrieved from: www.abc.net.au/4corners/special_eds/20090914/language/docs/Devlin_paper.pdf.

Fforde, C., Bamblett, L., Lovett, R., Gorringe S. and Fogarty, B. (2013). Discourse, deficit and identity: Aboriginality, the race paradigm and the language of representation in contemporary Australia. *Media International Australia*, 149: 162–173.

Fogarty, B. and Wilson, B. (2016). Governments must stop negatively framing policies aimed at First Nations people. *Sovereign Union*. Retrieved from: http://

nationalunitygovernment.org/content/governments-must-stop-negatively-framing-policies-aimed-first-nations-people.

Fogarty, W., Riddle, S., Lovell, M. and Wilson, B. (2017). Indigenous education and literacy policy in Australia: Bringing learning back to the debate. *The Australian Journal of Indigenous Education*. doi:10.1017/jie_2017.18.

Forde, S., Foxwell, K. and Meadows, M. (2009). *Developing dialogues: Indigenous and ethnic community broadcasting in Australia*. Bristol, UK: Intellect.

Freire, P. (1990 [1970]). *Pedagogy of the oppressed*. New York, NY: Continuum.

Gorringe, S. (2011). Honouring our strengths – Moving forward. *Education in Rural Australia*, 21(1): 21–37.

Gorringe, S. (2015). Aboriginal culture is not a problem. The way we talk about it is. *The Guardian*, 15 May. Retrieved from: www.theguardian.com/commentisfree/2015/may/15/aboriginal-culture-is-not-a-problem-the-way-we-talk-about-it-is.

Gorringe, S. and Spillman, D. (2008). *Engoori*. Presented at the Stronger Smarter Leadership conference. Stronger, Smarter Indigenous Education Leadership Institute, Bribie Island, Queensland.

Gorringe, S., Ross, J. and Fforde, C. (2011). '*Will the real aborigine please stand up': Strategies for breaking the stereotypes & changing the conversation*. AIATSIS Discussion Paper 28.

Guenther, J., Batt, M. and Osborne, S. (2014). Red dirt thinking on remote educational advantage. *Australian and International Journal of Rural Education*, 24(1): 51–67.

Harvey, D. (1990). *The condition of postmodernity: An enquiry into the origins of cultural change*. Cambridge, MA: Blackwell.

Hill, S. (2008). *Yolngu Matha and English learning at Galiwin'ku, an indigenous community in North-East Arnhem Land*. (PhD doctoral thesis), University of New England: Armidale, NSW.

Hoogenraad, R. (2001). Critical reflections on the history of bilingual education in Central Australia. In *Forty years on*, eds. J. Simpson, D. Nash, M. Laughren, P. Austin and B. Alpher, pp. 123–150. Canberra, ACT: Pacific Linguistics.

Jones, G., Lee, A. and Poynton, C. (1998). Discourse analysis and policy activism: readings and rewritings of Australian university research policy. In *Activism and the policy process*, ed. A. Yeatman, pp. 146–170. St Leonard's, NSW: Allen & Unwin.

Ladwig, J. and Luke, A. (2014). Does improving school attendance lead to improved school level achievement? An empirical study of indigenous education policy in Australia. *Australian Education Research*, 41: 171–194.

Lester, K., Minutjukur, M., Osborne, S. and Tijtayi, K. (2013). *Sidney Myer rural lecture 3: Red dirt curriculum: Re-imagining remote education*. 18 September, Alice Springs Northern Territory. Retrieved from: www.flinders.edu.au/ehl/fms/education_files/coreacom/SM%20Rural%20Lectures/Sidney%20Myer%20Rural%20Lecture%203%20-%20Karina%20Lester%20Makinti%20Minutjukur%20Sam%20Osborne%20Katrina%20Tjitayi-%20for%20Web.pdf.

Marika, R. (1999). The 1998 Wentworth lecture. *Australian Aboriginal Studies*, 1: 3–9.

Marika, R., Yunupingu, Y., Marika-Mununggirtj, R. and S. Muller (2009). Leaching the poison – The importance of process and partnership in working with Yolngu. *Journal of Rural Studies*, 25: 404–413.

McCallum, K. and Waller, L. (2017a). *The dynamics of news and indigenous policy in Australia.* Bristol, UK: Intellect.

McCallum, K. and Waller, L. (2017b). Indigenous media in Australia: Traditions, theories and contemporary practices. In *Minorities and the media in Australia,* eds. J. Buderick and G.S. Han, pp. 134–161. London, UK: Palgrave Macmillan.

McCallum, K., Waller, L. and Meadows, M. (2012). Raising the volume: Indigenous voices in news media and policy. *Media International Australia,* 142: 101–115.

Molnar, H. and Meadows, M. (2001). *Songlines to satellites: Indigenous communication in Australia, the South Pacific and Canada.* Leichhardt, NSW: Pluto Press.

Mundine, D. (1999). *Saltwater – Yirrkala bark paintings of sea country: Recognising indigenous sea rights.* Neutral Bay, NSW: Buku-Larrngay Mulka Centre.

Ngurruwutthun, D. (1991). The garma project. In *Aboriginal pedagogy: Aboriginal teachers speak out,* eds. R. Bunbury, W. Hastings, J. Henry and R. McTaggart, pp. 107–122. Melbourne, Australia: Deakin University Press.

Nicholls, C. (2005). Death by a thousand cuts: Indigenous language bilingual education programmes in the Northern Territory of Australia, 1972–1998. *The International Journal of Bilingual Education and Bilingualism,* 8(2&3): 160–177.

Northern Territory Government (2019). The Northern Territory Indigenous languages and cultures curriculum. Retrieved from: https://education.nt.gov.au/policies/indigenous-languages-and-cultures.

O'Regan, T. (1993). An Aboriginal television culture: Issues, strategies, politics. In *Australian television culture,* eds. T. O'Regan, pp. 169–192. St Leonards, NSW: Allen & Unwin.

Prosser, N., Litchfield, J., Dadleh, P. and Warren, T. (2015). Cultural identity and development within the community of Marree Aboriginal School in Australia. In *Identity, culture and the politics of community development,* ed. S. Wilson, pp. 17–23. Newcastle Upon Tyne, UK: Cambridge Scholars Publishing.

Prout, S. (2009). Policy, practice and the 'revolving classroom door': Examining the relationship between Aboriginal spatiality and the mainstream education system. *Australian Journal of Education,* 53(1): 39–53.

Rigney, L.I. (1999). Internationalization of an indigenous anti-colonial cultural critique of research methodologies: A guide to indigenist research methodology and its principles. *Wicazo Sa Review,* 14(12): 109–121.

Rigney, L. (2006). Indigenist research and Aboriginal Australia. In *Indigenous Peoples' wisdom and power: Affirming our knowledge through narratives,* eds. J. Kunnie and N. Goduka, pp. 32–50. Aldershot, UK: Ashgate.

Simpson, J., Caffery, J., and McConvell, P. (2009). Gaps in Australia's Indigenous language policy: Dismantling bilingual education in the Northern Territory. *AIATSIS Research Discussion Paper, 24.* Retrieved from: www.aiatsis.gov.au/research_program/publications/discussion_papers.

Smith, L.T. (2004). *Decolonising methodologies: Research and Indigenous Peoples.* London, UK: Zed Books.

Tafler, D.I. (2005). Rolling thunder: Changing communication and the Pitjantjatjara Yankunytjatara public sphere. *Pacific Journalism Review,* 11(1): 155–173.

Ungunmerr-Baumann, M.R. (2002). Against racism. *Compass,* 37(3). Retrieved from: http://compassreview.org/spring03/1.html.

Waller, L. (2012). Bilingual education and the language of news. *Australian Journal of Linguistics,* 32(4): 459–472.

Waller, L. (2017). Indigenous public spheres: From the ground up. *Critical Arts*, 30(6): 788–803.

Waller, L. (2018). Indigenous research methodologies and listening the Dadirri way. In *Ethical responsiveness and the politics of difference*, eds. T. Dreher and A. Mondal, pp. 227–242. London, UK: Palgrave Macmillan.

Waller, L. and McCallum, K. (2014). Don't cut off our tongues: Yolngu voices in news media and policymaking. *Communication, Politics and Culture*, 47(1): 18–31.

Waller, L., McCallum, K. and Gorringe, S. (2018). Resisting the truancy trap: Indigenous media and school attendance in 'remote' Australia. *Postcolonial Directions in Education*, 7(2): 122–147.

West, R., Stewart, L., Foster, K. and Usher, L. (2012). Through a critical lens: Indigenist research and the Dadirri method. *Qualitative Health Research*, 22(11): 1582–1590.

3 Forest rights act, local collectivisation and transformation in Korchi[1]

Neema Pathak Broome, Shrishtee Bajpai and Mukesh Shende

Introduction

The world over, Indigenous Peoples and other traditional communities and their habitats are facing destruction due to the demand for industrial growth and development. The peoples and the communities nevertheless are not only resisting the ongoing onslaught of 'accumulation by dispossession' but are also voicing the urgency of looking for fundamental alternatives to the current global order (Singh, Kulkarni and Pathak Broome, 2018). Korchi taluka an administrative sub unit of Gadchiroli district of Maharashtra State in India is one such region. Nearly 75.96% of the total geographic area in Gadchiroli is under forest cover, till recently under the jurisdiction of a highly centralised forest department.

Korchi taluka includes 133 villages or gram sabhas (village assemblies), which were traditionally divided into three *Ilakas* (feudal territories),[2] namely, Kumkot *Ilaka* including 60 gram sabhas; Padyal Job *Ilaka* including 30 gram sabhas and Kodgul *Ilaka* including 40 gram sabhas. Although officially the *taluka* is administered by Gadchiroli district administration, informally and independently the *Ilakas* continue to have their traditional village level to supra village level self-governance structures, mainly addressing socio-cultural issues. As per the 2011 census, the total population of Korchi was 42,844, of which 73% belonged to Scheduled Tribes (STs)[3] mainly Gond and Kanwar adivasi (tribal) communities. Around 8% of the total population is Scheduled Caste (SC).[4]

Almost the entire population of the taluka is heavily dependent on forest/forest resources for cash-based and subsistence livelihood. Collection of fruits, flowers, tubers, leaves, fodder, firewood, honey, wild fruits, wild vegetables, medicinal plants, tubers, meat, for self-consumption and sale of non- timber forest produce (NTFP) such as Bamboo, tendu leaves or bidi leaf (*Diospyros melanoxylon*), mahua flowers (*Madhuca indica*), among others is important for local economy, subsistence and community health. Livelihood is supplemented by daily wage labour on other farms or migration to cities. Dependence on the outside markets for food is minimal, most food requirements are met from agriculture and forests. In addition to forests being important for economy and livelihoods, they are an integral part of the adivasi socio-cultural practices and ceremonies and hence their political identity (Koreti, 2016).

90 out of 133 gram sabhas in Korchi have come together to form a collective that they call Maha Gramsabha (MGS) (a federation of gram sabhas). Similarly, women's self-help groups have formed a federation (Mahila Parisar Sangh) to address traditional discrimination, exclusion and violence against women and to increase women's voice in local traditional and contemporary decision-making institutions. These collectives have also been drivers behind the resist against mining which is being proposed by the state in the sacred forests of some of the villages in Korchi. These collectives are emerging as models of direct democracy and playing a critical role in transforming many local situations such as localising control over economy, reviving cultural identity, raising social and equity concerns, questioning existing models of development, monitoring local health and education, among others.

In Korchi, as in many other parts of India, historically injustices have been perpetuated by external factors such as centralised forest bureaucracy denying local access and use rights, and corporate and state nexus appropriating land and resources; and internal factors such as traditional systems of patriarchy and caste, class discrimination. The processes in Korchi enable us to understand that the existing underlying conditions of overtly unresisted conflict situations arising from these internal and external factors create a situation of dissatisfaction and a need for change. A direct conflict (in this case proposed mining leases) creates a situation of urgency for resistance. And a change in legal environment through laws like the STs and Other Traditional Forest Dwellers (Recognition of Rights) Act 2006 and Panchayat Extension to Scheduled Areas Rule (Maharashtra) 2014 (PESA) driven by conducive causes and conditions could become the enablers for alternatives to emerge. In this chapter, we will look at the emergence of such alternative processes and the factors that enabled their emergence. Finally, we will use the Alternative Transformation Framework (ATF) (Kothari, 2014) as an analytical tool to understand the elements and characteristics of these alternatives.

Methodology

This article is based on the report of a collaborative documentation of the multidimensional process taking place in Korchi. The study was carried out in 2017–2019, by Kalpavriksh (an environmental action group based in Pune, www.kalpavriksh.org) in collaboration with Amhi Amchya Arogayasathi (a local rural health-based organisation) and the MGS (the executive committee of the federation of village assemblies in Korchi). The study was carried out as part of a global project, the Academic-Activist Co-generation of Knowledge on Environmental Justice or ACKnowl-EJ (www.acknowlej.org).

The methodology of this case study developed at the backdrop of addressing the social issues within the wider framework of indigenous methodologies and the need to have ethical guidelines. Hence, the initial few months were spent in discussions with members of Ami Amchya Arogyasaathi (AAA), MGS and local activists about the objectives of the study and its relevance for the local processes. After many discussions, it was decided that the study will focus on the brief history of the social movements in the region, the emergence of the MGS at the backdrop of it, the women's collective at the level of the taluka and the visions of well-being that underlie these processes. The documentation of local history and detailed compilation of the MGS process was required by the community to keep it as a record that can be used as an awareness tool among the people and especially the youth.

The deeper understanding of the context was gained by looking at three villages in detail, namely, Zendepar, Bharitola and Sahle. The three villages were selected keeping in mind time and resource constraints, along with below four pertinent reasons-

a   Zendepar village is directly affected by the proposed mining conflict in the village and has been strongly resisting it.
b   Being immediate neighbours, Bharitola and Sahle although not yet directly impacted by proposed mining stand threatened and are actively supporting the local resistance.
c   All three villages actively involved in building local governance institutions, rules and regulations and are part of the MGS.
d   The local leaders of these villages are also very active and found semblance to the research objective and were willing to contribute to the research process.

In terms of methodologies, various elements like tracing the family genealogy for the three villages, compiling the history of the region, helping in biodiversity mapping in the three villages and helping in other local processes were added after consultation with the MGS members and AAA. To begin with, each Gram Sabha passed a resolution to contribute towards the research process by helping in documenting the history of the village, carrying out bio-diversity surveys, and socio-economic mapping among others. The respondents were suggested and collectively selected by the MGS, AAA members and the authors. The data of socio-economic status, bio-diversity mapping, and data on sale from NTFPs was collected by AAA with the help of MGS members. The methodology involved group discussions, detailed interviews, participation in cultural activities, particularly the village yatras (annual gathering and ceremonies), walking through the forests with the local people and participation in other local activities whenever possible. As part of the study over two years, the authors visited Korchi villages six times between September 2017 and April 2019[5] where general, non-structured conversations were carried out with communities guided through rough draft of questions put together for the study. A total of 30 semi-structured interviews were conducted with MGS activists, community members, AAA members, Mahila Parisar Sangh members and a few forest department officials. Apart from the interviews, there were around ten focused group discussions (FGDs) held with the executive committee of MGS, village assemblies, women's self-help groups and village committees. The authors also attended MGS monthly meetings, regular strategy meeting and meetings between the MGS and cluster level representatives. To gain understanding of women's perspective, a gathering of women from 30 villages in Korchi taluka and also neighbouring areas was organised wherein representatives from AAA, Mahila Kissan Adhikar Manch[6] and Kalpavriksh also participated in addition to the men from these villages.

Apart from FGDs, the authors had multiple conversations in the local gathering and meetings organised by MGS. The study was also supplemented with some secondary literature. A consultative process was followed all along the research to ensure that the ideas are continuously exchanged and the key results were presented back to the MGS and AAA for feedback.

Conceptual framework for analysis

"Across the world, there are a number of processes by communities, organisations, government bodies, movements and business that are trying to tackle various dimensions of unsustainability, inequity and injustice. Many of these processes are challenging structural forces such as capitalism, statism, patriarchy, racism, casteism and anthropocentrism. In this sense, they can be seen as *alternatives* to the currently dominant system. It is proposed that alternatives are built on the following spheres (or overlapping spheres) seen as an integrated whole; in this or other forms, these have been expressed by many in the past but are re-emerging in the new contexts of the 21st century: radical and delegated democracy, social well-being and justice, economic democracy, cultural diversity and knowledge democracy and ecological integrity and resilience (these are explained further in the note referred to below) (Figure 3.1).

The above approach is part of (and detailed further in), an evolving note 'In Search of Radical Alternatives', laying out a framework to imagine pathways and visions that are fundamental alternatives to today's dominant economic and political system, taking us towards equity, justice and ecological sustainability.[7] This document has emerged from an ongoing process called the Vikalp Sangam (Alternative Confluence)[8] that aims at bringing together practitioners, thinkers, researchers and others working on alternatives to currently dominant forms of economic development and political governance. It aims to create a cross-sectoral platform on alternatives (or constructive work) to share, learn, build hope, collaboration and to dream and deliberate towards an alternative future,

One of the issues faced by movements working towards radical transformation is that many actions being claimed as alternatives are actually

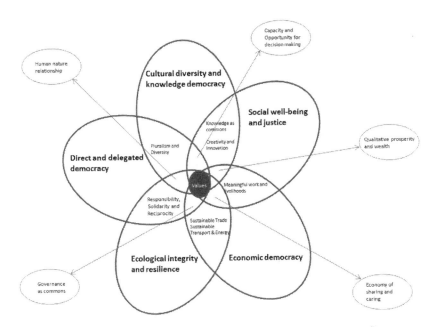

Figure 3.1 Spheres of alternatives transformation.
Note: the topics mentioned in the overlapping areas are only indicative, not exhaustive.

dealing only with the symptoms (e.g. recycling waste rather than challenging its generation and the economic forces that create it), rather than bringing in radical or transformative changes. In addition, they might be fundamentally challenging one dimension of transformation but might be negatively impacting other dimensions of transformations. In order to understand these and other complex issues, a tool called the Alternatives Transformation Format (ATF) has been developed as part of ACKnowl-EJ, the Academic-Activist Co-generation of Knowledge on Environmental Justice Project (www.acknowlej.org).[9] The ATF (Kalpavriksh, 2017) notes

> across the world there are initiatives by communities, civil society organisations, government agencies, and businesses to tackle the challenges of unsustainability, inequity, and injustice. Many of them confront the basic structural reasons for these challenges, such as capitalism, patriarchy, state-centrism, or other inequities in power resulting from caste, ethnic, racial, and other social characteristics; we call these transformative or radical alternatives.

The ATF helps to get an understanding of whether changes are taking place towards greater direct or radical democracy (where people on the ground are core part of decision-making), more control over the economy by the public (not the state or corporations) and the revival of relations of caring and sharing, sustaining or reviving cultural and knowledge diversity and the commons and greater equality and justice on gender, class, caste, ethnic, 'race' and other aspects, all of this on a base of ecological resilience, sustainability and fundamental ethics of co-existence amongst humans and between humans and nature."

The alternatives framework and the ATF together set the background for analysis of various initiatives at transformation in India that Kalpavriksh is undertaking case studies on. This is part of an ongoing process in Kalpavriksh to understand myriad attempts at generating and practicing alternatives that not only challenge the dominant 'development' paradigm but provide viable pathways for human well-being that are ecologically sustainable and socio-economically equitable. Apart from this case study, ATF was used for the first time in India to look at a craft from multiple dimensions (economic, socio-cultural, political, ecological and ethical) and understand multiple dimensions of transformation taking place in the lives of *vankars* (weaver) community of Kachchh, Gujarat, India linked to an overall revival of the handloom weaving (*vanaat*) craft from a time when it was in sharp decline.

Background

Across India, forests were taken over by the Colonial British government in 1865 by enacting the Indian Forest Act and constituting an elaborate and centralised forest bureaucracy to manage the forests. Colonial interests in these forests were commercial, and customary governance was considered an encumbrance in maximising benefits for the colonial state. These customary uses, therefore, were either extinguished completely or allowed as privileges rather than rights. Local forest use continued but remained dependent on bribes in kind or cash and to the whims and fancies of the forest bureaucracy (Guha, 1994). The colonial and draconian forests laws, policies and bureaucracy have continued in Independent India (Pathak Broome et al., 2014). Much like the tribal and other traditional forest dwelling communities across India, in Gadchiroli district also, forest-dependent tribal and non-tribal villages have been severely affected by the centralised and oppressive forest bureaucracy and denial of use and access rights. Forests in Gadchiroli also have commercially important forest produce, particularly Bamboo and *tendu* leaves. 85% of Maharashtra state's Bamboo comes from the forests of Gadchiroli. Extraction and trade of these commercially important forest products has till recently been a monopoly of the state with local people only earning the daily wage income (Maharashtra CFR-LA, 2017). Consequently, the district has seen a number of resistance movements rooted in different ideologies including socialist, Gandhian and even armed Maoist movements demanding village self-rule. Among the most important of these resistance movement has been the one in the mid-1980s against government plan to build an extensive network of 17–18 hydro-electric dams over an important rive Indravati flowing through the district. The movement called the 'save people and save forests movement' demanded greater tribal autonomy, control over decision-making and rights related to forests and its resources. This deepened the self-rule movement in the district, with villages such as Mendha-Lekha declaring de facto village self-rule and inspiring many others to do so (Pathak Broome, 2018). Asserting self-rule, however, remained an uphill task for villages across the district in the absence of any legal and policy support and State's policies of commercial exploitation continued. By the 1990s, the underground mineral potential of the district became evident and forests of Gadchiroli gradually began to be leased out for mining despite strong local opposition. As of 2017, 25 mining proposals were sanctioned or proposed in the district, collectively impacting 15,946 acres of dense forest directly and over 40,000 acres indirectly through allied activities (Pathak Broome and Raut, 2017). Twelve of these mining proposals are in Korchi taluka impacting about 1032.66 ha of forests. The presence of armed Maoist in the region has become a reason for heavy militarisation of the district and frequent encounters between the police and Maoist (real and suspected). Political economy of the region has led to an intense politics of violence.

In this context, a radical change in the legal environment came in 2006, after a long-standing grassroots struggle of the forest-dependent Tribal communities across India. The Parliament of India enacted a landmark legislation – The STs and Other Traditional Forest Dwellers (Recognition of Rights) Act 2006 also called Forest Rights Act of India for short (herein referred to as FRA). The FRA for the first time in the history of Independent India acknowledged the historic injustice on forest dwelling communities in colonial and post-colonial times. The Act provided for recording and recognition of 14 pre-existing forest rights, including the rights of the local *gram sabhas* (village assemblies) ***to claim rights to use, manage, and conserve their traditional forests (here on Community Forest Resource or CFRs) and protect them from internal and external threats***. The Act also provides for Free Prior Informed Consent (FPIC) of the *gram sabhas* before their traditional forests are diverted for non-forestry purposes, including mining. Considering its potential to turn forest governance on its head by making *gram sabha's* consent mandatory for diversion of forests, the Act has faced stiff opposition from existing power centres including the forest department. Consequently, till 2016 – over one decade after its enactment – only about 3% of the Acts minimum potential had been nationally met (CFR-LA, 2016). Because of multiple factors, mainly the people's movement, Gadchiroli has fared much better with about 38% of the total forests in the district already under the control of local *gram sabhas* by 2018 (Maharashtra CFR-LA, 2017).

Process towards alternative transformation in Korchi

We explore below how in the above-mentioned backdrop of historical injustice, conflict situations, resistance movements and various transformative processes unfold, particularly after the enactment of the Forest Rights Act 2006 (FRA) and Panchayat (Extension) to Scheduled Areas Act 1996 (PESA).

Alternative transformative format (ATF) and processes in Korchi

The conflict situation of mining stemming from the historic conditions of injustice and un-sustainability triggered the need towards greater political empowerment and collectivisation of *gram sabhas*. Using the ATF, we try to understand *gram sabha* empowerment in turn triggered transformative processes towards greater economic security, economic and social equity, re-building ecological consciousness and cultural revitalisation, impacting structural root causes of injustices in three major ways:

1   Bringing greater political autonomy by facilitating *gram sabhas* empowerment towards exercising direct democracy in matters concerning their village and holding is state and non-state actors accountable.
2   Gaining control over means of production (the forests in this case) and localising forest-based economy with ecological rejuvenation and long-term sustainability at the root.
3   Addressing gender, caste and class gender inequities, particularly in decision-making.

The flower of ATF spheres below depicts the interweaving of the Korchi process towards protection, conservation and reclaiming control over forest resources with that of reconstruction of local governance institutions, localising control over livelihoods, reviving cultural identity and raising social and equity concerns. At the root of being able to achieve these are underlying principles and values which include, open and transparent dialogue and deliberation, consensus-based decisions making; openness and respect for diverse opinions, learning by doing; maintaining transparency, accountability, inclusiveness, equity, respect for freedom, principle of sustainability, a sense of enoughness, maintaining non-violence, and finally as a gondi proverb *says Changla Jeevan Jage Mayan Saathi Sapalorukoon Apu Apuna Jababdarita Jaaniv Ata Pahe* (To achieve well-being everyone needs to know what their responsibility is) (Figure 3.2).

Addressing political decentralisation through direct, inclusive, transparent and delegated democracy

The roots of the most recent processes towards transformation in Korchi lie in multiple sequential events. These include a strong women-led resistance to the proposed mining leases in the early 2000s, the enactment and implementation of the Forest Rights Act (FRA) of India in 2008, particularly the Community Forest Resource (CFR) Right which meant rights to use,

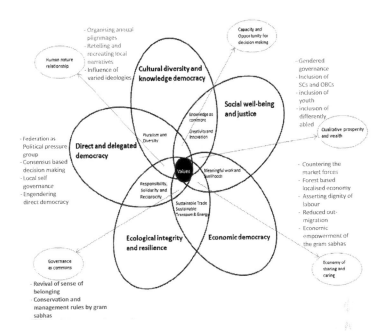

Figure 3.2 Korchi transformation flower.

sustainably manage and conserve their traditional forests; and the formulation of Maharashtra state rules under Panchayat (Extension) to Scheduled
Areas (PESA) Act of 1996 (Bijoy, 2012) in 2014. PESA had important and
empowering provisions for autonomy of the village *gram sabhas* (assemblies of all adult members of a settlement or a village). The formal political
and administrative unit for a village was a panchayat[10] (village executive
body at the level of a village and its multiple hamlets) through elected representatives. The traditional decision-making bodies on the other hand were
at the village and *Ilaka* levels but invariably included only male elders of
the community, thus excluding women, youth and non-tribal castes and
communities.

After the implementation of FRA and PESA rules, in Korchi, as in the
rest of Gadchiroli district, multiple factors such as strong grassroots movements, active and process-oriented nongovernmental organisations (NGOs)
and some supportive government officials led to better implementation of the
two enabling laws. By 2012, 87 out of 133 village *gram sabhas* in Korchi had
claimed and received legal titles over their traditional forests. The local social leaders and activists in Korchi used the opportunity provided by PESA
rules and FRA enactment to initiate village and taluka-level discussions on
what was meant by an empowered *gram sabha*? And what role could the acts
like FRA and PESA play in strengthening the *gram sabhas*? Over a period
of time, multiple debates and discussions on *gram sabhas* and processes of

self-rule were organised, including during village and *Ilaka*-level cultural gatherings. Influenced by these open public debates and discourses, villages in Korchi began to organise *gram sabha* meetings, formulated rules and regulations of local governance, opened up bank accounts and became effective institutions to deepen direct democracy.

In 2016, a taluka-level meeting was organised in which people from all communities, political ideologies, local formal and informal institutions and diverse other backgrounds were invited. After an intense debate and discussion in this meeting, it was felt that a supra level body was needed to support and facilitate mutual learning among the *gram sabhas*. Individual *gram sabhas* by themselves were not strong enough to prevent exploitation by external market forces as they ventured into collection and trade of NTFP. A larger *gram sabha* collective, which would be more inclusive, equitable and transparent than any of the existing taluka or *Ilaka* level institutions, was needed. It was decided to constitute a federation of all 90 *gram sabhas*, called the Mahasabha gramsabha. Unlike the traditional institutions, the MGS would include people from both tribal and non-tribal communities, different castes and women.

By 2017, *gram sabhas* at the village level and MGS at the taluka level emerged as institutions of self-governance. Individual *gram sabhas* began organising regular village-level meetings, while the MGS started meeting once a month in Korchi town. Member *gram sabhas* formally wanting to join the MGS would pass a resolution to this effect after a detailed discussion within their village, select two women and two men to represent them in the MGS general body and agree to pay a membership fee of Rs 5,000 per annum towards MGS functioning (earned from the sale of the NTFP). To facilitate greater interaction between neighbouring *gram sabhas*, 10–12 villages would meet in clusters. MGS executive body is of 15 members, including one woman and a man from each cluster (of seven clusters) and one person with disabilities. The 14 members represent all social groups (caste, class and gender) as per their population in Korchi taluka.

1   Addressing social inclusivity, well-being and justice

Indian society in general has been characterised by moderate to severe inequities within and between communities, related to caste, class, patriarchy and masculinity, age or generational domination, and others. Addressing these equities is fundamental to addressing root causes of injustice and hence achieving meaningful transformation and well-being for all concerned.

Gender: In Korchi, the women collectivisation (Mahila Parisar Sangh or a federation of 40 women's self-help groups) and their struggle against discriminatory and oppressive traditions within their community began in the 1990s. Women leaders emerging from these struggles and movements had a significant role to play in the resistance against mining. By 2016, when discussions on *gram sabhas* empowerment and self-determination were initiated at the taluka level, women leaders realised that discussions on women's participation in decision-making and their economic empowerment from the sale of forest produce were negligible. Women leaders raised the concern that while they are always at the forefront of resistance, they were not included in decision-making processes. This led to the decision that all local formal and informal institutions, including the MGS would have 50% representation by women (legally it is required for all local formal bodies such as the panchayats). The fact that discussions and decisions are now happening at the *gram sabhas* and not the Panchayats, already provides a much higher opportunity for women's participation. Some *gram sabhas* have made special efforts to ensure that meetings are held at times suitable for women. *Parisar sangh* also ensured that Korchi *taluka* is one of the few in the country with a focus on the rights of women under the FRA and Panchayat Extension to Scheduled Areas (PESA) Act, 1996.

Ethnicity: As the processes towards *gram sabha* strengthening were gaining momentum, conversations around empowerment of *gram sabhas*, and STs under PESA, began brewing discontent among the minority non-tribal population in the taluka, particularly the STs[11] and the Other Backward Classes (OBCs).[12] This issue was squarely addressed in the taluka meeting called by the local leaders in 2016, for which people from different castes, communities, political ideologies, formal and informal institutions and backgrounds were invited. After much discussion and clarifications, all participants agreed that empowerment of *gram sabhas* and their federation the MGS was needed for real transformation and it must be inclusive. These discussions converted a potentially significantly damaging conflict situation between different ethnic groups (adivasis and non-adivasis) to an opportunity for creating dialogue towards a more open and inclusive institutional arrangement indicating the maturity, adaptability and wisdom in the process. In this delicate situation while it was critical to take into account the concerns of the minority ethnic groups, equally important was to take into account the fears and insecurities of the traditional leaders and elders of falling into insignificance. It was therefore ensured that traditional elders get the traditional respect and included in various capacities, including as advising elders but do not become the only voice of or for the community.[13]

Youth: Gramsabhas gaining control over forest and forest produce has meant that the *gram sabhas* are now also ensuring livelihoods and economic benefits. Many young people from the community are involved in the harvest of the forest produce, forest management and conservation, and in administrative activities of the *gram sabhas* which require accounts keeping, record maintenance, networking and alliance building, among others. However, there is still a large youth population particularly who have been through higher education outside the villages, caught in a tussle between these unfolding local processes and the lure of the market, the outside cultures and the pull of right-wing religious elements. MGS has made special efforts to engage with the youth associations and groups to initiate debates on the local processes and their impact. Integration of these youth, however, remains a challenge.

2   Ensuring control over means of production, forest-based economy and equitable benefit sharing

The political empowerment is closely linked with the economic process of ensuring forest-based localised economy and gaining control over local livelihoods. In many ways, in fact the sustainability of the processes in Korchi is dependent on *gram sabha's* and MGS's capability to ensure a sustained control over forests and forest-based economy and addressing challenges posed by external market forces. The collection and sale of tendu-patta and bamboo by the *gram sabhas* began in 2017 (until then it was exclusively controlled by the forest department). The *gram sabhas* were helped by the MGS in understanding the process of auctioning and facilitating negotiations with the traders. Neighbouring *gram sabhas* were organised into smaller clusters and each cluster fixed a uniform rate for their forest produce, which was then negotiated with the traders.

In 2017, Korchi *grams sabhas* collectively received Rs. 107,987,970 (1,526,871 USD) as profit in addition to the daily wage collection fees to the individual families and all other expenses covered. The total turnover from tendu and bamboo is currently at about Rs. 160 million or USD 2 million annually. Of this amount, the *gram sabhas* have retained about 5 to 20% as administrative overheads while equally sharing the remaining with all families who participated in the collection, including women. *Gram sabhas* have maintained detailed and meticulous records of collection, people employed and amounts disbursed. This has meant 70–80% increase in income at the family level and 100% increase in income of the *gram sabhas* (which till then had no income or funds), empowering them financially to undertake activities for village well-being. Family income which has conventionally been in the name of the male head has in some villages been given to the woman. Directly participating in the activities related to trading, marketing, record maintenance and other allied activities has also resulted in increased awareness and skill enhancement among the *gram sabha* members (including women). The overall revival and localisation have resulted in reducing the distress outmigration which was rampant till a few years back.

Control over forests and forest-based economy has also helped the MGS to demystify the job and development promises being made by the mining companies. Local leaders' calculations have indicated that local livelihoods and well-being are most assured with a combination of options that villagers currently have. Food needs are largely met with the agriculture and forest, and cash requirements are being met with NTFP trade from the forests and other allied activities, leaving villagers with time to participate in community and collective cultural and political activities. Mining companies can only employ a handful of local people, mainly men and largely in unskilled sector while destroying the forests and forest-based income, affecting agriculture, causing water and air pollution and creating insecure and un-safe environment for women and children.

3   Addressing ecological wisdom, integrity and resilience

Rights and ownership over forests has revived a sense of ownership and a need for ensuring ecological sustainability towards the forests which had eroded over the years because of alienating colonial policies. Local elders remember that forests were rich, dense and supported many wildlife species (including mega fauna) till three decades ago. Slowly, forests began to degrade because of unregulated extraction for self-consumption, increasing populations, growing towns and their fuelwood needs and illegal extraction by outsiders. After receiving right under the FRA, some *gram sabhas* have started making rules and regulations for management and protection of forests, including a system of regular forest patrolling. Controlling fires has resulted in greater regeneration and richness in the forests. FRA requires all *gram sabha* to formulate management plans and strategies for the forests over which their rights have been recognised, such a planning would be required for sustainable harvest and sale of the commercially important NTFP. Under a Tribal Development Department programme, some *gram sabhas* have initiated drafting the management plans. With or without management plans, many villages have carried out successful plantations of diverse local species. In almost all cases, extraction of NTFP is carried out on rotation (ensuring that not all parts of the forest are extracted at one go). Using the free prior informed consent clause of the FRA, villagers have already registered their rejection of the mining proposals. Mining threat, however, is not over.

4   Use and revival of cultural spaces and addressing cultural vibrancy

Assertion of cultural identity has been a crucial part of the overall transformation in Korchi. Community leaders in fact used elements of existing cultural practices to strengthen *gram sabhas*, such as the system of community elders sitting together to discuss community issues. Regular ceremonial community gatherings have been very significant and crucial forums to discuss and develop collective strategies. Traditional cultural spaces such as *yatras* (an annual pilgrimage to a Sacred Natural Site) in Korchi have emerged as platforms to resist mining, initiate dialogues on issues of centralised governance, patriarchy, discrimination in traditional systems, definitions of 'being civilised vs being backward', definitions of 'development', electoral politics, among others.

Enablers for resistance and transformative processes

One distinct feature in the current process in Korchi is the supportive legal environment because of enactment of the FRA and PESA Rules for Maharashtra. However, it also suggests that mere enactment of the law cannot bring about transformation. This is particularly so with radical laws such as FRA and PESA for which the state's political and administrative will towards implementation remains abysmally low resulting in nationally limited or tardy implementation. There were multiple reasons why there was a better implementation of this Act in Korchi and rest of Gadchiroli. It is therefore important to understand enabling agents and factors that led to realisation of the potential of these legal provisions and emergence of the transformative processes. Some of these are described below:

Social capital embedded in adivasi culture, including setting aside time for the commons and community activities including community celebrations and festivities and engagement with community welfare activities is very much part of tribal culture. The community-oriented culture of the adivasis helped in multiple ways in moving towards transformative alternatives. The culture encourages viewing benefit of others intricately linked with the people coming together for a larger cause along with greater emphasis on collective practices, traditional systems of leadership (even if gender biased) and the culture of respecting community elders which provides an environment for emergence of community social leaders. Such leaders have played an important role in anti-mining resistance movement, efforts towards empowerment of *gram sabhas*, formation of MGS and other transformative processes in Korchi.

Long history of political mobilisation and debates on 'development' in Gadchiroli district have led to emergence of many resistance movements. Movement towards self-rule after Save Human Save Forests Movement in the 1980s led to self-rule experiment in many villages including Mendha-Lekha which continues to influence and inspire local people and leaders (Pathak Broome, 2018).

Local co-production of knowledge and co-learning- District level study circle: a district-level study group (*Abhyas Gat*) set up by civil society actors historically involved in resistance and transformative movements in the district contributed to transformative processes and effective FRA implementation. The study group discussed the FRA, its implications and procedures for claiming the rights. They also helped with evidence generation to support the claims. Discussions in the study group ensured that the much-forgotten existing record of rights was provided to all the villagers by the district administration. Mendha-Lekha started the process of filing claims and became the first *gram sabha* in the country to have their rights recognised, paving the way for hundreds of others in the district and in the country (Pathak Broome, 2018).

Peer learning and support from other taluka level *gram sabha* federations in Gadchiroli: In the recent time, another forum for mutual learning have also emerged which largely include the *gram sabha* members instead of civil society groups. Much like the federation of *gram sabhas* in Korchi, federations of *gram sabhas* have emerged in other talukas of Gadchiroli since 2016. These federations are important source of support for each other, particularly when faced with larger district-level challenges, including exploitative markets and traders. The federation members consult, advice and support each other while also financially helping each other in difficult times by offering loans and disaster relief.

Role of AAA: AAA, a local NGO, has been present in Korchi for a few decades and has worked towards health, forest management and women's empowerment. AAA has also supported local social leaders, including women as *karyakarta* (village activists) under various projects and provided them opportunities to interact with actors at the district, state and national levels, and be part of various discussions and debates. This has helped enhance their existing levels of awareness, information and leadership skills and gain respect and acceptability within the larger community. AAA has also provided timely help in accessing information and capacity building through various training programmes.

Characteristics of transformative processes through Korchi's Lens

The analysis below is specific to the context of Korchi in particular and Gadchiroli district in general. We understand that resistance and transformation are contextual and dynamic processes and what is relevant in this context may or may not apply to other areas and situations. Yet we believe there would be many common underlying characteristics connecting resistance and transformation across situations.

Continuous yet episodic and spiral – keeping political consciousness active

Political, social, economic and ecological alternative transformative processes in Korchi indicate that resistance and transformation are continuous and yet episodic. Political economy and resultant conflicts are evidenced from the historical events in this district also indicating that **conflict is often an integral part** of the process of transformation. The tribal lands of the central Indian forests have been at the heart of conflicts through the history as the people have constantly resisted these ingressions of precolonial, colonial and post-colonial rulers. Independence of India in 1947 did not mean greater autonomy or freedom of decision-making for the adivasi and other local communities. The country continued to follow extractivism and capitalism-based development; centralised and top-down forest governance; and exclusive and representative electoral democracy. All of the above stand in direct contradiction with the worldview, socio-political organisation of the adivasis. These contradictions have been historically and currently the underlying causes of a continuous environment of conflict, within which some events, policies or actions trigger stronger episodes of resistance.

The environment of resistance has kept the political awareness and consciousness alive, leading to emergence of collectives like Mahila Parisar Sangh and the MGS. Such autonomous, organic, inclusive and discussion-based collectives are crucial in creating an inherent understanding that resistance alone is not enough to challenge the root causes of injustices. The local processes towards strengthening self-rule are critical to impact the political economy of the region. Some of the past transformative actions have continued to sustain and inspire new ones while others have been co-opted and undermined by the established power structures. So, while the progression may appear to be circular as similar events arise over a period of time, coming apart and reinventing themselves they are not exactly the same in their reinvented form.

Scalar, temporal and evolutionary

We see that the transformation is an evolutionary process having both scalar and temporal dimensions. Multiple factors emerging at various points in time through the history can be transformative at different levels, e.g. individuals within the community, individual villages, taluka as a whole and at the level of the district. These transformations are subjective and do not impact the society uniformly at all points in time. Instead, they contribute to the overall evolution of the transformative processes particularly when these differently transforming processes and actors come together. Thus, transformative process is a result of evolution over a period of time as also coalition of or friction between various individuals, ideologies, civil society groups, deliberative process at different scales at any given point in time. District-level study circle and its influence in the process in Korchi, taluka-level federations and their interactions, individual villages like Mendha-Lekha located in other talukas but influencing processes in Korchi (and getting influenced by them) are the scalar dimensions of learning and evolution of the transformation process in Korchi.

Locally rooted but also addressing traditional and customary discriminatory practices

The transformation process in Korchi is definitely embedded in local socio-cultural and political values, conceptions of well-being, principles and histories. Simultaneously, these processes and practices have also incorporated many modern and contemporary ideas of political economy, human ecology, equity and social justice. For example, while the principle of consensus-based, inclusive decision-making and collective community action are integral to the adivasi traditions, greater emphasis on gender participation in decision-making, women being equal or primary beneficiaries of local economic activities, inclusion of non-adivasis (particularly scheduled castes) in decision-making bodies are newer inclusions.

Within a transformation process conceptions of well-being can be internally diverse and conflicting

The conceptions of well-being or transformation are not universally accepted conceptions in all 90 villages. There are several diverse and internally contradictory views and influenced by different actors and factors. The capitalist and extractive economy and its propaganda machinery have been effective in influencing a large part of the population, particularly the youth. The existing state education system further alienates them from their own culture, creates consumptive and career-based aspirations, motivating them to support mining and the promised jobs. The right-wing religious groups have also influenced a large part of the population and their agenda aligns more closely with the growth-based model of development. Considering the presence of multiple ideologies and conceptions of well-being, which ideology will influence the dominant processes at any point in time would depend on multiple causes and conditions. In many ways, the transformative processes in Korchi are continuously impacted and evolve because of the dialectics of these multiple conceptions of well-being.

Non-static and no fixed recipes

Even though in this analysis we are making an attempt to theorise and articulate the characteristics of the process of resistance and transformation in Korchi, the process itself does not have a self-articulated 'theory of change'. All processes are dynamic and non-static, continuously changing and evolving towards the larger goal of greater local autonomy and greater systemic accountability to be able to achieve equity, justice and well-being. Gram sabha members, Parisar Sangh members, MGS members have to continuously deal with newer challenges and opportunities. The unarticulated theory of change as it appears to us is asking we walk, walking we learn, learning we change **(Zapatista ref to be added)**.

Ever-alert, agile, multi-dimensional and responding to threats

The processes of resistance and transformation in Korchi have been ever-alert, agile and responsive in real time. This is evident in the manner the local leaders responded to the social discontent on inclusion of other castes and women's participation. Strategies are decided based on the need of the hour and importance of the issue in the monthly meetings. These could include any social and political issue at any scale, i.e. village, cluster, taluka or district. The process of transformation constantly faces internal contradictions and external threats which the regular and transparent discussion in the monthly meetings attempt to address.

Located in and dependent on inherently contradictory context

Also, within the processes of resistance and transformation, there are many inherent internal contradictions. Among the most significant being heavy dependence on the state and its adopted exploitative capitalistic model of economy and representative electoral democracy. *Gram sabhas,* the institutions of direct democracy, remain dependent on state institutions which remain centralised in their spirit and disconnected from local issues. Similarly, NTFP trade such as tendu leaves and bamboo which are the main stay of the people in the region and have been crucial in causing a radical shift in the local economy are themselves dependent on the external capitalist markets. Market fluctuations and vagaries have serious impacts on their sustainability.

Sustainable development goals and alternative transformative processes in Korchi

We believe the processes in Korchi hold important lessons for the global Sustainable Development Goals (SDGs) (SDGs, 2015). Two main goals that SDGs have set out to address are *eliminating poverty* and *achieving ecological sustainability*. In their preamble, the SDGs declare

> We envisage a world of universal respect for human rights and human dignity, the rule of law, justice, equity and non-discrimination.... A world in which consumption and production patterns and use of all natural resources are sustainable, one in which humanity lives in harmony with nature and in which wildlife and other living species are protected.

Although these SDG goals and preamble have been much appreciated, yet globally there have been doubts about their being truly realised. Ironically, the mechanism envisioned for achieving the SDG goals is in direct conflict with the goals themselves. This is because of three fundamental (among other) lacunae in the mechanism that has been envisioned to achieve SDGs (Kothari, et al., 2018). These are

1   The SDGs are envisioned to be achieved by reliance on existing economic order and prevalent model of economic growth, which are the very fundamental basis for the root causes leading to the very injustices and inequities that the SDGs intend to eliminate. The current economic model sustains itself on concentration of economic resources and political power in the hands of a few, mainly the state and private corporations. Such concentration of power and resources is supported by and in turn supports, at all levels, systems that support patriarchy, class and caste divides, and communal divisions.
2   The SDGs continue to depend on national governments and their centralised state agencies as the main drivers and decision-makers related

to the goals, targets and activities. This again contradicts with another root cause of ecological degradation and social inequity, the top-down and centralised decision-making processes. Like many international targets, the SDGs have also ignored decentralised decision-making institutions and processes of direct democracy.

3   Last but not the least is the absence of clarity on what basic set of ethical values or principles would underlie the processes in place to achieve all goals, targets and activities within the SDGs.

The alternative transformative processes in Korchi are among the many other alternative pathways across the globe (**add red ref**) which could help achieve the main goals and the intention of the SDGs. By creating local institutions of direct democracy, which include social and ecological justice and equity, economic self-reliance and equity and cultural and social vibrancy, they help achieve SDGs meaningfully and effectively. The processes in Korchi have in fact emerged as a response to the ecological degradation and social injustices resulting from growth-led development, centralised and top-down decision-making. The above-mentioned three fundamental lacunae in the SDGs Framework are addressed in many ways by the processes in Korchi as described in sections above.

Politically, the processes towards empowerment of *gram sabhas* and women's self-help groups and formation of their federations are towards achieving greater direct democracy with people in collectives having the power to take or significantly influence decisions impacting their lives. Through these collectives, the local people are now better empowered to hold outsiders, including state agencies, more accountable. Economically, the *gram sabhas* have gained control over the means of production and localised forest-based economy, thus enhancing local livelihood opportunities and affecting distress outmigration. Ways have been devised for equitable benefit sharing, including the rights and benefits to women. Caring and sharing for each other, helping and learning from each other and supporting each other as a community are at the core of these economic relations. While achieving better and equitable economic benefits, they have resisted and rejected models of ever-increasing economic growth which come at the cost of destruction through mining and other extractive means. Not only have they used their political and economic empowerment to resist mining and other forms of ecological degradation but have also put in place local systems of self-regulation, ecological restoration and forest patrolling to ensure ecological well-being and long-term sustainability of the forest resources.

While building processes towards political decentralisation and direct democracy and strengthening local economy by gaining control over means of production, social relationships have been delicately addressed based on mutual compassion and respect, cooperation instead of competition and with a central focus on qualitative well-being for all. This has been achieved including by changing traditional patriarchal systems to include women in decision-making and by taking into account the concerns of the non-tribal STs and OBCs. While doing so, respect for traditional elders has also been maintained.

Cultural spaces have been maintained and enhanced during the process, reflecting respect for cultural diversity and a stress on the knowledge commons. These achievements in five spheres or dimensions of life, including social, cultural, ecological, economic and political, themselves rest on a foundation of values and principles, such as subsidiarity, open and transparent dialogue, consensus-based decision making, openness to new and diverse ideas and opinions, openness to learning by doing, transparency, accountability, inclusiveness, equity, respect for freedom, mutual respect, right to information, sustainability, enoughness, non-violence, among others.

Acknowledgement

The authors would like to thank all gram sabhas, MGS, and Mahila Parisar Sangh members from Korchi and Amhi Amchi Arogyasaathi. Special thanks to Mahesh Raut who is one of the co-authors of the original report but could not contribute to this chapter because of extraneous circumstances.

Notes

1 The authors of this report would like to thank members of Maha Gramsabha, Korchi, Amhi Amchaya Arogayasathi and community members of Salhe, Bharitola, Zendepar, Bodena, Phulgondi, Padyal Job, Kodgul and Tipagarh village assemblies.
2 An administrative unit under the control of one traditional feudal lord or a *Zamindar.*
3 The government of India does not accept the term Indigenous People. Tribal groups have been enlisted as in one of the schedules of the Constitution of India and given a special status. All the listed tribes are called Scheduled Tribes.
4 Legal term used for the caste historically considered to be 'lower' and hence discriminated against in the Hindu caste system. Many such castes have been provided special protection and incentives in the Constitution of India. The castes which are listed under this category in one of the Schedules in the Constitution are referred to as the Scheduled Castes.
5 Bharitola, Zendepar, Salhe, Phoolgondi, Bodena, Padyal Job, Kodgul and Tipagarh villages of Gadchiroli district.
6 MAKAAM is a nation-wide forum working towards securing due recognition and rights of women farmers (https://makaam.in/)
7 www.vikalpsangam.org/about/the-search-for-alternatives-key-aspects-and-principles/
8 www.vikalpsangam.org
9 ACKnowl-EJ is a network of scholars and activists engaged in action and collaborative research that aims to analyse the transformative potential of community responses to extractivism and alternatives born from resistance. The project involved case studies, dialogues and analysis on transformation towards greater justice, equity and sustainability in several countries.
10 The executive committee or a Panchayat is elected from a cluster of villages. The decisions are taken at the level of the cluster gram sabhas where only a handful

of people from constituent gram sabhas are able to attend and invariably few women can attend. Often decisions are therefore taken by 5–7 member executive committees or the Panchayat itself. Increasingly, panchayats across the country are strongly influenced by party politics and their agendas. They have also been marred by corruption. Gram sabhas as envisioned under the FRA and PESA, however, are village assemblies of each village, hamlet or settlement, which can be held at regular intervals, within the village and at times most convenient for the villages and provide much better opportunities for all including women and youth to participate.

11 The term "Scheduled Tribes" is referred to specific Indigenous Peoples in different states in India who are defined in Article 342 of Indian Constitution and whose status is recognised by national legislation. They have been provided special protection in the Constitution of India which lays down some principles of positive discrimination for STs and Scheduled Castes (SCs). To know more on this read: The Constitution of India, Article 366 (25) and Article 342. A

12 Other Backward Class (OBC) are 'socially and educationally disadvantaged classes' other than SCs and STs who are entitled to 27% reservation in public sector employment and higher education.

13 At the same time, the *jat panchayats* also continue to exist parallelly. They have not remained untouched from the social debates and discussions. Also, many of the critical actors involved in the process are also members of the *jat panchayats* and have carried the discussions with them. *Jat panchayats* have therefore made some significant changes in the oppressive socio-cultural practices including the excessive expense in cash and kind the families had to bearing during marriage ceremonies, among others.

References

Bijoy, C.R. 2012. *Panchayati Raj (Extension to Scheduled Areas Act of 1996): Policy Brief.* UNDP. www.undp.org/content/dam/india/docs/UNDP-Policy-Brief-on-PESA.pdf (accessed on September 15th, 2019).

CFR-LA. 2016. *Promise and Performance: Ten Years of the Forest Rights Act in India. Citizens' Report on Promise and Performance of The Scheduled Tribes and Other Traditional Forest Dwellers (Recognition of Forest Rights) Act, 2006, after 10 years of its Enactment. December 2016.* Produced as part of Community Forest Rights-Learning and Advocacy Process (CFR-LA), India, 2016 (www.cfrla.org.in).

Guha, R. 1994. Colonialism and Conflict in the Himalayan Forest. In R. Guha (Ed.), *Social Ecology* (pp. 275–302). Delhi: Oxford University Press.

India, Census. 2011. *Census India, Maharashtra Gadchiroli.* www.censusindia2011.com/maharashtra/gadchiroli-population.html (accessed on June 15th, 2019).

Kalpavriksh. 2 February 2017. *Vikalp Sangam.* www.vikalpsangam.org/static/media/uploads/Resources/alternatives_transformation_framework_revised_20.2.2017.pdf (accessed June 15th, 2019).

Koreti, S. 2016. Socio-Cultural History of Gond Tribes in Middle India. *International Journal of Social Science and Humanity,* 6(4), 288.

Kothari, A. 2014. Radical Ecological Democracy: A Path Forward for India and Beyond, Development, 57(1), 36–45, www.palgrave-journals.com/development/journal/v57/n1/full/dev201443a.html. Also see http://kalpavriksh.org/index.php/alternatives/alternatives-knowledge-center/353-vikalpsangam-coverage

Kothari, A., Salleh, A., Escobar, A., Demaria, F. and Acosta, A. 2018. *Why We Need Alternatives to Development.* http://wordpress.p288574.webspaceconfig.de/?p=239

Kothari, A., Bajpai, S., and Padmanabhan, S, 2020. *Ladakh Autonomous Hill Council -Leh, How autonomous, How democratic?* Pune. India. Kalpavriksh

Maharashtra CFR-LA. 2017. *Promise and Performance: Ten Years of the Forest Rights Act in Maharashtra. Citizens' Report on Promise and Performance of the Scheduled Tribes and Other Traditional Forest Dwellers (Recognition of Forest Rights) Act, 2006.* Produced by CFR Learning and Advocacy Group Maharashtra, as part of National Community Forest Rights-Learning and Advocacy Process (CFR-LA). March 2017. (www.fra.org.in)

Pathak Broome, N. 2018. Mendha-Lekha- Forest Rights and Self-Empowerment. In M. Lang, C. Konig and A. Regelmann (Eds.). *Alternatives in a World of Crisis.* Global Working Group Beyond Development (pp. 134–179). Rosa Luxemburg Stiftung, Brussels Office and Universidad Andina Simon Bolivar, Ecuador.

Pathak Broome, N. and Raut, M. 2017. *Mining in Gadchiroli – Building a Castle of Injustices on the Foundation of One.* www.countercurrents.org/2017/06/17/mining-in-gadchiroli-building-a-castle-of-injustices/. (accessed on June 17th, 2017).

Pathak Broome, N., Desor, S., Kothari, A. and Bose, A. 2014. Changing Paradigms in Wildlife Conservation in India. In S. Lele and A. Menon. *Democratizing Forest Governance in India.* New Delhi: Oxford University Press (pp. 124–170).

SDGs. 2015. United Nations General Assembly. Resolution adopted by the General Assembly on 25th September 2015. www.un.org/sustainabledevelopment/ (accessed on September 15th, 2019).

Singh, N., Kulkarni, S. and Pathak Broome, N. 2018 (Eds). *Ecologies of Hope and Transformation: Post-development Alternatives from India.* Pune. India: Kalpavriksh and SOPECOM.

4 Food system transition in India

A political ecology analysis

Vandana

Introduction

The goals of sustainable development are based on the three critical pillars of economic development, environmental protection and social justice. These three elements are asserted to be of equal importance as evident from the framing of these goals. However, current economic and political systems and related policies have undermined both the environment and society to favour economic growth. Development polices at large have been argued to have compromised the interest of forest-dwelling communities in various ways. The report of The High-Level Committee on Socioeconomic, Health and Educational status of Tribal Communities of India published in 2014 mentions that the development process has pushed the *adivasi* communities to a situation worse than their original position. There is a built-in depressor in the way development has been pursued in tribal India which contributes to their deprivation. The economic growth led development model entails shifting of land from agriculture and forest use to industrial use (Sarkar, 2007). The conservation practices within this model of development have also been argued to be driven by the logic of the market that dominates economic thinking and other areas of policy (Gómez-Baggethun, E., & Ruiz-Pérez, M., 2011). In India, State forest practices aiming at conservation through scientific forest management have been opined to be inferior to practices of social forestry which entail community-led conservation measures (Gadgil, 1993). Due to these policies of development and processes of conservation, communities experience a loss of access to resources, and marginalization which has also culminated to insurgencies in some tribal areas in India. Furthermore, in the past decade, there has been an increase in scholarly works that connect this loss of access to and control over life-sustaining resources with a perception of declining health and well-being in the community (Richmond et al., 2005; Nichols, 2014). Motivated by this health and ecology connection this chapter examines the abysmal condition of malnutrition, as an indicator of well-being in the tribal population in India (See Figure 4.1), in the context of the broader changes in their living environment and changing access to local ecological resources. It studies the connection

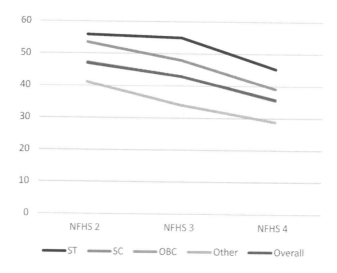

Figure 4.1 Prevalence of underweight across social groups.
Source: National Family Health Survey, multiple rounds.

between conditions of malnutrition and the changing food system reflective of changes in access to environmental resources.

The local food system which includes ways of agriculture or food production and also food consumption gets fundamentally impacted by changes in environmental resources. The Global Nutrition Report (2016) stresses the importance of food system in creating diet choices because it determines food availability, affordability, access and acceptability. Complementing this with the Global Food Policy (2016), it becomes evident that the current agriculture system is neither climate resilient nor is it inclusive to small farm holders, women and youth. This chapter is motivated by the increasing urge in the literature on the need to understand the intricate ways in which sustainability is relevant for food and nutritional security (Finley et al., 2017). It has been suggested that including sustainability in the agenda for food security would require consolidating a more holistic framework which brings together notions of sustainable agriculture, sustainable economy, sustainable food production and sustainable diets (Berry E. M. et al., 2015).

One important indicator bringing together sustainability and issues of food and nutrition is the Food Sustainability Index (2018).[1] It is broadly based on three categories of indicators to evaluate the food system: food loss and waste, sustainable agriculture and nutritional challenges and it ranks India at 33 among the 67 countries studied. Along with India, most of the other BRIC nations fare poorly as per this index. Though there has been positive improvement in the area of food loss and wastage, India scores below average in sustainability-related indicators and is among one of the worst in tackling nutritional challenges. Making agriculture 'nutritionally sensitive' has become a focus in policy literature in the past decade, with many studies researching the linkages between the two sectors and the pathways through which agriculture might improve nutritional outcomes (Arimond, 2011; Berti, 2003; Gillespie, 2012; Masset, 2011; World Bank, 2007). While much of the literature defines these emerging concepts of food system[2] and conceptual ways to transform it, limited work on barriers to this transformation and analysis of the inherent politics in food system transition has been pointed as a major research gap (Meeker, Haddad, & Chisholm, 2013). This chapter focuses on the transition in the food production and consumption ways based on the experiences of a tribal community in India, examining its policy context and analysing the political implication of the attempts of the State and non-governmental organizations (NGOs) to make the food system more climate resistant and nutrition sensitive. This enables a focus on the issues of justice and others ways of connecting with the environment as economic growth led sustainability development gets prioritized in the policy arena.

Even though India is food secure in terms of the food production levels, it is currently facing challenges related to crop diversification especially due to the shift to monoculture after the Green revolution (Dev, 2018). It is also suggested that the policies should be designed to be inclusive to the needs of small and marginal farmers. The agriculture policy in India focusing on rice/wheat dominated by the logic of monoculture drove out millets from the fields. Millets, which impart greater resilience to the cropping system against climate risk and are more nutritious compared to rice and wheat have faced a sharp decline in production over the years (Makkar, 2019). Millets and other coarse grains were traditionally grown in tribal areas. It is being suggested in several studies and by social activists working in the area of agriculture and nutrition that agriculture system in tribal villages has developed according to the local ecological conditions and comprises of a variety of nutritionally dense food crops.[3] The possibility of designing a more sustainable and nutrition sensitive food system is, therefore, explored recently based on the indigenous practices of agriculture in the tribal community.

Though the State policy related to food and agriculture has been modified at sub-regional levels to include millets, the policy process is far from being inclusive of issues of small farmers or any alternative system of agriculture production. It has been suggested in the past that food system and related changes should be examined within the context of creation of a complex network of actors, processes and related politics (DuPuis E.M. et al. 2006; Marsden et al., 1996; Winter, 2003). However, the current agri-food scholarship while being focused on the developed countries also remains disconnected from the political implications of food and agriculture changes (Sonnino et al., 2014; Moragues-Faus, 2017). Similarly, the extant literature on hunger and malnutrition have been framing it as a technical problem with a limited understanding of the related political economy factors (Nisbett et al., 2014). However, there has been a recent emergence of studies which explore the agriculture-nutrition linkage and highlight some of the impacts of agriculture interventions embedded in the broader policy priorities of development on nutrition outcomes. It has been pointed out that a focus on increasing income due to commercialization of agriculture may result in shifting from staples to cash crops which in turn will create a negative impact on nutritional status, especially in poor farming households (Pauw, Ecker, & Breisinger, 2011; Von Braun, 1995). The negative impact on nutrition due to such changes in food production system has led to a proliferation of local movements around food advocating for more radical alternatives to the globalized food regime which requires large scale commercialization of food production (Blay-Palmer et al., 2013; Marsden & Morley, 2014). Such changes have altered the way nature is experienced at the local level. Therefore, there has been a growing urge to analyse the politics of place and nature to understand the crisis of the current food system.

Building on this momentum to critically analyse the food system changes, this chapter uses a political ecology approach to understand the politics of changing crop pattern using the case of food production and consumption changes in a tribal community in India. It contributes to the current scholarship of food studies by bringing in a more politically sensitive approach to analyse the changing human–nature relationship through changes in food system. Linking the local specific conditions of food to policies operating at multiple scales as the analytical method inspired from political ecology works, this chapter builds a place-based understanding of the transitions in agriculture and food. This analysis aims is to focus on shifting power relations between State and community and on changing meanings around ecology within the community. As this chapter analyses the past and current policies impacting food system at the local level, it argues that even the initiatives claiming to be sustainable and nutrition sensitive would fail to impact the power position of nutritionally vulnerable farmer households. In the next section, the Political Ecology approach is discussed providing details of the analytical method adopted to build a place-based understanding of the food system transition. The policy context producing the changes in food system in the local level is explained in a later section. This is followed by a discussion on material and discursive changes related to human–nature interaction through food.

Place-based political ecology

Political Ecology (PE) as a field of study stresses on aspects of political economy, formal political institutions, environmental change, and stories about effect of that change on people. (E.g. Blaikie & Brookfield, 1987; Bryant, 1997; Zimmerer, 2000). In the past, scholars working in this area have advocated for better management of nature and rights of people. In the initial years of the development of this school of thought, the term 'political ecology' was used to refer in a general sense the politics of environmental problems without specific discussion of the 'ecology'. Bryant (1997, p. 13), for example, describes political ecology as an enquiry into 'the political forces, conditions and ramifications of environmental change', and may include studies of environmental impacts from different sources; location-specific aspects of ecological change; and the effects of environmental change on socio-economic and political relationships. Later on, a critical approach to political ecology was developed. This debated the 'ecology' within the political ecology approach. Instead of just focusing on politics regarding environmental problems, a 'critical' political ecology focuses on the politics of ecology by problematizing the way it scientifically legitimizes the prevalent environmental policy. Within this approach, there is no a priori adoption of concepts and explanations of environmental science (Forsyth, 2008, p. 4). All statements about ecology are assessed for their political construction.

Within later works of political ecology, transformations in the physical world was seen along with the transformation in meanings and discourses shaping those changes. Concepts like socio-nature are employed to understand how nature and society emerge in relationship with each other. This focus on changing relations between society and nature has been used in the past by agri-food scholars to broadly define the ecological dimensions of food system. However, there has been limited attention drawn to the aspect of power relations using concepts of political ecology within agri–food studies in the past. While the principles and concepts of agro-ecology recently promoted within agri-food studies embraces nature, science and society to be interconnected, it does not necessarily analyse its political dimensions (Moragues-Faus A. & Marsden T., 2017, p. 14). The analytical concept of 'place' from the field of political ecology can be utilized to explicate the politics in the transitioning food system in a tribal community.

'Place' as a concept has been used in the past to conceptualize the processes of globalization in a non-vertical way. It is understood as the site where the local and the global interacts. It is assumed to be constituted by nodes of local-global articulation (Biersack, 1999, p. 81) and is never simply local and sealed off from the outside (Moore, 1998, p. 347). Articulations are the crucial features of a 'place' and eventually produced by the distinct mix of wider and local social relations. As a concept, 'place' has both locational and relational aspects, hence, making it an amenable tool for both ecological as well as political analyses. This helps in developing a horizontal and dialectical perspective on local and global relations. It contributes to the overall understanding of policies of development as a place-based approach considers how the local or the grass-root responds to the forces extra-local factors like intervention of the State, NGOs and market. The concept of 'place' also includes exchange of images, values and meanings within the exchange between local and extra-local creating material/physical changes in the place. It has been argued that political ecology studies while focusing on struggles for rights of people and justice by resisting material changes need to also challenge existing meanings and representations associated with people and communities (Alvarez, Dagnino, & Escobar, 1998).

Thus, using the concept of 'place', this chapter builds a relational understanding of food system transition in a tribal community. This enables a contextual analysis of malnutrition as opposed to a bio-medical understanding

of it. By not confining to the local space, the concept of 'place' enables to examine processes operating at different spatial scales (Cummins et al., 2007)
and also investigates the creation of new meanings human–society interaction via changing food. It, thus, explains the material and notional ways
through which existing power relations gets reproduced through alterations
in the food system.

Using the concept of 'place', this chapter focuses on the following:

1   The State policies and NGO interventions operating at multiple scales
    making 'place': This brings out the policy context and practices of the
    State and civil society which interacts with the local living conditions
    crucial for its eventual transformation.
2   The changing power relations between the community and extra-local
    actors: Based on the narratives of people about their experiences of
    changing food production and consumption practices, this section ar-
    gues that through this making of 'place', the historically existing asym-
    metrical power relations gets reproduced.
3   The role of discourses, representations and meanings in process of tran-
    sitioning of food system: As the boundaries of local and the outside get
    blurred in the process of 'place making', new meanings about nature
    and society emerge in the community. These new meanings lead to new
    imaginaries of relations between society and nature further margin-
    alizing the traditional notions of human–nature connection exhibited
    through ideas about food.

Focusing on the above three aspects to build a place-based analysis of
changing food system, this chapter argues that the State food policy regime
creates new meanings of nature as it transforms the food system. In doing
so, it reproduces the historic power asymmetries and continues to margin-
alize alternative understanding of relations is nature. In the context of the
problem of malnutrition, this means that the tribal communities continue
to be vulnerable and pushed towards adopting agricultural practices which
have been criticised for being unsustainable and nutritionally insensitive.
This chapter examines the policy context perpetuating the problem of malnutrition as it discusses the practices of the State and civil society and its
impact on the power relation among State, community and ecology.

Methodology

The findings of this chapter are based on fieldwork carried out in the Indian
state of Jharkhand which involved engaging with the different developmental actors and members of the community. After the end of the *kharif* crop
season, which is the main agriculture season in India in rainfall-dependant
areas – between the months of October and December in 2016, interaction
with farmers, men and women of different age groups and profession was

undertaken. The research respondents were from the districts of Khunti, Latehar and Palamu in the State of Jharkhand. The selection of these places was based on the extent of the problem of malnutrition in the State of Jharkhand and the high proportion of tribal population in the State (see Table 4.1). Jharkhand has 32 out of the 700 Scheduled Tribes notified under the Article 342 of the Indian Constitution, and most of these tribes have a skill that was developed over centuries. This chapter focuses on one of the agricultural tribal communities in the State of Jharkhand called *Munda.*

The villages were chosen based on the accessibility to these areas as facilitated by an NGO based at Ranchi with program interventions in these villages. In addition to this, people of the Right to Food Network, which is the advocacy group whose work led to the formulation the National Food Security Act, 2013, were also interviewed to understand their vision and advocacy priorities. In the village, the semi-structured interviews conducted were focused around agriculture production, food consumption, health issues and their experience and perception of the related changes. In addition to this, their perception and experience of the NGO and government welfare and development programs were also discussed. The interaction with the NGO staff and the members of the advocacy group revolved around initiatives of millet revival undertaken in the past and their plan for future initiatives in this area. Their opinion about the government programs in this area was also discussed. Table 4.2 gives the details of the data source.

Table 4.1 Nutritional Status of Jharkhand

Indicator	Jharkhand	India
Stunting (Height for age) (Age <5 yrs.)	50.5	38.4
Underweight (Weight for age) (Age <5 yrs.)	45.7	35.7
Wasting (Weight for height) (Age <5 yrs.)	21.3	21.0
Anaemia (6–59 months old)	78.4	58.4
Women (BMI<18.5) Age 15–49 years	28.6	22.9
Population proportion belonging to ST group	26.2	8.6

Source: NFHS 4, Census 2011 and Clinical, Anthropometric and Biochemical (CAB) 2014 Jharkhand Factsheet.

Table 4.2 Interviews conducted in Jharkhand

Sector	Title	Total
NGO workers (n=15)	Field Workers	5
	Staff	4
	Senior Staff	6
Community Member (n=30)	Men	18
	Women	12
Government Staff (n=3)	Nutrition	2
	Agriculture	1

The analysis of the data is based on the themes that emerged from the narratives of people about the changes in food production, consumption and health. The themes that connected these sectors and conveyed about their perception about the changes in each of these areas were highlighted and have been used in this chapter.

Multi-scaled interventions making 'Place'

The current food regime in India evolved out of the food policies designed in the backdrop of the Bengal Famine of 1943. The basic goals of India's food policy then were to increase food production, stabilize food grain prices and maintain adequate stocks of food grain to avoid any situation of food crisis. This led to the creation of the Public Distribution System (PDS) which functioned in alliance with two bodies: The Food Corporation of India (FCI) and the Agriculture Price Commission (APC). The FCI procures, imports, stores and distributes food gains through village-level distribution centres. The APC controls and guides cropping pattern, land use and profitability in food grains through the minimum support price mechanism. In the post-1990s era, the food management system and delivery were overhauled which involved narrowing the target population of the program. PDS could no longer meet its stated objective of making food grain available among the poorest or reducing the government's food subsidy burden. Rapid economic growth and persistence of malnutrition hence became a confounding feature of the post-liberalization era. Hence, the 'rights-based paradigm' that emerged at the turn of the millennium advocated for legislatively guaranteed multi-sectorial approach towards food security. Intense debate has been brewed on issues related to food price inflation and corruption and leakages in the PDS since then.

A coalition of a non-governmental organization known as the Right to Food Campaign (RTFC), involving a myriad of advocacy groups – from tribal rights network to breast feeding promotion network eventually became successful in getting the National Food Security Act, 2013 passed after almost two decades of advocacy. Though it helped in achieving government's commitment to provisioning food grains for the poor, the approach continued assuming PDS as central in the food policy regime. This is because it has been an unquestioned intervention since India's initial efforts for ensuring food security, which began in 1937. Since then, the program has been expanded with additional objectives to fulfil. From being a war time food ration program to becoming a fundamental program for rural development in the 1970s and 1980s and thereafter, PDS in the current times as a major welfare program also gives political mileage to the government (Mooij, 1998). The reason behind the initiation of the policy of PDS by the state and the way it expanded and why it is now vital for food security has been described and the inter-link between the PDS and agriculture policy has also been elaborated (*Ibid.*). However, there remains scope to problematize the PDS centric approach in the food regime in light of the growing concern regarding marginalization of non-paddy food grains or coarse grains that have not been institutionalized in the PDS.

These coarse grains: climate resistant and nutri-dense were traditionally grown in tribal areas (Hariprasanna et al., 2014). As a result of lack of policy support, the cropped area and total production and per hectare yield of coarse grains have declined considerably. In order to meet the needs of a growing population, it is also important to assure that the measures suggested to improve agriculture does not worsen the existing situation by making the food system more unsustainable and insensitive to nutritional needs of vulnerable population groups. These measures mainly comprise of modernization of agriculture which has been critically examined and widely discussed as limitations of Green revolution (Falcon, 1970; Pingali, 2012). Though the National Food Security Act 2013 proposed to include millets in PDS, its operationalization remains pending.

While marginalization of a particular kind of food is a concern raised in the past, the policy process through which recent institutionalization of coarse grain is being carried out in certain districts is also problematic. In the past decade, several NGOs and State-run institutions have increased impetus on revival of the millets. Currently, production of millets suffers from bottlenecks related to low production, weak markets and difficult methods of processing and low consumer demand (Makkar, 2019). The NGOs interventions, though operating on a smaller scale, have been able to support farmers to produce millets through market linkages even in the absence of any minimum support price from the government. In past two years, the State government of Odisha has launched Millet revival Program in selected seven districts dominated by *adivasi* population and have plans of including it in the PDS and other programs like Integrated Child Development Scheme (ICDS) and Mid-Day Meal (MDM) which provide supplementary food to pregnant women and school children, respectively, through village-level centres. These government initiatives involve implementation support from the NGOs which is an important aspect within the overall millet revival policy process. Though it is a remarkable shift in the agriculture policy to include other kinds of food grains within the State-run food distribution system, it does not bring any radical change in power relations.

The next section describes the changes in food production and consumption ways in a tribal community focusing on power relations between State and community. It also discusses the recent initiatives of the NGOs to revive millets to argue how asymmetrical power relations will tend to get reproduced through recent millet revival policy initiatives.

Understanding power relations in food system transition: a case of **Munda** *tribes in Khunti, Jharkhand*

Khunti district in Jharkhand is predominately inhabited by *Munda* tribes who have traditionally been agriculturists. While in the past, they were widely distributed across the district they retreated to inner forest lands with the advent of people of other cultures in the district. Celebration of changing seasons is an integral part of their culture and they worship multiple deities associated with agriculture and hunting operations. Though it has been examined in other studies that *Munda* tribes have continued their cultural and religious practices even with the advent of modernization and industrialization in the nearby cities (Srivastava, 2007), there have been substantial changes in the food consumption practices in these communities. Traditionally, a paddy and millet producing and consuming area, the production and consumption of millets has declined substantially. As a woman explained, the daily food consumption behaviour of members of her family, she said:

> We used to eat lots of millets as young children. But our children do not like millets. They say it looks black; we don't want to eat it. They like eating rice. That is what we get in the anganwadi centres and in schools also. So, they like it.

> (Interview notes, Khunti)

Similar experience of change in consumption preference was revealed by women of several households. Furthermore, the farmer's group informed that they stopped growing millets as the sowing and harvesting cycle of millets coincides with that of the paddy crop that is now being cultivated in these areas. Since paddy cultivation involves an assurance of procurement due to the Minimum Support Price (MSP) declared by the government, most of the farmers have switched to cultivating paddy. Most of the families in the villages grow very small quantity of millets that is preserved to be consumed during festivals of religious importance. Moreover, in areas where millets are grown in large quantities, the ownership of land differs. As small farmers shifted to production of paddy, the farmers with bigger land, which generally belongs to people of other social group (non-tribal) began cultivating millets which is then marketed to the urban markets. As the farmer's group informed, millets are grown now in more quantity by the *sahukars* (trader caste/business caste). The recent impetus on consuming millets in urban population due to growing consciousness about health has moved millets from the farms of the *adivasi* farmers to the plates of urban population.

Several places in the state of Jharkhand have witnessed efforts of reviving millets in past decade. As it emerged from the experience of one of the NGOs which tried to revive millets five years ago, the main reason for failure is perceived to be lack of policy support from the government. As he explained:

> We took up the Millets Revival Program as part of a project supported by an international organization. Farmers grew millets for two years and the international organization procured the entire produce. So, farmers were happy. But once this organization stopped procuring

farmers were at a loss. There was no market available for selling the millets produce. Hence, after two years farmers stopped producing it.

(Interview notes, NGO, Palamu)

Other members of advocacy groups working towards the implementation of the National Food Security Act, 2013 also raised similar concerns. It is crucial to establish a market if millets are to be produced in large scale in these areas. Most of the NGOs and advocacy groups in Khunti and in other districts of the state of Jharkhand opine that building the market network is crucial for bringing back millets to the farms.

The current focus on the need for market to revive millets is rooted in the agriculture policy related to millets developed in the early years post-independence which was also driven by this logic of the market. The Indian Institute of Millet Research (IIMR) primarily focused on 'promoting economic growth by generating and disseminating technologies which create markets (for these grains).'[4] The research emphasis of this institute, founded in 1958, functioning under the Indian Council of Agricultural Research (ICAR), was to meet food security objectives by creating market-oriented production systems. This would create cash resources for the small-landholders and increase off farm employment for rural and urban poor. This focus of market in policy would require millets to be grown in large scale within the agriculture system of monoculture.

It is due to this reason that even in tribal areas, production of millets in large scale began to be carried out by the trader caste instead of tribal framers who operate at a relatively smaller scale. While inclusion of millets through various policies seem to be an initiative to include indigenous food grain in the food production system, reviving it through mechanism of monoculture continues to alienate the traditional knowledge system of farming. As the farmers informed, the traditional methods of mixed farming within which millet was traditionally grown can no longer be practised because of the promotion of rice or wheat through State policies. This indigenous knowledge related to agriculture based on principles of agro-ecology, thus continues to get marginalized even within the policy discourse related to millets.

Furthermore, these polices and understandings of millet revival would also fail to change the consumption pattern in nutritionally vulnerable communities. Increase in urban demand and marketing mechanisms which forms the basis of the current millet revival model could bring better prices for farmers but that could also lead to lack of consumption of millets by these very farmer households which are nutritionally vulnerable. This would reproduce the urban ways of consumption, and hence, continue its dominance over any local understanding of the relationship between nature, food and human health. The relations between the State, market and community would hence remain unchanged as households would depend on forces of the market to decide what they would consume.

While the millet revival program does aim to ensure consumption of millets by the poor by including it in the government programs like PDS, ICDS and MDM, much needs to be done to improve the implementation of these existing programs. In the past, these policies have received much criticism due to inadequate storage facilities for government procured grains, issues of corruption and low quality of grains supplied through these government programs (Drèze & Khera, 2015; Khera, 2006, 2011). Due to this, there has been a strong urge to replace PDS with cash transfer in the past few years. In this backdrop, a reliance on government procurement and storage services to supply millets to the poor would not ensure the distribution of good quality grains to the poor since demand is also created parallelly in urban centres that would fetch better prices and hence attract higher quality grains. Therefore, the current millet revival initiatives fail to take into cognizance these issues within the existing structure of PDS in its design and implementation. Additionally, it also ignores the crucial dimension of changing consumption patterns in communities with alarming levels of malnutrition.

As preference for food consumption has shifted to emulate the urban diet, millets have increasingly been denigrated as poor man's food. The current food policy while wiping out millets from the farms has created a 'caste system' of food grains. A focus on only improving the production of millets would not necessarily ensure consumption of millets in *adivasi* communities with abysmal nutritional conditions. As a woman explained, changing diets has impacted their condition of nutrition and overall health.

> Our method of farming has changed. We now use chemicals in farming and have been consuming food that is grown using these chemicals. Thus, we need to the hospital to treat us. This was not the case earlier.
>
> (Interview notes, Khunti)

This implied connection between method of agriculture and perception of declining health is indicative of an entwined nature–food–health relationship. Food that is grown using chemicals are perceived to hampering health and nutritional conditions. Despite this understanding, the food preferences have been changing as discussed above. The society–nature relation in the community expressed through food production methods and health connection urges for a need to revisit the concept of nature as understood within food studies. It helps in conceiving food (and nature) not as inanimate matter as is done in the agro-industrial model. On the contrary, it brings out the ways in which nature (in this case, food) impacts human health. This means that nature is an animate participant in human society, and there exists a reciprocal relationship between society and nature (Singh, 1992). An inanimate conception of nature has been argued to be one of the impediments in emergence of more ecologically and materially sustainable food production and consumption models (Bennett, Peterson, & Gordon, 2009).

In addition to this, the changing food consumption preferences reveal the process through which ideas related to neoliberal consumption circulate and alter the local society–nature relations. Food system changes envisioned by the state and NGOs/advocacy groups are also based on the elements of neoliberal discourse like market development and reliance of support from external agents like State or private businesses (Chapman, 2017). Thus, any alternative way of understanding of nature–society relation gets dominated by the neoliberal logic, and new meanings of nature and society relation emerge. The next section describes the creation of these new meanings and marginalization of any alternative world-view as a particular representation of the tribal community dominates.

The tribal representations and changing meanings

> You see, it's a tribal area... so the people here have faulty food habits. They do not eat properly and do not understand that child need to be fed as per their growth needs. We try to make them aware about nutrition but their habits do not change. Hence, they suffer from malnutrition.
>
> (Interview notes, State Nutrition Officer, Ranchi)

The government programs and practices are designed and implemented based on a particular representation of the tribal community as evident from the quote above. The community is perceived to be ignorant and lacking basic ideas of nutrition. Later in explaining about the food habits of the tribal community, the government officer mentioned about the lack of availability of protein-rich food like milk for which the government is trying to launch a program to include eggs in the meals for children and mothers. In this particular understanding of food, certain items are perceived as ideal food. This has been problematized in the past in the scholarship related to food and nutrition based on the analysis of cultural factors of milk consumption (DuPuis's, 2000) and also by looking at the intersection of politics and science of nutrition.

While the conflict between narratives and counternarratives has been clearly drawn in problematizing the global corporate food system, there remains scope to note how these narratives are being increasing joined by other discourses related to eating and the body (Lucy Jarosz, 2015). The science of nutrition has largely escaped scrutiny and has instead been seen as a trusted ally by academics, public health authorities and activists trying to bring out the negative consequences of highly processed fast food or industrially farmed food. For example, some food has been criticized for their high fat or calorie content, while others are celebrated for being rich in micro nutrients and anti-oxidants. This has happened to the extent that there seems to be an exploitation and misuse of the nutrition science by companies to sell their products or create dietary guidelines. Even though the constitutive element of food (viz; fat, calories, carbohydrates, protein or vitamins), which has to bear the brunt of criticism for various forms of Malnutrition and lifestyle-related problems keeps shifting, this approach of reductionism in nutrition has hardly been questioned. It was only recently that this dominant paradigm has been challenged (Jacobs & Steffen, 2003; Pollan, 2008; Scrinis, 2002). This key feature has been referred to as the ideology of *nutritionism* that has played a major role in dietary guidelines and food marketing since 1980s (Scrinis, 2012).

Furthermore, this reductive approach to nutrition informs the larger policies to deal with the problem of malnutrition, explaining it as a problem due to insufficient calorie intake or inadequate food intake combined with poor sanitation, low-income or inefficient agricultural practices. This language of nutrition sanitizes the discussion of hungry and malnourished and maintains a certain social order exerting the power of one kind of knowledge over others (Escobar, 1998). As Arima Mishra (2010) in her anthropological study of hunger and famine in Kalahandi in indigenous communities examines the process of creation of poverty and conditions of hunger, she also challenges the practice of externalizing the blame on faulty food practices prevalent among the local government functionaries. Such a reductionist approach to nutrition aligns with the mainstream approach to agriculture development and also millet revival focusing on building a market-oriented food system.

In the backdrop of this politics of creation of these meanings around certain food items new imaginaries of human–nature relationships are created. Creation of these new imaginaries is part of the process of 'place making'. As a young man from the *Munda* community, now working in a local NGO explains,

> In this area people used to eat millets in the morning and then work for the entire day in the fields. They would not feel hungry for the entire day. So, millets are good. But you see, other foods-like the rice given by the government was not there then. So, there was less food also. Hence, we ate few times in a day. Now we have more food, so we can eat several times in a day.
>
> (Interview notes, Khunti)

The above quote brings out the perception of the people regarding the food system changes. Though millet is understood to be more nutritious providing energy for an entire day's work, the state policy of food is seen to have created an unprecedented abundance of food. This abundance is believed to be brought through State policies. This is in contrast with the food and ecology connection that existed earlier in the community. As is evident from an excerpt from a folklore on *Munda*, paddy and millets were perceived to be given by the gods of heaven and earth for their sustenance and well-being.

"......He led them onto the place.
They found the mat and baskets full of paddy,
The boy said, 'The gods in the heaven have given us paddy
The gods on earth have given us millet
For our sustenance, our well-being......"

(See, Singh, 1992)

Thus, in the past, food was closely related to ecology, symbolized here by the gods of earth, and was crucial for their well-being. A close connection among religious beliefs, nature and food has ensured the consumption of millets even today during festivals. However, millets are no longer consumed as a food of preference. Food has been reduced only to a nutrient providing entity, an important instrument of the State policy and hence lost its connection with ecology. The changes in relationship between society and nature become clearer as food consumption abandons its ecological roots and gets determined by the policies of the State. Thus, it is not only the food production practices promoted through State agriculture policies but the new food consumption ways that have also lost its connection with ecology.

Conclusion

In this chapter, the current policy regime related to food, agriculture and nutrition is reviewed along with the policy process of revival of millets. In the recent past, millet revival has been undertaken by the rising concern to make agriculture system more nutrition centric and climate resilient. Though the recent agro-food scholarship analyses the ecological impact of these efforts to bring in alternative food, it fails to analyse the inherent politics in seemingly inclusive policies of the State. This chapter argues that the policy initiatives of State and NGO programs are driven by the market-oriented neo-liberal logic of development and alienate any alternative society–nature relations. Using the concept of 'place' within a political ecology approach, this chapter explicates the process in which 'place' is made through extra local factors operating at multiple scales. With the advent of multiple development and welfare interventions of the State, any alternative notion of human–nature interaction, shown here through the example of food, gets marginalized. The market-driven welfare policies of the State and civil society organizations while enable expansion of the necessary poverty alleviation policies, it fails to improve the existing inequality in power relation between State, market and communities. Policies are designed based on the dominant knowledge system about agriculture, nutrition and food, the traditional ways of understanding food in connection with ecology continue to remain marginalized. Cereal crops supported through policies of the State have been argued to be state making projects and hence is inherently political (Scott, 2017). It's a major instrument in transforming the rural landscapes and subjectivities of people. This chapter demonstrates the changing subjectivity of people by means of changing food production and consumption preferences. It supports the argument elsewhere that the knowledge production in the area of agriculture has been favouring genetic engineering but locking out innovation related to agroforestry innovation based on traditional ecological knowledge (Pimbert, 2017). The analysis produced in this chapter about the making of 'place' shows the process in which the imagination and lifeworld of the tribal community gets altered. It highlights that policies of millet revival are also not inclusive of traditional knowledge related to methods of agriculture and food. With a focus on the inherent politics of food production and consumption changes, this chapter suggests that there is an urgent need to rethink the existing policy mechanisms that aim to develop a more inclusive and sustainable nutrition-sensitive food system.

Notes

1 Available at http://foodsustainability.eiu.com/ accessed on 10. November. 2019.
2 The idea of food system includes not only food production or agriculture activities but food distribution and transformation, retail as well as consumption behaviour (HLPE, 2017).
3 Bharat Dogra & Baba Mayaram. "Cash Free Farming" available at www.civilsocietyonline.com/static/media/static/2016/02/06/December_2015.pdf.
4 See website http://www.millets.res.in/about-institute.php accessed on 10. November. 2019.

References

Achadi, E., Ahuja, A., Bendech, M. A., Bhutta, Z. A., De-Regil, L. M., Fanzo, J., & Kimani, E. (2016). *Global nutrition report 2016: From promise to impact: Ending malnutrition by 2030.* Washington: International Food Policy Research Institute.
Alvarez, S., Dagnino, E., & Escobar, A. (1998) "Preface and acknowledgments." In *Cultures of politics/politics of cultures: Re-visioning Latin American social movements,* ed. S. Alvarez, E. Dagnino, and A. Escobar, xi–xiii. Boulder: Westview Press.
Arimond, M. H. (2011). *Agricultural interventions and nutrition: Lessons from the past and new evidence.* Rome: FAO.
Bennett, E. M., Peterson, G. D., & Gordon, L. J. (2009). Understanding relationships among multiple ecosystem services. *Ecology Letters, 12*(12), 1394–1404.
Berry, E. M., Dernini, S., Burlingame, B., Meybeck, A., & Conforti, P. (2015). Food security and sustainability: Can one exist without the other? *Public Health Nutrition, 18*(13), 2293–2302.
Berti, P. K. (2003). A review of the effectiveness of agricultural interventions in improving nutrition outcomes. *Public Health Nutrition, 7,* 599–609.
Biersack, A. (1999). "Porgera—Whence and whither?" In *Dilemmas of development: The social and economic impact of the Porgera gold mine, 1989–1994,* ed. C. Filer, 260–279. Canberra: National Research Institute and Asia Pacific Press.
Blaikie, P., & Brookfield, H. (1987). Defining and debating the problem. Land degradation and society/Piers Blaikie and Harold Brookfield with contributions by Bryant Allen...[et al.].

Blay-Palmer, A., Landman, K., Knezevic, I., & Hayhurst, R. (2013). Constructing resilient, transformative communities through sustainable "food hubs". *Local Environment, 18*, 521–528.

Bryant, R. L. (1997). *Third world political ecology*. London and New York: Routledge.

Chapman, A. M. (2017). The neoliberal economy of food: Evaluating the ability of the local food system around Athens, Ohio to address food insecurity (Doctoral dissertation, Ohio University).

Cummins, S., Curtis, S., Diez-Roux, A. V., & Macintyre, S. (2007). Understanding and representing 'place' in health research: a relational approach. *Social Science & Medicine, 65*(9), 1825–1838.

Dev, S. M. (2018). *Transformation of Indian Agriculture? Growth, Inclusiveness and Sustainability* (No. 2018-026). Indira Gandhi Institute of Development Research, Mumbai, India.

Drèze, J., & Khera, R. (2015). Understanding leakages in the public distribution system. *Economic and Political Weekly, 50*(7), 39–42.

DuPuis, E. M. (2000). Not in my body: BGH and the rise of organic milk. *Agriculture and Human Values, 17*(3), 285–295.

DuPuis, E. M., Goodman, D., & Harrison, J. (2006). Just values or just value? Remaking the local in agro-food studies. *Research in Rural Sociology and Development, 12*(06), 241–268.

Escobar, A. (1998). Whose knowledge, whose nature? Biodiversity, conservation, and the political ecology of social movements. *Journal of Political Ecology, 5*(1), 53–82.

Falcon, W. P. (1970). The green revolution: Generations of problems. *American Journal of Agricultural Economics, 52*(5), 698–710.

Finley, J. W., Dimick, D., Marshall, E., Nelson, G. C., Mein, J. R., & Gustafson, D. I. (2017). Nutritional sustainability: Aligning priorities in nutrition and public health with agricultural production. *Advances in Nutrition, 8*(5), 780–788.

Forsyth, T. (2008). Political ecology and the epistemology of social justice. *Geoforum, 39*(2), 756–764.

Gadgil, M. A. (1993). *This fissured land: An ecological history of India*. Berkeley: University of California Press.

Gillespie, S. (2012). The agriculture-nutrition disconnect in India: What do we know? IFPRI Discussion Paper 01187.

Gómez-Baggethun, E., & Ruiz-Pérez, M. (2011). Economic valuation and the commodification of ecosystem services. Progress in Physical Geography, 35(5), 613–628.

Hariprasanna, K., Gomashe, S., Ganapathy, K. N., & Patil, J. V. (2014). Millets for ensuring nutritional security. *Popular Kheti, 2*(3), 170–175.

HLPE. (2017). Nutrition and food systems. A report by the High Level of Experts on Food Security and Nutrition of the Committee on World Food Security. Rome.

IFPRI. (2016). *Global food policy report*. Washington: International Food Policy Research Institute (IFPRI).

Jacobs Jr, D. R., & Steffen, L. M. (2003). Nutrients, foods, and dietary patterns as exposures in research: A framework for food synergy. *The American Journal of Clinical Nutrition, 78*(3), 508S–513S.

Jarosz, L. (2015). Contesting hunger discourses. In *The International Handbook of Political Ecology*. Bryant, R. L. (Ed.). Edward Elgar Publishing.

Khera, R. (2006). Mid-day meals in primary schools: Achievements and challenges. *Economic and Political Weekly, 41*(46), 4742–4750.

Khera, R. (2011). India's public distribution system: Utilization and impact. *Journal of Development Studies, 47*(7), 1038–1060.

Makkar, S. (2019). Millets in the Indian plate: A policy perspective. *Economic and Political Weekly, 54*(36), 49–55.

Marsden, T., & Morley, A. (Eds.). (2014). Current food questions and their scholarly challenges: Creating and framing a sustainable food paradigm. In *Sustainable food systems*, 17–45. Abingdon: Routledge.

Marsden, T., Munton, R., Ward, N., & Whatmore, S. (1996). Agricultural geography and the political economy approach: A review. *Economic Geography, 72*(4), 361e375.

Masset, E. H. C. (2011). *A systematic review of agricultural interventions that aim to improve nutritional status of children*. London: EPPI Centre, Social Science Research Unit, Institute of Education, University of London.

Meeker, J., Haddad, L., & Chisholm, N. (2013). A state-of-the-art review of agriculture-nutrition linkages. An AgriDiet Position Paper, (August).

Mishra, A. (2010). *Hunger and famine in Kalahandi: An anthropological study*. New Delhi: Pearson Education India.

Mooij, J. (1998). Food policy and politics: The political economy of the public distribution system in India. *The Journal of Peasant Studies, 25*(2), 77–101.

Moore, Donald S. (1998). Subaltern struggles and the politics of place: Remapping resistance in Zimbabwe's eastern highlands. *Cultural Anthropology, 13*(3), 344–381.

Moragues-Faus, A. (2017). Problematising justice definitions in public food security debates: Towards global and participative food justices. *Geoforum, 84*, 95e106.

Moragues-Faus, A., & Marsden, T. (2017). The political ecology of food: Carving 'spaces of possibility' in a new research agenda. *Journal of Rural Studies, 55*, 275–288.

Nichols, C. E. (2014). Hidden hunger: A political ecology of food and nutrition in the Kumaon hills. *Geoforum, 64*, 182–191.

Nisbett, N., Gillespie, S., Haddad, L., & Harris, J. (2014). Why worry about the politics of childhood undernutrition? *World Development, 64*, 420–433.

Pauw, K., Ecker, O., & Mazunda, J. (2011). *Agricultural growth, poverty, and nutrition linkages in Malawi*. Washington: International Food Policy Research Institute (IFPRI).

Pimbert, M. P. (Ed.). (2017). *Food sovereignty, agroecology and biocultural diversity: Constructing and contesting knowledge*. London: Routledge.

Pingali, P. L. (2012). Green revolution: Impacts, limits, and the path ahead. *Proceedings of the National Academy of Sciences, 109*(31), 12302–12308.

Pollan, M. (2008). *In defense of food: An eater's manifesto*. New York: Penguin.

Richmond, C., Elliott, S. J., Matthews, R., & Elliott, B. (2005). The political ecology of health: Perceptions of environment, economy, health and well-being among 'Namgis First Nation'. *Health Place, 11*(4), 349–365.

Sarkar, A. (2007). Development and displacement: Land acquisition in West Bengal. *Economic and Political Weekly, 42*(16), 1435–1442.

Scott, J. C. (2017). *Against the grain: A deep history of the earliest states*. New Haven: Yale University Press.

Scrinis, G. (2002). Sorry, marge. *Meanjin, 61*(4), 108.

Scrinis, G. (2012). Nutritionism and functional foods. *The Philosophy of Food, 39*, 269.

Singh, K. S. (1992). The *Munda* epic: An interpretation. *India International Centre Quarterly, 19*(1/2), 75–89.

Sonnino, R., Moragues-Faus, A., & Maggio, A. (2014). Sustainable food security: An emerging research and policy agenda. *International Journal of Sociology of Agriculture Food, 21*(1), 173e188.

Srivastava, M. (2007). The sacred complex of *Munda* tribe. *The Anthropologist, 9*(4), 327–330.

Von Braun, J. (1995). Agricultural commercialization: Impacts on income and nutrition and implications for policy. *Food Policy, 20*(3), 187–202.

Winter, M. (2003). Geographies of food: Agro-food geographies making reconnections. *Progress in Human Geography, 27*(4), 505e513.

World Bank. (2007). *From agriculture to nutrition: Pathways, synergies, and outcomes*, Report No. 40196-GLB. Washington: The World Bank – Agriculture and Rural Development Department.

Xaxa, P. V. (2014). *Report of the high-level committee on socio-economic, health and educational status of tribal communities in India*. New Delhi: Ministry of Tribal Affairs, Government of India.

Zimmerer, K. S. (2000). The reworking of conservation geographies: Nonequilibrium landscapes and nature-society hybrids. *Annals of the Association of American Geographers, 90*(2), 356–369.

5 The political ecology of the Tabasará river basin

Ginés A. Sánchez Arias

Introduction

As cities' hinterlands expand without oversight, they threaten the cultural legacy, territory, and overall quality of life of 370 million indigenous people currently living in the world (Cultural Survival 2018).[1] This tragic reality shows the systematic injustice that comes from neighboring unsustainable, resource extractive societies. In just the last 20 years, Tido and his family have had to protest mining projects (Gjording 1991; Wickstrom 2003), hydroelectric dams (Evans 2015), a weak rule of law, corrupt judges (Cansari and Gausset 2013), development banks and carbon credit opportunism (Hofbauer 2017), human and indigenous rights violations (Pérez et al. 2016) and even conspicuous cartographic practices at the hands of Panamanian government institutions (Smith, Ibañez, and Herrera 2017). These forces amount to a new toolkit of colonialism, hence forth referred to as coloniality. It appears to be ubiquitous that bureaucratic processes exploit time to weaken indigenous people's stamina (Tuhiwai-Smith 2012, p. 24), use mapping tools to uncover their resources (Monmonier 1996; Scott 1998), and sponsor relationships with private industries that in turn profit from their loss (Pérez et al. 2016). This relationship can get progressively worse due to the constant need to leave crops unattended in order to march, and occupy roads, to resist outsider encroachment (Gudynas 2009; Swyngedouw 2004). This chapter uses a political ecology approach to analyze the indigenous resistance movement against extractivism and corruption in Panama. I argue that the Ngäbe ran a successful resistance, even though their river valley was destroyed. Their struggle became known worldwide, pushing the Panamanian government to admit wrongdoing and ultimately inspiring a generation of local NIMBY activists, who continue to advocate for sustainable development in Panama (Figures 5.1 and 5.2).

Methods

In 2013, I started visiting the Comarca Ngäbe-Buglé for extended periods of time, in order to begin assessing sites prior to starting a Ph.D. program at Louisiana State University. For this purpose, I lived with the Ngäbe of the

Figure 5.1 Opening the way for the dam's reservoir in the Tabasará River and point of resistance.

Figure 5.2 Goejet, M10's president, can be seen next to the trunk of a dead Espavé tree. Photographs by the author, December 2013.

Tabasará River basin, specifically, in a hamlet known as Kiad. I attended more than 50 protests on the streets of Panama City, the towns of Tolé and Viguí, and on the Pan-American Highway. As part of a critical ethnographic approach, I became an active witness in the encounters between the Ngäbe, the police, and several government officials. Through the lens of actor-network theory, my study weaves a path through a complex network of actors, including indigenous leaders, government officials, environmentalists, NGOs, political parties, school teachers, a dam, and businesses. Most importantly, I attended and participated in rallies within the Comarca, which gave me insight on the various strategies used by the Ngäbe. I traveled along with locals across mountains and valleys, meeting people, and chatting with them about their livelihoods. My interviews were mostly done informally in order to distance myself from institutional types. I took notes, anecdotal evidence, film, and recordings of some conversations throughout five years of research. At the heart of my fieldwork methods, was becoming a student of Ngäbere, the local language. Learning the language of my hosts became the most valuable part of my approach in studying the political ecology of the Tabasará.

Geographical context: a river, a dam, and a resistance movement

Out of the 52 watersheds in the Isthmus of Panama, the Tabasará river basin is the 24th largest and the 7th longest. This river is born in the Comarca Ngäbe-Buglé, an indigenous territory located in western Panama. It meanders south through the eastern-most hills and marshes of Chiriquí province, making its way to the Pacific Ocean. In 1997, the same year that the Comarca became a recognized territory, a hydroelectric power consortium was created to develop two dams in the Tabasará river. In 2000, the Supreme Court of Panama suspended the project given its failure to obtain the consent of the neighboring communities. But by 2011, Panama's energy demand had grown substantially, and a new concession contract entered into between the National Authority of Public Services (ASEP) and the hydroelectric company, Generadora del Istmo, S. A. (GENISA) gave way to a controversial study of environmental impact (EIA) that was anyhow approved. The situation became truly alarming when an addendum to the construction plans would allow an expansion of the dam's generation capacity, which would mean a taller wall, and the future flood level of the reservoir would increase to the point of inundating houses, crops, fruit gardens. In direct response, the Ngäbe of the Tabasará created *el Movimiento 10 de Abril* (M10), an organization to fight for the health of their river.

M10 slowly became a well-known indigenous environmental movement. Its slogan was to defend the "life, traditions, ecosystem, cultural, and intellectual patrimony of the Ngäbe and Buglé of Panama" (interview with Goejet, M10's president in 2015). M10 not only attracted people directly affected by the damming but also national and international non-indigenous activists. The group eventually built a network of technical supporters (biologists, academics, and conservationists), many of whom helped proof the human right abuses and ecological overstepping in many public debates with government officials.

The case of GENISA's "Barro Blanco dam" has been well documented in national and international news outlets, NGOs (e.g. CIEL, CIAM, and CMW), several Human Rights Commissions, and researchers in environmental justice, policy, and finance (Cansari and Gausset 2013; Evans 2015; Hofbauer and Mayrhofer 2016; Pérez et al. 2016). After more than seven years of failed negotiations, constant protests became an everyday part of life. Due to their relentless resistance, M10 managed to stop the construction of the dam several times, but in the end, the government, admitting to all the faults, anyway, decided that Panama needed the hydropower plant, and offered to pay reparations to those affected by the project. These have not been accepted. Tensions have now waned, and the conflict remains with animosities on all parts. The courts ruled against the indigenous people, and the project completed its construction in August 2016.

Indigenous movements have a unique vantage point. That is, the position of not being fully engulfed by the state's administrative apparatus. At the center of my analysis is the state capitalism's construction of exploitable difference from the borders it creates. In this sense, borders can be drawn where accumulation by dispossession occurs, but also where a "divide and conquer" tactic helps the state redraw borders. This chapter analyses coloniality, capitalism, and poverty in three parts. The first part looks at the cultural border. The second, looks at indigenous resistance and their digital presence, which also looks at mechanisms that help to empower similar struggles dealing with capitalist borders and exploitation. The last part focuses on the legibility of borders, the lack of oversight and institutional presence hinders indigenous representation in politics, which is followed by some conclusive remarks on the aftermath.

Analysis Part 1: remote global capitalism

The hills where indigenous people live are globalizing faster than ever before. This process is happening via the expansion of telecommunication systems, satellite mapping, energy grid expansion, and population growth. The global economic, political, and cultural program that drives colonization is capitalism (Peet, Robbins, and Watts 2011, p. 203). Neo-Marxist approaches in political ecology (Biersack 2006, p. 10; Bryant 1998, p. 80; Watts 1983, p. 267) help articulate this landscape with attention to political economy (Barnes, Peck, and Sheppard 2016). Global capitalism has an ideological appearance: it promises to encourage freedom and creativity, but its systematic exploitative and competitive structure engulf everyone, making them either tools or losers. The cultural dimension of capitalist expansion promises to welcome all peoples into free interactions but works to homogenize cultures at the periphery. The following analysis looks more closely at capitalism at a particular shifting frontier, where it currently tries to absorb new subjects. Following this logic, some Ngäbe can be seen as semi-proletariat, seasonal workers, somewhat-dependent on the cash economy. Many already live or commute to work as household servants or with informal contractors. Some have access to their extended family's agricultural plots, which are do not run as enterprises, while others partially rely on the remittances of family members.

Since colonial expansionism began, capital used brute force to instill the commodity-form into the indigenous populations (Cleaver 1979, p. 86). Since this moment, indigenous people would always be forced to participate in market relationships but from an original position of disempowerment. As numbers of indigenous people dramatically decreased, the colonial governments would create "money taxes" to create a dependency relation (Sauer 1966). Other mechanisms of colonial rule would displace indigenous people to poor quality land (Blaikie 2016, p. 54). Today, the Ngäbe live on one of the worst soils in the entire country (Gordon 1982, p. 4). There are other complexities at play about the current condition of indigenous people's poverty or powerlessness. Refusal to do work for pay was called backwardness by economists of capital, while the necessity of "civilizing" primitive peoples grew (Cleaver 1979, p. 87). This same xenophobic stance still prevails today. The problem comes when hubris overpowers people to act in superior stance to others. Hubris elicits this threshold with regard to development: "Development always entails looking at other worlds regarding what they lack and obstructs the wealth of indigenous alternatives" (Sachs 1999, p. 7).

Indigenous communities' direct ties to the land, forest, or water ecosystems have been shown as examples for living sustainably, which in some parts of the Andean region has been synonymous with *buen vivir* in Spanish or *sumak kawsay* in Quechua (Gudynas 2011; Santos 2014; Walsh 2010). *Buen vivir*, I argue, is an alternative form of "a good quality of life," but given racism, paternalism, and other colonizer manifestations of violence, cannot be allowed even, it seems, the most basic right: to exist. In general, hydropower development affecting indigenous lands has a recent historical precedent as a hybrid neoliberalization process, where private and state institutions sell formerly collective resources to feed urban electrification and international carbon markets (Finley-Brook and Thomas 2010). We can call this process a type of modernized poverty, which derives from scarcity (Sachs 1999, p. 11). This capitalist exploitation of indigenous lands can also be read as the modern colonization of the built boundaries driven by a necessity of economic growth for the metabolism of cities (Gandy 2004, p. 369). An early colonizer's strategy was claiming the alleged vast availability of land in the New World, which prompted the enclosure of territories and restriction of land availability to the colonized (Cleaver 1979, p. 86). Today, the legacy of such practice takes the form of systemic segregation, inequality, marginalization, and pollution.

In the case of the Barro Blanco dam, the poverty produced is as an aggregate of the river overflowing, the reservoir area shifting, the implementation of forced reforestation programs, and in deploying the police to use force to push them out. Risk-assessments from a developmental point of view dismiss the fact that indigenous people end up dealing with the full weight of a dam's externalities, while cities reap all of the benefits (Gandy 2004; Kaika 2003;

Swyngedouw 2009). By damming the flow of the river, a hydroelectric plant also creates an imminent threat for local plant and animal species, that will deal with a change too drastic to adapt to, resulting in extinction (Lansing, Lansing, and Erazo 1998). The "more-than-human world," the unaccounted for, are not even part of the *demos*, and due to having limited mobility across ecosystems, plants and animals suffer hazards and experience disasters even more so than the human inhabitants. In a different plane, indigenous people face exogenous pressures like coloniality and extractivism, thus, in mutual aid, many resistance strategies of indigenous people make use of environmentalism as a political discourse. Since indigenous people's stewardship of nature begins from their alternative relationship to the "more-than-human world," it stands to reason, that any development effort, if it sustainable, can learn from cultures like the Ngäbe (Figure 5.3).

Bakker and Bridge (2006, p. 12) write, "Conceding that commodities do indeed have their origins in social relations that are largely obscured by the commodity form [...] through their circulation, exchange, and use [...] resources perform myriad social functions as 'things in motion.'" Water as energy is one of these obscured commodities. In this darkness, Barro Blanco's maximum capacity of only 28 megawatts of energy outweighs the social cost of impoverishing several hundred people, archaeological sites, places of ritual and pilgrimage, fauna, flora, sediment flows, water regime, land tenure, and mature forests. Panama's National Energy Secretariat in 2007 published that 56% of Panama's installed energy capacity came from hydropower. In 2016, the hydroelectric capacity had doubled to 1,768 MW,

Figure 5.3 Moneni ritual at the petroglyphs (now underwater). This yearly ritual, that can no longer occur on this site of pilgrimage, was evidence of the vital connection of the Mamatada cosmology with the river. This site was on the Tabasará River, 200m from Kiad. Photograph by the author, February 2016.

while remaining at similar share (60%) of gross consumption compared to other types of energy. The energy demand keeps increasing and the grid must adapt to the demand of skyscrapers, hospitals, and other buildings where constant energy flows are indispensable (Interview with the Secretary of Energy in 2014).

Analysis Part 2: #TabasaráLibre

On the digital front, M10 seeks to inspire indigenous people to strive to protect their quality of life, ecosystem, cultural, and intellectual legacy. As M10 matures, it informs itself, more by the global network of empathizers than by the national *status quo*. Their internet hashtag movement became known as #TabasaráLibre. The scope of action in cyber-activism focuses on "freeing the river" from the Barro Blanco hydroelectric project (Hofbauer and Mayrhofer 2016). The hashtag's discourse focuses on the calamities of the centralized economic structure of development where minorities are unrepresented. The hashtag covers various themes concerning colonization: from paternalism, misconceptions of the extreme poverty, indigenous culture priorities, human rights, peace with nature, and nonviolent resistance. #Tabasarálibre also connects an array of actors and news outlets that aim to update the public about the current status of indigenous and peasant communities, and meeting points for workshops and rallies in various parts of the Comarca and surrounding areas.[2]

M10 is largely composed by Mamatada believers, which is fundamentally a non-violent religion (field notes and Guionneau-Sinclair 1987, p. 90), making unlikely clashes with the anti-riot police. Tido, a Mamatada practitioner, does not get involved with street protests, while new generations, who are more active and study their civil rights more closely, do tend to want to fight. Some practitioners helping with the resistance against GENISA come from all over the Comarca. Even though they do not live in the Tabasará basin, they have settled on the project's gates, to pray every day for years without stop. Clementina Perez is their leader, and they call themselves *Movimiento 22 de Septiembre* (M22). M10 and M22 have grown and maintained their cause also supporting other indigenous groups and communities, as with helping other indigenous groups (e.g. Chan 75 dam in the Changuinola River, in Bocas del Toro province).

The internet, provided by telecommunication companies, are rapidly gaining momentum in the Comarca. WhatsApp has already become an established means to organize rallies and meetings, replacing summoning people by traveling across the valleys and mountains. This technology has also helped spread indigenous leaders' voices in real time to news channels and radio shows. Possibly due to the extent of globalization, M10 has centered their campaign for indigenous rights very closely to the United Nations' (UN) declarations of sustainable development goals. Throughout the years, their campaign became ever more articulate under the parameters of environmental justice, possibly given the help of the conservationists who worked in solidarity with them. Their digital presence has been unprecedented among Panama's environmental movements. M10 fliers read "522 years of resistance" and are carried out in opposition to the celebration of the 12 of October (Columbus Day).

Barro Blanco is erected barely outside the Comarca or rather quite literally on the border with it. Its real border is a fluid mass. Indigenous resistance must articulate this evasive boundary. Their campaign must capture the concept of a capitalist hinterland and translate into something that the public opinion can empathize with. By causing habitat loss and fragmentation up and downstream in the aquatic ecosystems, capitalist expropriation simultaneously creates and removes borders to exploit people and the environment. Conversely, GENISA tries to convince the public of the utility they provide and how "green" and desirable they are. Regardless of what is said, land grabbing and land transformation by capitalism's border expansion produce externalities, which ultimately allow for the exacerbation of negative feedback loops in the ecosystem. All types of deforestation, such as mono-crop plantations, have brought about pests that eat that proliferate on the fields of the indigenous communities (Gordon 1982, p. 140). This negative flow prompts indigenous people to leave the highlands and enter the cash economy to survive. In the Comarca, people also have resorted to buying pesticides to protect their crops. In turn, petrochemical pollution enters their ecosystem and water they consume. A diverse forest served as buffer zone protecting the crops but at the current rate of deforestation and the expanding neighboring cattle ranches are just two of the factors that work against indigenous people.

Also, on the digital front, European development banks finance projects encouraging companies to rebrand their slogans of natural resource exploitation to address their discourse towards helping vulnerable peoples in coping with Climate Change or promoting development that helps locals get out of poverty. Non-binding human rights international regimes, like the UN Declaration on Indigenous Rights, offer hope for victims, but human rights treaties also find resistance, as state regulations are not forced to follow them (Murphy 2013, p. 1217; Pérez et al. 2016). Those affected by GENISA's Barro Blanco, campesino and indigenous alike, held dozens of workshops with environmentalists and lawyers to help the many communities understand the long-term implications of the dam. Not the abundance of available information, but the constant use of it in media outlets, forced GENISA to face many setbacks and lose a lot of money and backing, as protests emphasized the many infractions the company had already committed. This, however, backed fired, because public opinion ended up blaming the company and not the spirit of the project. The government was able to join in condemning GENISA, yet still arguing for the national importance of dam, which was even promoted as "green development" and as "renewable energy."

Analysis Part 3: legibility of borders

Most national policies until recently embodied the prejudices of colonial governments, which looked upon indigenous forest-dwellers not as resource managers who possessed sophisticated ecological knowledge (Gordon 1982, p. 158), but as "primitive" peoples who should be pacified, civilized, and eventually incorporated into Western culture (Davis and Wali 1994). Before the Comarca Ngäbe-Buglé existed, *colonos* (colonists) and Ngäbe had a troubled relationship characterized by informal claims to the land, swayed by deception and aggression. The official delimitation of borders of 1997 gave Ngäbe indigenous communities a new level of protection but now under the Panamanian state. It follows, thus, that the state is responsible for protecting indigenous people's property (Wainwright and Bryan 2009, p. 160). Who in power determines when is suitable to respect the boundaries of the disenfranchised? The legibility of borders is at the core of disputes, and still supersede claims over the health of the environment.

With the advent of Climate Change along with capitalist societies' growing understanding of environmental degradation, a special space grew for indigenous people to perform the role as stewards, as conservationists. With the Green Revolution, indigenous people could embody a new identity as protectors of nature and, at the same time protect their territory. Being "closest to nature," they could become the default caretakers of the world's fragile ecosystems (Herlihy and Knapp 2003, p. 308). This can be read as a new environmental determinism that readily assigns Indigenous Peoples to a civilizational job in the network of a "sustainable capitalism." Subsequently, mapping indigenous territory with a participatory twist grew out of the idea that vulnerable landscapes could be protected through a joint effort whereby local communities could map their knowledge of the landscape to make it legible, ultimately protecting it and themselves in the process (Corbett and Keller 2005; Nietschmann 1995). The main problem with legibility and mapping is: who is ultimately empowered my map making? Indeed, mapping initiatives can lead to confusion, or what I call cross-pragmatic incompatibilities (Sánchez-Arias 2015). Tido said in an interview in 2016 (Figure 5.4):

> Once given to the Ngäbe, later it [the Comarca] came to be ignored. In other words, this [delimitation] is not really a law. So, this [boundary post] serves only to entertain. Moreover, who could enforce this [boundary post]? Nobody. Because the same people who make the laws, ignores them.

Maps can be weapons, that for better or worse inform those in power about the exploitable elements of the landscape (Bryan and Wood 2015). Participatory mapping, however, has the potential to be countermapping by providing an institutionally validated means to make clear to the larger society which elements of their indigenous landscape are important to them.

Figure 5.4 Tido on borders. This *hito* (marking) is now underwater. Located 30 mins walk downriver from Kiad. Photograph by the author, June 2016.

The saying goes, "if you cannot beat them, join them" or like Karl Offen (2009) put it, "O mapeas o te mapean" (Map or be mapped). Away from the paradoxical nature of participatory mapping, geographers who help map indigenous landscapes see an emancipatory potential, imperceptibly against the risk of more colonization (Smith et al. 2017). Considering the many examples of cross-cultural political debacles across the world, the less powerful actors either conform, perish, or learn how to play the game (Rocheleau, Thomas-Slayter, and Wangari 1996). Many human geographers and critical cartographers support participatory research because the activity itself is believed to reduce the power imbalances inherent in the historically hierarchical researcher/researched dichotomy (Kelly et al. 2010; Smith et al. 2017). The idea of leveling the playing field with "participation" may give researchers greater insight into the target culture's inner workings. Others claim that giving into the systemic logic might be altogether a cultural defeat (Elwood 2010; Kim 2015). Researchers and participants have been engaging as partners for decades, seeking to undermine monopolies of knowledge (Kindon 2010, p. 519) and since population numbers of many indigenous groups have made a comeback (Gordon 1982, p. 40), they have a better chance in proving continuous presence on the land. Nevertheless, urbanization continues apace, keeping pressures on "remote" ecosystems and cultures. The map, as an antidote, seeks to make borders comprehensive and legible, an inter-linguistic bridge, where nature's stewards and civilized society become harmonic partners. However, in "context-dependent local discourses" about environment and development, "each has lessons to teach and problems to avoid" (Peet and Watts 1996, pp. 15–16).

With participatory mapping, research projects seek to validate indigenous knowledge and experience by combining research with legal action, as well as jumpstarting remote communities into the process of participation in research so they themselves seek mapping as weapon of defense (Davis and Wali 1994). Mapping landmarks with spiritual meaning ends up giving purpose to the participatory countermapping process. One clear example can be seen with the creation of the Comarca. Its districts and place names are in Ngäbere (e.g., Besiko, Mirono, Tabasará). Insights about the cultural landscape as represented through conceptual maps suggest the combination of "genealogical histories and symbolic attributions of place with some form of geographical representation" (Butzer and Williams 1992, pp. 256–257). Moreover, glyphs, runes, and cultural symbols also inform of the importance given to cultural interpretations by indigenous elder's memories and hopes. The importance of looking at these maps is the very politically charged landscape superimposition that results from the "process," the practice of making maps cross-culturally, while inside a colonial landscape.

In opening up mapping as both a didactic activity and legal action, participatory countermapping requires indigenous groups and researchers to appeal to bureaucrats, judges, and government executives for legitimation. However, in Panama, substantial illegal activity operates under cover or by circumventing due process. As a minority group, this task is thus all the more difficult. In this case study, international organizations like the UN have stepped in but have seldom succeeded or wanted to. Countermapping efforts end up neglected in practice. This is the point when and where the scholar-activist must enter the scene. Scholars are trained to dwell within contentious intellectual and technical atmospheres. While "map or be mapped" exemplifies the obvious urgency, academics need to be in the forefront of innovating methods to plan for the failure of conventional means.

Nietschmann (1995, p. 7) writes "[A well-designed map] has transcendental power, because it can be easily translated by everyone everywhere." However, indigenous languages and cultures have developed ontologies that make humanity diverse but at the same time create non-communicable or illegible worlds, which modern states do not care about —unless they can extract value. So, has mapping worked for the betterment of indigenous people's rights and land tenure? (Bryan and Wood 2015). In Panama, participatory research sought to breach the gap between Ngäbe existentialities and those of the Westernizing policymakers in Panama (Smith et al. 2017). Escape from modernity does not seem an option anymore; even the remote areas of the world are scarce, and the question of population growth remains. On top of that, there is a clear need for conservation. Rising internal populations add to the pressures on the biologically diverse environments but also challenge indigenous groups to focus their campaign against outside encroachment. Kiad is a clear example of this.

Making knowledge, not just toponyms, legible can leak sensitive information. Barro Blanco and M10 are just two players under Panama's vast sea of problems with indigenous people. Even while having maps available to them, public opinion never settled the notion of boundaries about the dam or the reservoir. A utilitarian mindset always ran over the facts of borders and law. In this manner, nation-states act to tame indigenous political action with innovations in the bureaucratic processes (Scott 1998), which protect or emulate capitalism, adapting new technics to expand its reach and control. Clerks from "independent" government branches like the Defensoría del Pueblo (Ombudsman) assist Indigenous Peoples to document claims and help them pursue legal action, while at the same time, working as a mirage of hope, dilating time and building new distances between the indigenous people and the perpetrators.

Traditional–modern dichotomies tend to leave Indigenous Peoples on the far side from modernity reflecting a "racial dualism" where indigenous rights are rooted in their status as tradition-bound and stuck in time and against the modern state's seemingly benign intentions to spread wealth (Gordon and Hale 2003; Sletto 2009, p. 256). Such prevailing racial ideologies (and versions of them) are "common sense" in much of Central America (Mollett 2006, p. 1237). Lorde (1984, p. 112) so aptly put it, "[t]he Master's tools will never dismantle the Master's house." Inverting this logic: What but the Master's tools could dismantle the Master's house? "The Master" employs the more powerful tools; if one were to learn how they work, then would one be able to dismantle his house, his capitalism, his borders? This is the caveat with the legibility of maps.

Conclusion: aftermath

As mineral deposits and untapped rivers of Panama become mapped in detail, what is left to ask is: who has the power to cultivate and harvest the map's potential in making the landscape legible? A map contains a summary of all the valuable vectors and anyone in the world can see them and seek to influence a purchase with local authorities. There are laws in place that protect the rights of humans and non-humans, including Indigenous Peoples, but in a landscape determined by corruption, the map is made up of valuable information that can instead be used to plan national projects that will always seem too big for minorities to combat. GENISA knew about this landscape because of maps produced by the state and hoping the "Indians" would quickly surrender, sought to profit and deliver a much-valued service: electric power. In the end, it did not matter that the map showed the political boundary of the Comarca's territories.

The mapped landscape that is cultural, discursive, political, economic, and spiritual helps the group with more resources to make and remake borders that best conform to the maker's agenda. Indeed, the Tabasará has been made substantially more uneven. Borders on a map become a new semiotic landscape for those affected by them. Primitive accumulation of "undiscovered" land for productive efforts and for capital's propagation became the story of modernity: "to legally organize the colonial conquest and expansion of European powers" (Neilson and Mezzadra 2013, p. 32). Now, "a theory of legal pluralism is required" (Teubner 1997, p. 7). Fragmentation of the pluralist possibilities of a World Society become blurred because the border is a method for capital (Neilson and Mezzadra 2013, p. 280), which means that the jurisdictional reaches of the hinterlands draw the limits of the city (Cronon 1992). Thus, the city ends where its extractive capabilities reach. Moreover, the city's networks of influence are not solely economic or energetic. These can also be cultural and psychological.

The process of accumulation by dispossession is closed, static, and unidirectional, serving the people who have the ability to utilize nature for profit. A legible landscape has irreversible consequences (Elwood 2010; Rundstrom 1995), as the Barro Blanco case has shown in relation to of the Comarca's borders. To shift from ontology (how things are) to ontogenesis (how things become) "is a conceptual shift in how we think about maps and cartography" (Del Casino and Hanna 2006, p. 104), in other words, it is legibility. Capitalism creates its own legibility, as it commodifies Ngäbe space: as with the privatization of bodies of water "built around the logic of public law and public goods" (Neilson and Mezzadra 2013, p. 278), can also be considered as an enclosure within a map's jurisdiction. A map's very being is to have a becoming or a process, emphasizing the means over its end goal (Smith et al. 2017, p. 57). The most lingering conceptual misunderstanding during the whole Barro Blanco debacle was the question: where does the dam end? Proponents of Barro Blanco talk about the wall itself, while the ecologically minded look at the reaches of the waterscape.

If both parties hold the same maps at all times, when they come together to dialogue about proposed development projects, what variables and tactics will be used? What policy can exist that helps conserve indigenous valued places? Intended or not, boundary making to secure people in place, wherein people and their cultures are presumed as primordial and static, risks the re-introduction of the "spatial incarceration of the native" (Appadurai 1988, p. 36). The day that the dam started its operations, it meant a direct indigenous right to the ecosystem of the river (Wickstrom 2003, p. 44). A glimpse of the aftermath can be seen in Figure 5.4. Indigenous communities like Kiad keep looking for ways to alleviate these catastrophes with hopes of progressing towards a political arena when uneven power relations will not dictate their fate. This case study also sheds light on how sustainable development needs the rule of law, because illegitimate development, even if a country's majority favors it, still promotes injustice, which further erodes peace. The UNs' 16 SDG, "Peace, Justice and Strong Institutions," is at the crux of the solution. I would argue, also, that SDG #1 "No poverty" can also be addressed in case studies where poverty is not confused with lacking cash, for instance. Modernity is not a requirement for sustainability, and indigenous people can live a dignified life and have the right to exist (Figure 5.5).

In retrospect, the Barro Blanco dam could be seen as the most significant setback against one of the most ambitious cultural revitalizations in the region. In deciding how to become legible as indigenous people, the aftermath of the dam leaves behind the urgent need to decolonize. To this worry, on the banks of the Tabasará River, there is the school that holds the key for a Ngäbe

Figure 5.5 The dam adds new stress to the river ecosystem and to the regrowth forests that ease the slash and burn agriculture of the locals. Regrowth forests must now be sacrificed for food production after the loss of fruit gardens near the fertile banks of the river. The reservoir also fills and recedes leaving a muddy shoreline, complicating human passage. Photograph by the author, February 2017.

adaptive strategy. That is, linguistic innovation from a unique Ngäbe orthography already developing a pedagogy. This opens a new chapter for political ecology's considerations on how written language can inform the struggle for power. For months at a time, Tido walks the comarca teaching reading and writing, spreading his message: the desire to change the fate of the Ngäbe by giving new meaning to their linguistic group. The autonomous indigenous writing system could simultaneously make the Ngäbe a legitimate part of the map of education in Panama, and at the same time allowing an illegible critical literacy to protect the Ngäbe from colonial mentality and extractivism.

Notes

1 See "Alteridad+" on YouTube, a nine-minute documentary comparing the indigenous people of the Tabasará and the people of the affluent neighborhood

of Altos del Golf in Panama City. I made this video to show how narratives about quality of life and corruption across two very different communities can, in practice, be complementary to each other.

2 San Felix, Soloy, Chichica, Cerro Venado, Bajo Mosquito, Llano Palma, Cerro Caña, Llano Culebra, Maraca, Cerro Maíz (in the districts of Tolé, Müna, and Besiko).

Bibliography

Appadurai, A. 1988. Putting Hierarchy in its Place. *Cultural Anthropology* 3(1): 36–49.

Bakker, K., and G. Bridge. 2006. Material Worlds? Resource Geographies and the 'Matter of Nature'. *Progress in Human Geography* 30(1): 5–27.

Barnes, T.J., J. Peck, and E. Sheppard. 2016. *The Wiley-Blackwell Companion to Economic Geography*. Hoboken, NJ: Wiley.

Biersack, A. 2006. Red River, Green War: The Politics of Place along the Porgera River. In *Reimagining Political Ecology*, eds. A. Biersack and James B. Greenberg. Durham, NC: Duke University Press, 233–280.

Blaikie, P. 2016. *The Political Economy of Soil Erosion*. New York, NY: Routledge.

Bryan, J. and D. Wood. 2015. *Weaponizing Maps: Indigenous Peoples and Counterinsurgency in the Americas*. New York, NY: The Guilford Press.

Bryant, R.L. 1998. Power, Knowledge and Political Ecology in the Third World: A Review. *Progress in Physical Geography* 22: 79–94.

Butzer, K.W., and B.J. Williams. 1992. Addendum: Three Indigenous Maps from New Spain Dated Ca. 1580. *Annals of the Association of American Geographers* 82(3): 536–542.

Cansari, R., and Q. Gausset. 2013. Along the Road: The Ngäbe-Buglé Struggle to Protect Environmental Resources in Panama. *The International Indigenous Policy Journal* 4(3). Retrieved from: http://ir.lib.uwo.ca/iipj/vol4/iss3/5

Cleaver, H. 1979. *Reading Capital Politically*. Austin: University of Texas Press.

Corbett, J.M., and C.P. Keller. 2005. An Analytical Framework to Examine Empowerment Associated with Participatory Geographic Information Systems (PGIS). *Cartographica* 40(4): 91–102.

Cronon, W. 1992. *Nature's Metropolis: Chicago and the Great West*. New York, NY: W. W. Norton & Company.

Cultural Survival. 2018. "Issues." *Cultural Survival, Inc.* Retrieved from: www.culturalsurvival.org/issues Accessed Oct. 10, 2019.

Davis, S.H., and A. Wali. 1994. Indigenous Land Tenure and Tropical Forest Management in Latin America. *Ambio* 23(8): 485–490.

Del Casino Jr., V.J., and S. Hanna. 2006. Beyond the 'Binaries:' A Methodological Intervention for Interrogating Maps as Representational Practices. In *The Map Reader: Theories of Mapping Practice and Cartographic Representation*, eds. M. Dodge, R. Kitchin, and C. Perkins. Hoboken, NJ: John Wiley & Sons, Ltd., 102–107.

Elwood, S. 2010. Thinking Outside the Box: Engaging Critical Geographic Information Systems Theory, Practice and Politics in Human Geography. *Geography Compass* 4(1): 45–60.

Evans, K.R. 2015. "TabasaráLibre: A Case Study of Carbon Colonialism in Panama's Barro Blanco Hydroelectric Project". Honors Theses – All. 1522.

Finley-Brook, M., and C. Thomas. 2010. From Malignant Neglect to Extreme Intervention: Treatment of Displaced Indigenous Populations in Two Large Hydro Projects in Panama. *Water Alternatives* 3(2): 269–290.

Gandy, M. 2004. Rethinking Urban Metabolism: Water, Space and the Modern City. *City* (8)4: 363–379.

Gjording, C.N. 1991. *Conditions Not of their Choosing: The Guaymí Indians and Mining Multinationals in Panama*. Washington, DC: Smithsonian Institution Press.

Gordon, E.T., and C.R. Hale. 2003. Rights, Resources, and the Social Memory of Struggle: Reflections and Black Community Land Rights on Nicaragua's Atlantic Coast. *Human Organization* 62(4): 369–381.

Gordon, L.R. 1982. *A Panama Forest and Shore: Natural History and Amerindian Culture in Bocas del Toro*. Pacific Grove, CA: Boxwood Press.

Gudynas, E. 2009. *El mandato ecológico: Derechos de la naturaleza y políticas ambientales en la nueva Constitución*. Quito, Ecuador: Editorial Abya-Yala. Kindle Edition.

———. 2011. Buen vivir: Germinando alternativas al desarrollo. *América Latina en Movimiento* 462: 1–20.

Guionneau-Sinclair, F. 1987. *Movimiento profético e innovación política entre los Ngobe (Guaymí) de Panamá: 1962–1984*. Panamá, PA: Universidad de Panamá.

Herlihy, P., and G. Knapp. 2003. Maps of, By, and for the Peoples of Latin America. *Human Organization* (62)4: 303–314.

Hofbauer, J. 2017. Operationalizing Extraterritorial Obligations in the Context of Climate Project Finance – The Barro Blanco Case. *Journal of Human Rights and the Environment* 8(1): 98–118.

Hofbauer, J., and M. Mayrhofer. 2016. Panama "Barro Blanco" Case Report. COM-CAD Arbeitspapiere: Working Paper No. 144.

Hughes, T. 1988. *Networks of Power: Electrification in Western Society, 1880–1930*. Baltimore, MD: John Hopkins University Press.

Kaika, M. 2003. Constructing Scarcity and Sensationalising Water Politics: 170 Days that Shook Athens. *Antipode* 35(5): 919–954.

Kelly, J. H., P. Herlihy, A. R. Viera, et al. 2010. Indigenous Territoriality at the End of the Social Property Era in Mexico. *Journal of Latin American Geography* 9(3): 161–181.

Kim, A.M. 2015. Critical Cartography 2.0: From Participatory Mapping to Authored Visualizations of Power and People. *Landscape and Urban Planning* 142: 215–225.

Kindon, S. 2010. Participation. In *The SAGE Handbook of Social Geographies*, eds. S. Smith, R. Pain, S. Marston et al. London, UK: SAGE, 517–545.

Lansing, J.S., P.S. Lansing, and J.S. Erazo. 1998. The Value of a River. *Journal of Political Ecology* 5(1): 1–22.

Lorde, A. 1984. The Master's Tools will Never Dismantle the Master's House. In *Sister Outsider: Essays and Speeches*, eds. A. Lorde. Santa Cruz, CA: The Crossing Press, 110–113.

McSweeney, K. 2005. Indigenous Population Growth in the Lowland Neotropics: Social Science Insights for Biodiversity Conservation. *Conservation Biology* 19(5): 1375–1384.

Mollett, S. 2006. Race and Natural Resource Conflicts in Honduras: The Miskito and Garifuna Struggle for Lasa Pulan. *Latin American Research Review* 41(1): 76–101.

Monmonier, M. 1996. *How to Lie with Maps*. Chicago, IL: University of Chicago Press.

Murphy, A.B. 2013. Territory's Continuing Allure. *Annals of the Association of American Geographers* 103(5): 1212–1226.

Neilson B., and S. Mezzadra. 2013. *Border as Method, or, the Multiplication of Labor*. Durham, NC: Duke University Press.

Nietschmann, B. 1995. Defending the Miskito Reefs with Maps and GPS: Mapping with Sail, SCUBA, and Satellite. *Cultural Survival Quarterly* 18(4): 34–37.

Offen, K. 2009. O Mapeas o Te Mapean: Mapeo Indígena y Negro en América Latina. *Tabula Rasa* 10: 163–189.

Peet, R., and M. Watts. 1996. *Liberation Ecologies: Environment, Development, Social Movements.* London, UK: Routledge.

Peet, R., P. Robbin, and M. Watts. 2011. *Global Political Ecology.* London, UK: Routledge.

Pérez, B.F., J.A. Hofbauer, M. Mayrhofer, and P.V. Calzadilla. 2016. Rethinking the Role of Development Banks in Climate Finance: Panama's Barro Blanco CDM Project and Human Rights. *Law, Environment, and Development Journal* 12(1): 1–17.

Porter, P.W., and E.S. Sheppard. 1998. *A World of Difference: Society, Nature, Development.* New York, NY: Guilford.

Rocheleau, D., B. Thomas-Slayter, and E. Wangari, eds. 1996. *Feminist Political Ecology: Global Issues and Local Experiences.* New York, NY: Routledge.

Rundstrom, R.A. 1995. GIS, Indigenous Peoples, and Epistemological Diversity. *Cartography and Geographic Information Science* 22(1): 45–57.

Sachs, W. 1999. *Planet Dialectics: Explorations in Environment and Development.* New York, NY: Zed Books.

Sánchez-Arias, G.A. 2015. Alternative Geographies in the Age of Globalization: On Contradiction and Simultaneity. Revista Panameña de Política N° 19.

Santos, B. de S. 2014. *Epistemologies of the South: Against Epistemicide.* Border, CO: Paradigm Publishers.

Sauer, C.O. 1966. *The Early Spanish Main.* Berkeley: University of California Press.

Scott, J.C. 1998. *Seeing Like a State: How Certain Schemes to Improve the Human Condition have Failed.* New Haven, CT: Yale University Press.

Sletto, B. 2009. 'Indigenous Peoples Don't have Boundaries': Reborderings, Fire Management, and Productions of Authenticities in Indigenous Landscapes. *Cultural Geographies* 16(2): 253–277.

Smith, D.A., A. Ibañez and F. Herrera. 2017. The Importance of Context: Assessing the Benefits and Limitations of Participatory Mapping for Empowering Indigenous Communities in the Comarca Ngäbe-Buglé. *Panama Cartographica* 52(1): 49–62.

Swyngedouw, E. 2004. *Social Power and the Urbanization of Water: Flows of Power.* Oxford, UK: Oxford University Press.

———. 2009. Troubled Waters: The Political Economy of Essential Public Services. In *Water and Sanitation Services: Public Policy and Management*, eds. J.E. Castro, and L. Heller. London: Zed Books, 22–39.

Teubner, G. 1997. Global Bukowina: Legal Pluralism in the World Society. In *Global Law without a State*, ed. G. Teubner. Aldershot, UK: Ashgate, 3–38.

Tuhiwai-Smith, L. 2012. *Decolonizing Methodologies: Research and Indigenous Peoples.* New York, NY: Zed Books.

Wainwright, J., and J. Bryan. 2009. Cartography, Territory, Property: Postcolonial Reflections on Indigenous Counter-mapping in Nicaragua and Belize. *Cultural Geographies* 16(2): 153–178.

Walsh, C. 2010. Development as Buen Vivir: Institutional Arrangements and (De) colonial Entanglements. *Development* 53(1): 15–21.

Watts, M.J. 1983. *Silent Violence.* Berkeley: University of California Press.

Wickstrom, S. 2003. The Politics of Development in Indigenous Panama. *Latin American Perspectives* 131(4): 43–68.

6 Indigenous ecological knowledge in the Colombian Amazon – challenges and prospects for a more sustainable use of local forest fauna

Torsten Krause, Maria Paula Quiceno Mesa and Uldarico Matapí Yucuna

Introduction

For millennia, people have used forest and forest products, created and managed forest ecosystems for their benefit but also degraded or transformed forest areas to other land-uses (Roberts et al. 2017). Across the world, people adapted to living in and with forest ecosystems resulting in an intricate and complex interconnection between people and forests (Sharpe 1998, Roosevelt 2013), which resulted in complex social-ecological and adaptive systems (Messier et al. 2015).

Intact forest ecosystems provide a wealth of benefits and ecosystem services to humankind. Tropical forests are large terrestrial carbon sinks (Jackson et al. 2008), home to a myriad of plant and animal species (Antonelli et al. 2018) and the provider of numerous resources on which millions of people depend (Sunderland et al. 2013). The biophysical impacts of deforestation and forest degradation are manifold and include increased soil erosion (Pimentel 2006), the loss of biodiversity and genetic resources (IPBES 2019), changes in local climatic patterns and hydrological cycles (Jackson et al. 2008), but also lead to social-cultural impacts for instance the loss of ecological knowledge (Rodríguez et al. 2007) and cultural identity.

Many local groups and indigenous people around the world have developed an intricate way of using forest resources and managing forest ecosystems in ways beneficial to people and supportive of what could be termed the environmental stewardship of forests (Reichel-Dolmatoff 1976; Aswani et al. 2018; Paneque-Gálvez et al. 2018). Traditional knowledge, local and indigenous knowledges all share that they are holistic and place based and different from positivist western science. In this chapter, we present the particular relational and situated knowledge of relationships of living beings with one another and with their environment, in our case tropical forests (Berkes 2010, 2018). We use indigenous ecological knowledge (IEK) since we work with an indigenous knowledge holder. Indigenous ecological knowledge can be regarded a sub-set of the broader indigenous knowledge that encompasses much more than the ecological aspects of the territory and includes cultural traditions, language, etc. (Berkes 2018).

Local beliefs and practices based on IEK are increasingly seen as an important source of information for the development of sustainable management practices across the Amazon (van Vliet et al. 2018) and beyond. Indigenous ecological knowledge also has practical advantages and can be used to assess the status of forest biodiversity (Meijaard et al. 2011), identify species and species abundance (Cummings and Read 2016) and species health (Berkes 2018). In addition, research from the Bolivian Amazon suggests that IEK is associated and spatially overlapped with forest conservation (Paneque-Gálvez et al. 2018). Nonetheless, globally there is an impoverishment and loss of IEK driven by globalization, modernization and market integration, particularly affecting medicinal and ethnobotanical knowledge (Aswani et al. 2018), but also ethnobiological practices as we will show in this chapter.

We present findings from collaborative research with a spiritual leader (Shaman) in the Colombian Amazon. Although the role of the spiritual leader is decreasing in many Amazonian indigenous groups, the shaman often still acts as the spiritual leader and a manager of scarce ecological resources, for instance forest fauna. A shaman is an intellectual, spiritual leader and indigenous knowledge holder at the same time, having acquired a wealth of first-hand knowledge by living it (Reichel-Dolmatoff 1999). In this chapter, we present indigenous ecological knowledge with a focus on forest fauna and draw on contemporary forest governance (laws, policies and programs) in Colombia and the interlinkages and challenges it poses for indigenous ecological knowledge.

The Colombian Amazon

The Colombian Amazon covers approximately 6% of the Amazon bioregion and about 42% of the Colombian territory (477,000 km^2). It is still relatively well preserved, due among others, to a low population density (DANE 2011) but also due to the more than five decade long armed conflict which prevented large-scale infrastructure developments and industrial exploitation of mineral and forest resources (Sanchez-Cuervo and Aide 2013). However, since the peace agreement with the FARC-EP and the Colombian government was signed deforestation in Colombia soared, particularly because of the expanding agricultural frontier in the Amazon (IDEAM 2017).

Beginning in the 1980s, the government started to title indigenous reserves (span.: *resguardos indígenas*) based on the notion of collective land rights. Although these do not necessarily reflect the ancestral lands of specific groups, the strive for clarifying land tenure and forest ownership was also an opportunity for many indigenous groups to claim rights to lands they have settled in. Therefore, it is important to understand that the designation of indigenous reserves in Colombia oftentimes does not coincide with the territories that were previously managed via shamanic knowledge since the contemporary reserves are the result of the historical displacement that occurred during the rubber boom and later on also the Colombian armed conflict. The now demarcated reserves represent a de facto formalization of land ownership according to western ideas of formalized land and property. However, the ownership does not infer that the resources of the territory can be freely used or commercialized. For instance, the commercialization of timber outside of the reserve is illegal under Colombian law unless it is done with a permit that can only be granted by the regional autonomous corporations (CARs). Game on the other hand can only be hunted for subsistence purposes and cannot be sold outside the reserve.

Nowadays, half of Colombia's forests are collectively owned by indigenous and local communities, the majority of these areas being located in the Amazon region (RRI 2017) (Figure 6.1). The Colombian Government officially recognizes 87 different Indigenous Peoples in Colombia with collective land titles for 710 indigenous reserves across the country (DANE

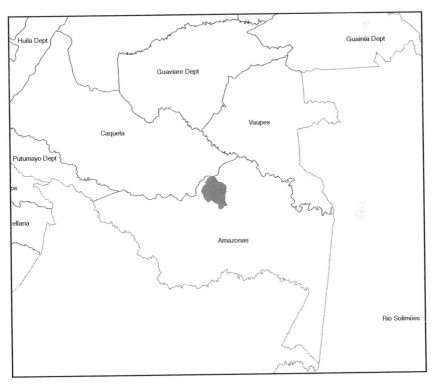

Figure 6.1 The location of the indigenous reserve Nonuya Villa Azul (in grey) in the Colombian Amazonas department.

Source: Googleearth.com

2007). In the Colombian Amazon, there are 56 Indigenous Peoples, including some Indigenous Peoples in voluntary isolation, living in 162 recognized indigenous reserves covering a total area of approximately 24.7 million hectares (OPIAC n/d). Of those, 59 reserves (nine million hectares) overlap with national parks. Indigenous reserves are collectively owned and are imprescriptible as well as inalienable and under autonomous management (Constitution of Colombia 1991).

Methods and material

We used an ethnographic research approach and worked closely with an indigenous knowledge holder from the Matapí[1] ethnicity (Uldarico Matapí Yucuna, who is also a co-author of this book chapter and who is considered to be the last shaman, or spiritual leader, of the Upichía) over several years. We carried out this work in the indigenous reserve Nonuya Villa Azul, located in the Amazonas department in south-eastern Colombia, because it is the home of Uldarico Matapí. Nonuya Villa Azul borders the Caquetá river to the south and the Yari river to the west and is for most part covered by lowland Amazonian rainforest. The reserve covers an area of approximately 2,600 square kilometers and is pluriethnic as it includes people from five different ethnicities – Matapí (Upichía), Nonuya, Muinane, Yucuna and Huitoto.

In June 2017, after several rounds of negotiations and being granted access to the reserve, we visited the reserve and had long conversations with both the traditional, elected authority of the reserve and the spiritual authority (i.e., Uldarico Matapí) that lasted over several days during our visit. While the traditional authority is elected by members of an indigenous reserve and acts as the legal representatives of the territory before the Colombian authorities, the shaman as the spiritual leader is not elected but his or her knowledge and role is passed down ancestrally.

We started to collaborate with Uldarico Matapí because he has worked extensively with Tropenbos International Colombia for more than two decades and published several reports and books on indigenous cartography, history of the ethnic group, inter-ethnic relations, the symbolic and shamanic aspects of traditional management (e.g., Matapí and Matapí 1997; Matapí and Yucuna 2012). While western cosmovision has been shaped by science, in the indigenous cosmovision, it is the spiritual leader of an ethnic group who organizes information into structured knowledge, he is thus the true supplier and transmitter of indigenous knowledge (Reichel-Dolmatoff 1999). Thus, Uldarico Matapí is regarded as a facilitator and mediator who translates, documents and interprets indigenous knowledge to the benefit of science and society, which facilitated this collaborative research tremendously. Moreover, while part of our collaborative work took place in the reserve of Nonuya Villa Azul, we also met on several occasions in Bogotá, due to difficulty in accessing the reserve.

Throughout this chapter, we draw on the collaborative work with him and much of what we write is based on his knowledge and the accounts of his experience. A major aim of our collaborative work is to document and share this knowledge and experience and to provide a brief account of the indigenous ecological knowledge, with a focus on forest fauna, and the contemporary challenges for forest governance in Colombia. Within the framework of our collaborative research, Uldarico Matapí also authored a report (in Spanish) on indigenous knowledges on which we draw, either through interpreting the report or by using direct quotes from the report itself (referenced as Uldarico Matapí 2018). This report documents the particular indigenous cosmovision and ecological knowledge on forest resources use and the contemporary challenges that pose a threat for the continuous existence of the IEK of the Upichía and other Indigenous Peoples. Furthermore, we also include the conversations we had with the traditional authority of the reserve of Nonuya Villa Azul (translated into English). We discuss how IEK on forest fauna can inform forest governance at large. Therefore, and in addition to the aforementioned reports and documents, we consulted available literature on IEK and forest fauna in the region and official texts including the national constitution, as well as laws and decrees published by the government relating to indigenous reserves and hunting.

The Amazon is a pluricultural region characterized by a tremendous diversity of ethnicities, languages and knowledges (Davis 1996). Although much of what we present is based on the cosmovision and knowledge of the Upichía, there are some similarities to the traditions and cosmovision of other ethnicities. However, the challenges and threats for IEK and indigenous reserves and territories encountered by other ethnicities are similar throughout the Colombian Amazon, albeit they may be conceived and analyzed in a different manner depending on the specific local context.

The colonial project and the implications for indigenous ecological knowledge

"In order to understand the present, we have to analyze and understand the acts of the past, which can also teach us the future" (Uldarico Matapí 2018). For centuries, the Amazon region has been eyed as a vast track of resources rich and unused land. The tropical forests of the Colombian Amazon, despite being among the most remote areas of this vast biome, have been exploited for more than two centuries (Davis 1996; Uribe 2017). Starting in the end of the 19th century and driven by growing industrial demand the extraction of rubber (e.g., *Hevea brasiliensis)* represented the first major wave of exploitation. In the course of the fateful rise in rubber extraction, rubber companies enslaved tens of thousands of indigenous people who suffered tremendously from violence and forced labor. During the rubber boom, a major reconfiguration of indigenous territories took place and many indigenous groups were displaced from ancestral territories, their numbers decimated or their peoples entirely extirpated (Hecht and Cockburn 2011), shaping the cultural geography of the north-western Amazon found today.

In the beginning of the 20th century, after the rubber boom ceded and rubber plantations in Asia replaced Amazonian rubber, another wave of exploitation started and lasted for several decades until the late 1970s (Antunes et al. 2016). Hunting of Amazonian animals reached industrial scales as the trade of Amazonian hides was a lucrative market and demand in Europe and the US was high. Most commonly hunted species were black caiman, giant and neo-tropical otters, jaguar and ocelot for the skin and fur trade (Payán and Trujillo 2006; Antunes et al. 2016). The trade in Amazonian hides is nowadays regulated and largely prohibited by national legislations, but harvesting for consumption and the illegal trade in wild meat continues to pose a threat to a range of species (van Vliet et al. 2014; Sarti et al. 2015). Although commercial hunting, that is for selling meat, animal parts or live animals, is officially prohibited in Colombia, subsistence hunting, that is for own consumption, is legal and forms an important part of indigenous cultural identity and daily livelihoods across the Amazon (Reichel-Dolmatoff 1976; Colombia 1991; Maldonado Rodríguez 2010).

Throughout history, the colonization of the Amazon was pursued as a project for national state-building, securitization of the national borders, expanding agricultural frontiers into 'empty and unused' lands, exploitation of natural resources and 'civilizing' the tribes of the hinterlands. In the wake of several economic booms, the colonization and state-building efforts, indigenous people were assimilated into the 'modern' way of life, often with the help of evangelical missionaries (Uribe 2017), who still operate almost unchecked throughout the Amazon region. The state-building still continues, for instance through state mandated educational programs that place indigenous children from more remote communities in residential schools where they are taught in Spanish. However, the wealth of indigenous knowledges (not just ecological knowledges for that matter), language and customs are restricted to the confined spaces of the respective indigenous reserves and left to the teachings of parents and elders, who often do not see their children for extended periods of time due to the distance of the residential schools.

Most recently, conservation and the expansion of national parks have become another disguise for the state to colonize the Amazon and to subdue Indigenous Peoples living in reserves overlapping or adjacent to national parks. This conservation bonanza ironically coincides with the increase in deforestation in the frontier areas of the Colombian Amazon and other state-led infrastructure and development projects that are pushed onto the land and also into indigenous territories. This has received strong critique by representatives of indigenous reserves in the middle Caquetá river area, who claim that "the state is negotiating with foreign companies and governments about resources and even about the forest without consultation" (Personal Communication – traditional authority, June 2017), undermining the constitutional rights to consultation and free prior and informed consent.

Colombia's institutional and legal framework support indigenous rights and land tenure. The Colombian Constitution establishes indigenous reserves (span. *resguardos*) grants a high degree of political autonomy and the right to self-governance (Constitución de la República de Colombia 1991, Art. 330) as well as the right to use natural resources sustainably (this excludes, however, mineral and other non-renewable resources) (Colombia 1991). According to the Colombian constitution, indigenous reserves cannot be subdivided or transferred in whole or in part (Colombia 1991, Art. 63) and indigenous reserves are recognized as territorial entities similar to departments or municipalities (Art. 286). Article 330 further stipulates the right of indigenous communities to participate in decisions taken on natural resource exploitation within the formalized boundaries of indigenous reserves. Nonetheless, these boundaries often do not match ancestral territories or sacred sites, which may be subject to mining and forestry exploitation.

In the wake of territorial legalization that started in the last decades of the 20th century and continues to this day, indigenous reserves (*resguardos*) were delineated but often resulted in the division of territories and respective territorial management that were previously considered as a unit managed through indigenous knowledge by the shaman and elders. The resulting reduction of previously larger and often fluid territories has significant implications to this day. Physically, it led to the establishment of fixed communities and settlements. Spiritually is meant the containment and restriction of knowledge to the boundaries of the now established reserves. As Uldarico notes "a geographical plot has no sense of indigenous cultural belonging" (Uldarico Matapí 2018).

Although indigenous knowledge and management are recognized by the government in theory, for instance in the recent National Development Plan (DNP 2018), in practice they are rendered insignificant as the state does not recognize these as valid forms of management, outside the reserves. Thus, indigenous management and knowledge systems are currently only respected within the boundaries of indigenous reserves. This also means that traditional forms of management exerted by shamans and spiritual leaders, and elders is being confused by the boundaries laid out by the state and restricted, for example by the designation of National Parks as state projects for conservation (Espectador 2017). Moreover, even inside the reserves, indigenous knowledge and management are at risk of being lost as it is practiced by a decreasing number of elders, indigenous knowledge holders and a few younger indigenous people who want to keep this knowledge alive.

Colombia has ratified two international agreements – the United Nations Declaration on the Rights of Indigenous Peoples (UNDRIP 2008) in 2009 and the International Labor Organization's convention 169 (ILO 1989) in 1991. In accordance with the ILO convention, indigenous people have the right to land and resources, to participation in decision-making, the right to self-determination and the right to consultation regarding any decisions or projects (private or publicly lead) that might affect their rights. Regarding hunting, the Colombian legal framework allows indigenous people to carry out subsistence hunting in indigenous reserves, but with the limitation that hunting should be practiced in a way that does not cause deterioration (Decreto 1076 2015). However, neither subsistence nor deterioration are defined in the legal frameworks. Some areas of indigenous reserves that overlap with protected areas and national parks are subject to special management regimes (REM – *régimen especial de manejo* requiring coordination between the state and indigenous authorities in order to regulate the use and management of natural resources jointly (MINAMBIENTE n.d.).

Although indigenous knowledge is recognized in the National Development Plan of Colombia (DNP 2018), the Colombian constitution only recognizes the use and customs of indigenous people and does not refer to indigenous ecological knowledge. This has implications to the designation of indigenous reserves which are defined by the state and demarcate territorial limits but not a particular ethnic territory nor ancestral territories, although they are often represented as ethnic territories. In reality, most of the indigenous reserves in Colombia are pluriethnic, that is there are more than one ethnicity living alongside one another. This is important, since the pluriethnicity of the reserves itself poses challenges in how to manage and govern the forest. Within the established reserves, indigenous people are allowed to practice their traditions, but outside of which these traditions and indigenous knowledges are rarely valid or recognized.

The significance of indigenous ecological knowledge on forest fauna

Indigenous ecological knowledge and the different ways in which indigenous people perceive and relate to their territory are the basis for indigenous cosmovision and culture (Reichel-Dolmatoff 1976). In the Amazon, animals are an integral part in indigenous cosmovision and subsistence hunting and fishing are a major component of local livelihoods and important cultural tradition, deeply connected to the integrity and management of the territory (van der Hammen 1992; Rodríguez and Van der Hammen 2003). Traditionally, indigenous communities have since time immemorial used a vast range of forest products and animals. The number of species that are consumed varies and depends on the particular cultural preferences of the ethnic groups and taboos. Certain species are recognized as fit for human consumption only during specific times of the year based on intricate ecological calendars and linked to the availability of forest fruits consumed by these. Likewise, hunting techniques vary and were adapted to the circumstances and ecological conditions, the time of the year and the species sought after. Local restrictions regarding meat also play an important role, for instance the restrictions in the preparation and consumption of certain species for pregnant and breast-feeding women (Bonilla Riveros 2014).

From a legal perspective, forest fauna has no human owner, and people cannot claim ownership over faunal resources. The absence of private ownership over an important material but also spiritual resource is, however, not a tragedy of the commons as it might be in other contexts where private ownership is considered key for effective natural resource governance.

In the cosmovision of the Upichía, it is first and foremost the existence of the forest and its flora what provides the basis of animal and people's existence. It is then the knowledge about the forest, the basis for all live, that moves the world and gives rise to any form of territorial management. This is reflected in the recognition of supranatural laws that are in place to manage the territory, laws that were not invented by people but originate in the very beginning of life. According to these laws, the forest, the trees and animals have owners with which one has to establish a relationship according to the law of origin (Fausto 2012; Echeverri 2016).

Traditional management based on other forms of ownership that is spiritual, i.e., the notion of the masters of the animals or owners of the game (*dueños*) is deeply entangled in the local cosmovision where every species is said to have a master or owner, who releases these slowly for hunting by humans. In that sense, the notion of extinction that is often used in the conservation context is not understood by people for whom animals are also 'people' and where hunting and the presence and availability of animals depend on the animals' owners (*dueños*) who release them after negotiation with the shaman. In the same context, the word management can also be misinterpreted, since it is the *dueños* who take care of the animals and what happens in the forest (Cabrera 2012).

Despite the onset of modernity and the introduction of firearms that changed traditional hunting practices substantially, IEK still plays an important role for local hunters, albeit it is no longer as important and respected as it used to be. For instance, knowing the location of salt licks that are frequented by different animals in the forest and what rules to follow when going to hunt at the salt licks is considered fundamental for a good hunter who is respectful of species hunted (Cabrera 2012). Some salt licks are sacred sites which are considered the home (the *maloca* of certain species, for instance the tapir) and respected as the dwellings of the owner or master of species, and hunting in these is prohibited or restricted to important occasions only (Cabrera 2012; Bonilla Riveros 2014). However, outside the sacred sites, animals can be hunted and in areas close to the river and in cultivated areas (in Spanish – *chagras*) without prior permission from the owner or master of the species.

The spiritual leaders of an ethnic group know, relate and transmit the history of the creation of the world by the creators (the Upichia refere to it as *Karipulaquena*). Being such an ancient science, it has its own language, which is a primitive language that only creators and other beings of that time understand. It is a clear and precise language that does not include lying. The importance of shamanism allows and facilitates the compliance, functioning, use and management of the natural resources of the forest. It also guarantees the continuous use of the forest and the cultural environment without causing any deterioration (see Matapí and Yucuna 2012).

The Upichía cosmovision recognizes and distinguishes four distinct forms of management of the territory, each having a specific place and meaning (Uldarico Matapí 2018).

1   Shamanic management – based on the spiritual knowledge and abilities that a shaman possesses – a shaman is identified in childhood and educated to be able to exert the knowledge and abilities – ancestral and indigenous knowledge; only passed on from shaman to shaman and not shared with others. Among many of the indigenous ethnicities in the Colombian Amazon and elsewhere, shamans are in charge of mediating between the supernatural world, natural resources and human beings, i.e., the people of the tribe and have been the spiritual authority that also provided spiritual protection.
2   Ethnic management – based on ethnicity (belonging to group) – indigenous knowledge often exerted among elders, which is distinct from shamanic knowledge
3   Cultural management – based on alliances forged during marriage – ability to manage knowledge across different ethnicities (in some of the ethnic groups of the Colombian Amazon exogamy was common and even required) (see (Davis 1996)),
4   Mythical management – passed from elders to children – based on stories and orally translated myths

Local indigenous governance for the Upichía is thus based on the sum of the different types of management as described above. Without being able to pass on the respective knowledge and management principles, the ability to govern the territory is eroding as one cannot govern and manage what is not known. Knowledge about the forest is crucial and is above everything else as the rules on how to manage the forest were established even before the origin of animals. It is the vegetation that constitutes the forest and that, through providing food, allows all other living beings to survive.

The importance of IEK is strongly related to the ecological calendars that indicate the seasonal changes and dictate the different activities that can be carried out during these seasons in response to the productivity of the forest (planting, harvesting, collecting fruits, fishing, hunting, etc.), which are influenced by climatic (e.g., rainfall and temperature), solar and lunar changes over the course of the year. The ecological calendars originate from the creators of the world and are inextricably linked to indigenous knowledge, without which it is not possible to manage the forest which, in turn, only exist due to the ancestral creation that is manifested by the ecological calendars.

The animals that live in the forest are pre-destined for human use (for food, medicine, art, or in spiritual meaning and myths) but must be respected. Hunters have to follow certain principles, for instance for planned hunting trips with the purpose to supply meat for special occasions (e.g., traditional celebrations) the shaman has to consults the owners of the species (*dueños*) and asks for permission prior to the hunt. If a hunter is not going on a planned hunt, he can hunt any animal that he encounters, as long as the ecological calendar is followed, since the encounter is a sign that the animal is given to the hunter as game by the respective owner. The ecological calendars in turn are based on intricate knowledge of the forest and how it changes over the course of a year. It gives clues as to when trees bear fruit, when the fish migrate, or when certain animal species can be taken (when they are fat) and when they cannot be hunted (when they are skinny), which depends on the availability of fruit and other foods.

The consumption of meat from forest animals is an obligation and a physical requirement for the nutrition of the body, but one must know when the meat provides that nutrition. If one knows how to handle and how to use the meat, then one nourishes the body. As described by one of the traditional leaders "The meat tastes according to what happens in the forest, if I don't eat it, I don't know where to go to look for seeds and fruits I need" (Personal Communication, traditional authority, 2017). Thus, knowledge about forest fauna, and what animals can be hunted, where and when to hunt them and how to handle their meat is crucial for the nourishment of the body, but also to maintain the relationship with the forest and to read and understand what is happening in the forest. However, as Uldarico recounts "today the links with and incorporation of other cultures erodes the traditionally prohibited consumption of certain species. Nowadays, it is much more, because we enter the white culture and consume without the authorization of anyone, forgetting our own customs" (Uldarico Matapí 2018). Indigenous ecological knowledge and local hunting can be an effective conservation measure since, in the words of Uldarico, "protecting and preserving for the Colombian Indigenous Peoples is not to prohibit, because to prohibit is to subject society to the destruction of things" (Uldarico Matapí 2018).

Discussion – the future of IEK in the Colombian Amazon

The socio-economic and ecological changes that affect the Amazon are not just a threat to the forest itself but also to the future existence of IEK. Along these lines, Uldarico Matapí identifies three main challenges for the future of indigenous knowledge. First and foremost, the existence of money which historically has brought destruction and violence, as evidenced by the rubber and pelt booms. The second challenge is the rapid advancement of contemporary technology, which despite its positive implications of allowing exchange and communication also radically transforms peoples' relationships with another and imposes a mainstream cultural ideal inspired by western culture. The third challenge is political power, represented by contemporary state policies and legal frameworks that affect indigenous territorial autonomy and decision to ever greater extents. As he eloquently frames "the destructor now makes the rules and imposes the conditions under which we now have to manage our territories and forests" (Uldarico Matapí 2018). This statement also speaks to the larger issue of a lack of indigenous participation in decision-making and state-driven pathways for a more sustainable development (Collen et al. 2016).

Indigenous people are often seen as environmental stewards and destructors at the same time. They are portrayed as stewards if they continue to keep their traditions and continue to live as they have in the past, but destructors if they dare to embrace demonized western lifestyles. The truth is that modernity and the market economy have expanded into the most remote corner of the Amazon and changes are inevitable. However, how this change can reconcile sound environmental management and respectful and sustainable forest resource use that is fundamental for indigenous cultures is a daunting task. This is particularly true if hunting continues to be stigmatized and portrayed as a clash with the western conservation mindset and the idea that forest protection and conservation often are understood and framed as human non-interferences in 'natural' processes. Yet, based on indigenous worldviews, the human presence and use of the territory are fundamental in order to maintain a cultural identity and to respect the resources nature provides. Not using these resources, for instance wild animals, leads to their extinction, since they are no longer part present in the mind and cultural memory. Consumption of wild meat is inherently necessary to maintain the human body and soul and not using resources of the forest to maintain one's body and those of one's family are the first step towards the loss of culture and ecological knowledge related to the different uses of forest resources.

Hunting is not just an important livelihood activity in the Colombian Amazon, it also has an important cultural meaning (Sirén 2012). However, contemporary forest governance continues to omit indigenous cosmovision around hunting and the traditional management of forest fauna, thus failing to take social conditions surrounding hunting into consideration. In traditional Amazonian worldviews, everything has or can have an owner and nature is domestic because it is the domus of someone (Descola 1986) and the non-human world neither belongs to everyone nor is it no one's land (Fausto 2012). Yet, this central feature of Amazonia indigenous worldview is in conflict with the modern state's ambition to continuously seek to define ownership over resources and impose a universal vision of conservation. An example of this is the legislation on fauna within current regulatory frameworks where all trade in wild meat is illegal, blurring the difference between the subsistence hunter who sells some of his harvest and capitalized commercial hunter (van Vliet et al. 2015). Indigenous ecological knowledge and its documentation and subsequent application in hunting management and practice can become an important cornerstone in the discussion whether or not to allow for hunting to become a legal source of income for indigenous people. This discussion and shift in state mandated hunting regulations can potentially counteract the current decline in IEK but also help to increase the respect for indigenous knowledge and management.

Given the extent of indigenous reserves in the Amazon, state mandated forest resources governance and conservation efforts must respect the traditional use and spiritual connection indigenous people have with the forests and animals that are an integral part of the territory and their ways of life. Up to date, the relatively low population densities in the Colombian Amazon (DANE 2011) and reasonably large and intact forest areas that are fairly remote from road infrastructure, larger rivers and urban centers have so far provided a refuge for terrestrial forest species. Although the pelt hunting era may be over, overharvesting of forest fauna, particularly large bodied mammals, is threatening animal populations, particularly those close to urban centers and markets, which are also affected by habitat loss and degradation (van Vliet et al. 2014). Faunal declines in turn affect local communities, decreasing their hunting efficiency and their ability to meet dietary needs and threatening food security (Nasi et al. 2011). Because wild meat is an important contributor to diets (Sarti et al. 2015) and has an important cultural significance (Sirén 2012), sustainable hunting management guided by IEK of wild forest fauna must be a crucial component of forest governance. Moreover, losing wild animals as an important food source increases the dependence of local populations on the market economy and may propel timber harvesting or other forest degrading activities, such as mining and livestock, in order to obtain necessary income to purchase food.

One of the main preoccupations expressed by Uldarico and other informants is that younger hunters no longer know and follow traditional rules, which is a serious threat to the continuous existence of IEK. This is a trend observed across many indigenous communities, where indigenous languages and cultures are slowly disappearing and with-it entire chapters of human history and knowledges that are invaluable (Davis 2009). The reasons for it are manifold and range from neoliberal state building and development projects extending into the most remote corners, to the loss of territory and rights over access to natural resources. Moreover, after the rubber boom in the Amazon, the more recent Colombian armed conflict coupled with the growing and trade of illicit drugs and illegal gold mining are still significantly affecting indigenous communities throughout Colombia and the Amazon (Rodríguez 2016). Although Colombia has signed international conventions that demand for instance free, prior and informed consent, the state continuously seeks to undermine territorial autonomy through neoliberal development projects, or through central education plans and teaching in Spanish. This also means that children from remote communities are often sent to schools where they stay in residential schools away from home during the week, without contact with the forest or their native language where they are taught based on a western curriculum and value system. Furthermore, with increasing access to social media and modern technology, elders are increasingly worried about the resulting shift in worldviews, oriented towards mainstream ideas of ways of life, which results in the undervaluing or even rejection of local traditions. Recognizing the interconnection between cultural and biological diversity is key as the loss of IEK threatens not only forest biodiversity (Aswani et al. 2018) but also of the tremendous cultural diversity that still exists today (Davis 2009).

The Amazon remains the largest continuous rainforest in the world, home to hundreds of ethnic groups. Moreover, in light of the global efforts to materialize and achieve the Sustainable Development Goals, the Amazon region is of particular importance. From a material perspective, it is a major carbon sink and thus plays a crucial role in the mitigation of climate change (SDG 13- climate action). Moreover, it is the habitat for the vast share of the world's known terrestrial species (SDG 15- Life on Land) and important in safeguarding biodiversity. However, from a more immaterial point of view, the different forms of indigenous knowledges that still exist are of immense value, in and by themselves, but also because they may be in fact useful for science and society. Current forms of development based on extractive industries and modernization often disregard these immaterial values. Moreover, the traditional indigenous people should not only be seen as beneficiaries of sustainable development but in fact as agents in driving and materializing sustainable development in their territories and beyond. It is therefore in the global interest to understand the social-ecological relations of the Amazon forests, and how indigenous people relate to the forest based on local ontologies, how they manage the resources of the forest and how the indigenous ecological knowledge that still exists can be safeguarded. Doing so requires an interdisciplinary and integrated way to study forest ecosystems to understand social-ecological relations. This is a task only achieved from multiple scientific angles and with respect to different ontologies and worldviews.

For attaining a truly integrated and holistic perspective, the very people who have lived in and whose cultures have adapted to forest ecosystems over centuries must be included. The indigenous "way of life reveals to us the possibility of a separate strategy of cultural development; ... it presents us with alternatives on an intellectual level and on a philosophical level. We should keep in mind these alternative cognitive models" (Reichel-Dolmatoff 1999). Yet, the powerful positivist model of science continues to dismiss other types of ontologies and epistemologies (Baptiste 2018), reducing forests to carbon in a utilitarian narrative about forests role in the mitigation of climate change (Nielsen 2014; Echeverri 2016). This is a worrying trend that not only fails to account for IEK that has been an integral way of life in the

Amazonian forests but also marks a decline in social-ecological relations forged over millennia.

Conclusion

In this chapter, we discussed how state policies and the establishment of indigenous reserves as a place for the different ethnicities to reside undermine traditional management of indigenous territories. Given that many indigenous groups in the Colombian Amazon have historically been displaced and forced to migrate, most of their ancestral territories do not coincide with the contemporary indigenous reserves that were established by the state. For indigenous knowledge holders and spiritual leaders such as Uldarico Matapí, this is crucial since they cannot manage a territory which they do not consider to be theirs and for which they do not have the necessary knowledge to exercise their responsibility.

Based on the insights that indigenous knowledge, particularly ecological knowledge, has to offer for a more inclusive, respectful and holistic approach to forest governance, it must be acknowledged and included in scientific endeavors, for instance in tropical forest ecology and management, but also in governmental initiatives that operate under the umbrella of forest governance. The work carried out by organizations such as Tropenbos International Colombia has to be acknowledged here. Continuing this work would allow us to understand more about social-ecological interlinkages that are recognized and articulated in IEK and learn from indigenous approaches to forest governance in the Amazon region.

Failing to recognize the importance of indigenous ecological knowledge undermines the long-term effectiveness and equity of global and local efforts to protect forests and to ensure the continuous existence of the tremendous biocultural diversity that is still present in the Colombian Amazon. Through collaborative work with local experts and especially with Uldarico, it becomes more evident that the understanding of social-ecological systems and the implications for management necessarily involves the actual use of resources and especially wildlife. The material and symbolic interactions are the source of knowledge and keep knowledge alive, ultimately allowing for the adaptation of management strategies. Herein, the documentation and understanding of local ecological calendars are fundamental to maintain and recognize traditional resource rules and the social ecological interrelations as well as the fluctuating ecological productivity which defines how indigenous people used and still use forest resources, plant their agroforestry fields or carry out fishing.

Finally, any research with indigenous communities must consider and respect the outstanding value of local and indigenous knowledge and create spaces for dialogue and collaborative forms of research. Only then will it be possible to communicate the rich indigenous knowledges to other researchers, society and decision makers that are geographically, culturally and spiritually detached from these local social-ecological systems in the Amazon region. However, working through meaningful collaboration requires that researchers commit and invest time and effort in the long term. The relative isolation of many Amazonian communities makes collaborative work difficult. Yet, without more permanent transdisciplinary research, the language and symbolic richness of the contributions from indigenous knowledges towards a more sustainable resource management are difficult to position in global dialogues and decision-making bodies that ultimately decide over the fate of the Amazon.

Note

1 The Matapí ethnicity is an ethnic group historically living in the area of the upper Mirití and Apaporis River, in north-western Amazonia. The Matapí refer to themselves as Upichía, which is an alternative name and throughout the chapter we use the word Upichía when we refer to the corresponding indigenous ecological knowledge.

References

Antonelli, A., A. Zizka, F. A. Carvalho, R. Scharn, C. D. Bacon, D. Silvestro, and F. L. Condamine. 2018. Amazonia is the primary source of Neotropical biodiversity. *Proceedings of the National Academy of Sciences* **115**:6034–6039.

Antunes, A. P., R. M. Fewster, E. M. Venticinque, C. A. Peres, T. Levi, F. Rohe, and G. H. Shepard. 2016. Empty forest or empty rivers? A century of commercial hunting in Amazonia. *Science Advances* **2**: e1600936.

Aswani, S., A. Lemahieu, and W. H. H. Sauer. 2018. Global trends of local ecological knowledge and future implications. *PLoS One* **13**:e0195440.

Baptiste, B. 2018. *Chamanismo: Brujería o Conocimiento? Todo es Ciencia.* Colciencias, Bogotá.

Berkes, F. 2010. Devolution of environment and resources governance: Trends and future. *Environmental Conservation* **37**:489–500.

Berkes, F. 2018. *Sacred Ecology.* 3rd edition. Routledge, New York.

Bonilla Riveros, T. A. 2014. *Usos, prácticas e ideologías socio-culturales de la cacería de dos comunidades Tikuna, ubicadas en el sur de la Amazonía colombiana.* Universidad Nacional de Colombia – Sede Amazonía, Leticia.

Cabrera, J. A. 2012. *Natural licks and people: Towards an understanding of the ecological and social dimensions of licks in the Colombian Amazon.* University of Kent, Kent.

Collen, W., T. Krause, L. Mundaca, and K. A. Nicholas. 2016. Building local institutions for national conservation programs: Lessons for developing Reducing Emissions from Deforestation and Forest Degradation (REDD+) programs. *Ecology and Society* **21**(2):4.

Colombia, C. d. l. R. d. 1991. Constitucíon de 1991 con reformas hasta 2009. Page 125. Corte Constitucional, Bogotá.

Cummings, A. R., and J. M. Read. 2016. Drawing on traditional knowledge to identify and describe ecosystem services associated with Northern Amazon's multiple-use plants. *International Journal of Biodiversity Science, Ecosystem Services & Management* **12**:39–56.

Dane. 2007. *Colombia una Nación Multicultural.* Departamento Administrativo Nacional de Estadística, Bogotá.

Dane. 2011. *Estimaciones De Población 1985–2005 Y Proyecciones De Población 2005–2020 Total Departamental Por Área.* Departamento Administrativo Nacional de Estadística, Bogotá.

Davis, W. 1996. *One river – Explorations and discoveries in the Amazon rainforest.* Vintage, London.

Davis, W. 2009. *The wayfinders – Why ancient wisdom matters in the modern world.* House of Anansi Press, Toronto.

Decreto 1076. 2015. Ministerio de Ambiente y Desarollo Sostenible. Government of Colombia, Bogotá.

Descola, P. 1986. *La Nature Domestique: Simbolisme et Praxis dans l'Écologie des Achuar.* Éditions de la Maison des Sciences de l'Homme, Paris.

DNP. 2018. Bases del Plan Nacional de Desarrollo 2018–2022. Page 945 *in* D. N. d. Planeación, editor. Government of Colombia, Bogotá.

Echeverri, J. Á. 2016. *Amazonia 2020, sin visión indígena. UN Periódico.* Universidad Nacional de Colombia, Bogotá.

Espectador. 2017. *Las críticas a Visión Amazonia.* El Espectador. El Espectador, Bogotá.

Fausto, C. 2012. *Warfare and shamanism in Amazonia.* Cambridge University Press, New York.

Hecht, S., and A. Cockburn. 2011. *Fate of the forest: Developers, destroyers, and defenders of the Amazon.* University of Chicago Press, Chicago.

IDEAM. 2017. Esfuerzos del país se concentran en alcanzar meta de zero deforestación.*in* MINAMBIENTE, editor. Sala de Prensa. *Colombian institute of hydrology, meteorology and environmental studies.* IDEAM, Bogota.

ILO. 1989. *C 169 Indigenous and tribal peoples convention.* International Labour Organization, Geneva.

IPBES. 2019. Global assessment report on biodiversity and ecosystem services of the Intergovernmental Science-Policy Platform on Biodiversity and Ecosystem Services. IPBES Secretariat, Bonn, Germany.

Jackson, R. B., J. T. Randerson, J. G. Canadell, R. G. Anderson, R. Avissar, D. D. Baldocchi, G. B. Bonan, K. Caldeira, N. S. Diffenbaugh, C. B. Field, B. A. Hungate, E. G. Jobbágy, L. M. Kueppers, M. D. Nosetto, and D. E. Pataki. 2008. Protecting climate with forests. *Environmental Research Letters* **3**:044006.

Maldonado Rodríguez, A. M. 2010. *The impact of subsistence hunting by Tikunas on game species in Amacayacu National Park, Colombian Amazon.* Oxford Brookes University, Oxford.

Matapí, C., and U. Matapí. 1997. *History of the Upichía.* Tropbenbos International, Bogotá.

Matapí, U., and R. Yucuna. 2012. *Cartografía ancestral yucuna-matapí: Conocimiento y manejo tradicional del territorio.* Tropenbos Internacional Colombia, Bogotá.

Meijaard, E., K. Mengersen, D. Buchori, A. Nurcahyo, M. Ancrenaz, S. Wich, S. S. U. Atmoko, A. Tjiu, D. Prasetyo, Nardiyono, Y. Hadiprakarsa, L. Christy, J. Wells, G. Albar, and A. J. Marshall. 2011. Why don't we ask? A complementary method for assessing the status of great apes. *PLoS One* **6**:e18008.

Messier, C., K. Puettmann, R. Chazdon, K. P. Andersson, V. A. Angers, L. Brotons, E. Filotas, R. Tittler, L. Parrott, and S. A. Levin. 2015. From management to stewardship: Viewing forests as complex adaptive systems in an uncertain world. *Conservation Letters* **8**:368–377.

Minambiente. n.d. *Línea temática de manejo: Regímenes Especiales de Manejo.* Parques Nacionales Naturales de Colombia. Parques Nacionales Naturales de Colombia, Bogotá.

Nasi, R., F. E. Putz, P. Pacheco, S. Wunder, and S. Anta. 2011. Sustainable forest management and carbon in tropical Latin America: The case for REDD. *Forests* **2**:200–217.

Nielsen, T. D. 2014. The role of discourses in governing forests to combat climate change. *International Environmental Agreements: Politics, Law and Economics* **14**:265–280.

OPIAC. n/d. Miembros de la OPIAC. National organisation of Indigenous People in the Colombian Amazon Bogotá.

Paneque-Gálvez, J., I. Pérez-Llorente, A. C. Luz, M. Guèze, J. F. Mas, M. J. Macía, M. Orta-Martínez, and V. Reyes-García. 2018. High overlap between traditional ecological knowledge and forest conservation found in the Bolivian Amazon. *Ambio* **47**:908–923.

Payán, E., and L. A. Trujillo. 2006. The tigrilladas in Colombia. *Cat News* **44**:25–28.

Pimentel, D. 2006. Soil erosion: A food and environmental threat. *Environment Development and Sustainability* **8**:119–137.

Reichel-Dolmatoff, G. 1976. Cosmology as ecological analysis: A view from the rain forest. *Man* **11**:307–318.

Reichel-Dolmatoff, G. 1999. A view from the headwaters. *The Ecologist* **29**:276–280.

Roberts, P., C. Hunt, M. Arroyo-Kalin, D. Evans, and N. Boivin. 2017. The deep human prehistory of global tropical forests and its relevance for modern conservation. *Nature Plants* **3**:17093.

Rodríguez, C. A., and M. C. Van der Hammen. 2003. Manejo indígena de la fauna en el Bajo y Medio Río Caquetá; tradición, transformación y desafíos para su conservación y uso sostenible. Page 14 *in V Congreso Internacional de Manejo de Fauna Silvestre en la Amazonia y Latinoamérico.* Fundación Natura, Bogota.

Rodríguez, C. A., M. C. van der Hammen, and M. Gruezmacher. 2007. Conocer para respetar: Principios Ecológico – Culturales Indígenas y el Enfoque Ecosistémico (UICN) en la Amazonia Colombiana. Page 89 *in* Á. Andrade, editor. *Aplicación del Enfoque Ecosistémico en Latinomérica.* Commission on Ecosystem Management & The World Conservation Union, Bogotá.

Rodríguez, G. A. 2016. *Los conflictos ambientales en Colombia y su incidencia en los territorios indígenas.* Editorial Universidad del Rosario, Bogotá.

Roosevelt, A. C. 2013. The Amazon and the anthropocene: 13,000 years of human influence in a tropical rainforest. *Anthropocene* **4**:69–87.

RRI. 2017. *Tenure data and tool – Colombia.* Rights and Resources Initiative, Washington.

Sanchez-Cuervo, A. M., and T. M. Aide. 2013. Consequences of the armed conflict, forced human displacement, and land abandonment on forest cover change in Colombia: A multi-scaled analysis. *Ecosystems* **16**:1052–1070.

Sarti, F. M., C. Adams, C. Morsello, N. van Vliet, T. Schor, B. Yag,e, L. Tellez, M. P. Quiceno-Mesa, and D. Cruz. 2015. Beyond protein intake: Bushmeat as source of micronutrients in the Amazon. *Ecology and Society* **20**:22.

Sharpe, B. 1998. Forest people and conservation initiatives: Ihe cultural context of rain forest conservation in West Africa. Pages 75–97 *in* F. B. Goldsmith, editor. *Tropical rain forest: A wider perspective.* Springer Netherlands, Dordrecht.

Sirén, A. 2012. Festival hunting by the kichwa people in the ecuadorian amazon. *Journal of Ethnobiology* **32**:30–50.

Sunderland, T. C. H., B. Powell, A. Ickowitz, S. Foli, M. Pinedo-Vasquez, R. Nasi, and C. Padoch. 2013. *Food security and nutrition: The role of forests.* Center for International Forestry Research (CIFOR), Bogor, Indonesia.

UNDRIP. 2008. *United Nations declaration on the rights of Indigenous Peoples.* United Nations.

Uribe, S. 2017. *Frontier road – Power, history, and the everyday state in the Colombian Amazon.* Wiley Blackwell, Oxford.

van der Hammen, M. C. 1992. *Managing the world – Nature and society by the Yukuna of the Colombian Amazonia.* Tropenbos, Colombia.

van Vliet, N., J. Fa, and R. Nasi. 2015. Managing hunting under uncertainty: From one-off ecological indicators to resilience approaches in assessing the sustainability of bushmeat hunting. *Ecology and Society* **20**(3):7.

van Vliet, N., L. L'haridon, J. Gomez, L. Vanegas, F. Sandrin, and R. Nasi. 2018. Chapter 26- The use of traditional ecological knowledge in the context of participatory wildlife management: Examples from indigenous communities in Puerto Nariño, Amazonas-Colombia. Pages 497–512 *in* R. R. Nóbrega Alves and U. P. Albuquerque, editors. *Ethnozoology.* Academic Press, Cambridge.

van Vliet, N., M. P. Quiceno Mesa, D. Cruz-Antia, L. J. Neves de Aquino, J. Moreno, and R. Nasi. 2014. The uncovered volumes of bushmeat commercialized in the Amazonian trifrontier between Colombia, Peru & Brazil. *Ethnobiology and Conservation* **3**:1–11.

7 A dialogue of knowledges – what can we bring home from the plurivers?

Roy Krøvel

Introduction

This chapter draws on experiences from participating in a joint university project between Oslo Metropolitan University and three indigenous and communitarian universities in Colombia, Ecuador and Nicaragua. During the project, 45 master students and 5 PhD students from the three indigenous and communitarian universities received scholarships to complete masters degrees or PhDs. Additionally, a series of workshops and conferences was organized to develop indigenous and communitarian research methodologies. Master students, PhD students and academics from the indigenous and communitarian universities employed the research methodologies made at these workshops in various research projects.

In this chapter, I wish to explore the possibility of mutual understanding between very different traditions of science. There are of course many philosophies, views or perspectives on science in Norway, but I will place the tradition I identify with, within the framework of the thinking of philosopher Arne Næss and the deep ecology movement.

The Nordic environmental movement that emerged in the 1970s was closely associated with "deep ecology." The movement sought to counter increasing materialism, consumerism, and struggled against expansive industrial development projects such as dam building on indigenous people's traditional territories. According to the Deep Ecology platform, the well-being and flourishing of human and nonhuman life on Earth have value in themselves (synonyms: inherent worth, intrinsic value, inherent value). "Richness and diversity of life forms contribute to the realization of these values and are also values in themselves" (Næss and Sessions, 1984).

Before becoming a full-time environmentalist, Arne Næss spent four decades as a university professor of philosophy. No Norwegian scientist have had such an impact on the development of Norwegian universities as Næss. Næss developed obligatory introductory courses to philosophy and science that formed and informed generations of Norwegian academics.

In Latin America, the indigenous movement is also closely related to resistance against expansive capital, defence of territories and unfair exploitation of natural resources. The emerging network of indigenous universities in the continent is closely related to the indigenous movement. To what extent can these seemingly parallel movements learn from each other? Can Deep Ecology be helpful as a bridge to understand the philosophies of the emerging indigenous universities in Latin America?

According to Escobar, the concept of "Buen Vivir" embraces the "inseparability and interdependence of humans and nature" (Escobar in White, 2018). Concepts such as "Buen Vivir" are informing "critiques of the prevailing development model, confronting basic assumptions about progress, competition, consumerism, and materialism." Indigenous organizations are rejecting anthropocentricism as well as capitalist and socialist forms of development because both "are destructive of both humans and ecological systems." (White, 2018). Critique of anthropocentrism and the interdependence of humans and nature were key themes also for deep ecologists. The chapter draws on documents published by indigenous and communitarian universities in Nicaragua, Colombia and Ecuador to discuss and analyze how indigenous researchers in the network of indigenous universities (RUIICAR) discuss issues related to nature and society. A comparison will be made with key documents from the Deep Ecology movement. The purpose is to explore similarities and differences between deep ecology and indigenous people's knowledges with the hope of understanding both better.

The Network of Indigenous, Intercultural and Community Universities of Abya Yala (RUIICAY)

The universities discussed in this chapter are members of the Network of Indigenous, Intercultural and Community Universities of Abya Yala (RUIICAY). RUIICAY is an example of a transnational network uniting forces in the struggle to build and defend locally self-governed institutions of higher education.

Three members of RUIICAY took part in a project funded by The Norwegian Programme for Capacity Development in Higher Education and Research for Development (NORHED) that forms the background for the experiences discussed here.

The Pluriversidad Amawtay Wasi in Ecuador and the Universidad Autónoma Indígena Intercultural (UAIIN) in Colombia were both founded by indigenous organizations with roots going back to the early 1970s. The third member of the project is University of the Autonomous Regions of the Nicaraguan Caribbean Coast (URACCAN) in Nicaragua. The common trait in the historical context of these three institutions is that Indigenous Peoples and minorities have gained rights and autonomy only over the last three decades, and only after protracted and often violent struggles. However, the struggle to build autonomous systems for higher education continues and has been an ongoing issue throughout the course of the NORHED project.

For the RUIICAY-universities, the concept *interculturality* plays an important role. For these universities, interculturality refers to communication between different cultures that contribute to building equity and mutual respect. In the literature, interculturality is often related to ideas of "hybrid" identities and "fusion cultures." These terms seek to capture the ways people and groups create and recreate new cultural patterns integrating new elements of formerly distinct and separated norms, values, behaviors, and lifestyles. As the universities explain in documents describing the cooperation in the network, humanity is confronted with a set of global challenges such as climate change and loss of natural diversity that can only be solved if individuals, groups, and cultures manage to build mutual understanding across cultures and experiences.

Methodology – a dialogue of knowledges

The research presented here is not "objective" in the meaning "disinterestedness" (Merton, 1942). I have been working with some of the indigenous and communitarian universities for 20 years, in addition to having a close relationship with some of the indigenous organizations mentioned in this article. At the same time, I have participated in environmental activism with some of the Norwegian deep ecologists mentioned here. Instead of being "disinterested," I try to draw on these experiences to reflect from the inside with the goal of building mutual understanding between the two traditions. As such, the methodology is inspired by what the indigenous and communitarian universities (RUIICAY) call "Dialogue between knowledges" ("Diálogo de Saberes"). As one group of academics and activists (fittingly named "Diálogo de Sabers") explains the rationale of diálogo de sabers:

> All knowledge is incomplete (of course, also science), so reciprocity is necessary to share experiences and improve them. However, reciprocity from the premise of equality (...). Therefore, we need a translation exercise among these knowledges to make them mutually intelligible.
>
> (Diálogo de Saberes)

To explore deep ecology in light of indigenous concepts such as "Buen vivir" and the "pluriverse," I will explore qualitatively key documents from the two traditions of knowledge. On the one hand, I select texts from the indigenous universities that expand on research methodologies, pedagogy, and philosophy, in addition to 45 master theses that seek to follow the guidelines set out in the first documents. On the other hand, I have selected texts published by Arne Næss explaining deep ecology in addition to texts by other environmentalists that engage with and criticize Næss' deep ecology from different ecological perspectives.

The analysis will focus on aspects that relate to nature and environment and how dissimilar ontologies contribute to producing different worldviews (cosmovisión) and "knowledges." I explore these texts to make an informed systematic analysis building on my interpretation of the texts.

A short presentation of the texts:

- CCRISAC is a jointly produced documentation of indigenous science and research methodologies titled "Base Document for Cultivation and Nurture of Wisdom and Knowledge" (Gutierrez, 2019). It sums up methodologies used by indigenous and communitarian researchers at the participating universities. The CCRISAC was produced at a long series of workshops held at the three universities over a period of three years. More than 20 researchers, including myself, were involved in the process.
- The second document I will draw on is also the result of a long and participatory process. Ten indigenous researchers jointly authored an introduction to the philosophy of the indigenous university of Ecuador: Kapak Ñan Pedagógico: Filosófico de la Pluriversidad "Amawtay Wasi" (The Great Road of Learning: The philosophy of the Pluriversity "Amawtay Wasi") (Sarango et al., 2017).
- In addition, I have systematized 45 master theses submitted and defended during the project. The research projects for the master theses were done following the principles set out in the CCRISAC. Feedback from the students played an important role as the CCRISAC was revised and a second version published in 2018.

In addition, I have selected texts from various perspectives related to Deep Ecology that can help shed light on the (possible) relationships between Deep Ecology and Indigenous Knowledges from CCRISAC perspectives.

- The first text selected to "represent" Deep Ecology is the Deep Ecology Platform published by Næss and Sessions in 1984 (Næss and Sessions, 1984). Næss had already published his original Deep Ecology Paper at a conference in 1972 that became the start of a philosophical movement. However, the Deep Ecology Platform is even more concise and elegantly sums up the thinking behind the movement.
- In *Ecology, Community, and Lifestyle: Outline of an Ecosophy*, Arne Næss examines the "relevance of philosophy to the problems of environmental degradation and the rethinking of the relationship between mankind and nature" (Næss, 1990).
- Sigmund Kvaløy Sætreng was a fellow mountaineer, deep ecologist, philosopher, and friend. Nevertheless, he held a slightly divergent view on holism, harmony, and conflict, a view that is relevant when trying

to understand the social and political context of the indigenous and communitarian universities. I will in particular draw on arguments put forward in the article "Complexity And Time: Breaking the Pyramid's Reign" printed in Reed (1993).

- Finally, Murray Bookchin was a fierce critic of Deep Ecology from an alternative ecological perspective. The "social ecologist" Bookchin argued that deep ecologists failed to account for the social and economic root causes for current ecological crisis, a perspective that can help us understand why the indigenous universities are so preoccupied with capitalism and market liberalism (Bookchin, 1993).

Indigenous Peoples in Nordic eco-philosophy from Næss to Vetlesen

From the outset, deep ecology was inspired by non-western thinkers. Næss, for instance, published a book on Gandhi's political ethics (Næss, 2000). In addition, deep ecologists such as Næss, Sigmund Kvaløy Setereng, and Nils Faarlund were influenced by the Sherpa culture they encountered when traveling or climbing in the Himalayas. It was the environmental protests and the attempt to blockade the hydroelectric dam in the river Alta that led to the most intimate cooperation with Indigenous Peoples (the Sámi). Drengson expressed the relationship with Indigenous Peoples by deep ecologists in the following way in the article called Some Thought on the Deep Ecology Movement:

> If we do not accept the industrial development model, what then? Endorsing the Deep Ecology Platform principles leads us to attend to the "ecosophies" of aboriginal and indigenous people so as to learn from them values and practices that can help us to dwell wisely in the many different places in this world.
>
> (Drengson)

More recently, the theme of Indigenous Peoples and a perceived sensitivity towards nature and environment has been taken up by a new generation of philosophy professors such as Arne Johan Vetlesen.

Eduardo Viveiros de Castro, meanwhile, explains that what falls under the domain of social andhuman relations for … Amazonian peoples' is very broad. In fact, "animals, plants, spirits are all conceived as persons" so that "modern distinctions between nature and culture, animals and humans, and even descent and marriage ties are effectively inverted" (Skafish, 2013, p. 15). The difference between "occidental" and Indigenous Peoples ontologies are perhaps deeper than what can be captured by or imagined based on the above description of deep ecology.

The deep ecology platform

Deep ecology as environmentalism in general emerged as a popular grass-roots political movement inspired by the publication of Rachel Carson's book Silent Spring (Carson, 1962). In the early 1970s, Arne Næss came to believe that two different forms of environmentalism were emerging. He called the first one "long-range deep ecology movement." The second he called the "shallow ecology movement." The a "deep" movement engaged in deep questioning of our purposes and values, right down to fundamental root causes for ecological degradation. The "shallow" movement, on the other hand,

> stops before the ultimate level of fundamental change, often promoting technological fixes (e.g. recycling, increased automotive efficiency, export-driven monocultural organic agriculture) based on the same consumption-oriented values and methods of the industrial economy"
>
> (Drengson)

The deep ecology platform consists of eight points formulated by Næss and George Sessions and published in 1984. For the purpose of this chapter, some of the points are particularly relevant.[1] The first point reads "The well-being and flourishing of human and nonhuman life on Earth have value in themselves" (Næss and Sessions, 1984). The second point highlights the significance of diversity: "Richness and diversity of life forms contribute to the realization of these values and are also values in themselves." The political component arises from the point stating, "Present human interference with the nonhuman world is excessive" and "Policies must therefore be changed. The changes in policies affect basic economic, technological, and ideological structures. The resulting state of affairs will be deeply different from the present." Political change is not enough without appropriate ideological change. "The ideological change is mainly that of appreciating life quality." Næss laid out his view on life quality in "Ecosophy T" which originally was presented as his personal philosophy. Ecosophy T has "self-realization" as its core. To realize oneself, however, is not understood in a traditional Western way such as "Fulfillment by oneself of the possibilities of one's character or personality" (Merriam-Webster, 2019). Through this capitalized Self, according to Næss, in distinction to realization of man's narrow selves, the realization of ourselves as part of an ecospheric whole contribute to the blossoming of every being.

The call for deep change, including the ways we appreciate life quality, links Næss to the indigenous concept "buen vivir" – a term is used by indigenous movements to promote well-being of human and nonhuman life. It includes critique of Western development theory as well as promoting alternatives to development emerging from indigenous traditions. The full richness of the term is difficult to translate into English as it includes "quality of life" in a form that is only possible in community. Nature is understood to be an integral part of this community.

> Buen Vivir embraces the inseparability and interdependence of humans and nature. In the current development debates, Buen Vivir has informed critiques of the prevailing development model, confronting basic assumptions about progress, competition, consumerism, and materialism. It rejects anthropocentricism and critiques capitalist and socialist forms of development because both, albeit in different ways and to different degrees, are destructive of both humans and ecological systems. The ethos of Buen Vivir centers on fostering harmony between humans and nature, quality of life, and conviviality.
>
> (Escobar in White, 2018, pp. 3–4)

The critique of development models, basic assumptions about progress, competition, consumerism, materialism, anthropocentricism, and capitalist as well as socialist forms of development, in many ways echoes deep ecology.

Environmental conflict and ecology in indigenous regions

To deepen our understanding of indigenous perspectives of "Buen Vivir" in community including nature, let us now turn to the master students taking part in the RUIICAY master program. In one assignment, we asked the students to go back to the home villages and hometowns and make interviews with at least three local leaders. Two thirds of the students were indigenous. The rest were either Afro-descendants or Mestizos living in regions with a significant indigenous population.

The students could freely select local leaders but were asked to make qualitative interviews about nature, environment, and/or exploitation of natural resources. The vast majority of students included community leaders alongside employees of national or international Non-Governmental Organizations working in the area. Most interviews quickly started to revolve around issues of trust and mistrust between local communities and outsiders working for nongovernmental organizations (NGOs).

After completing the task, we systematized the interviews. Three categories emerged based on the quality of intercultural communication and understanding between the actors. The first category contains strongly conflicting perspectives and struggles over fundamentally conflicting views of the world. The second category describes a situation with less conflict but with serious challenges affecting potential collaboration. The third category contains descriptions of alliances reflecting mutual understanding based on respect.

Many community leaders express frustration and concern over the presence of multinational companies in or around their territories. The main criticism is that the extractive industries show little or no understanding of how the natural resources are crucial to the communities' survival, and since the companies are not directly affected by the contamination or destruction their activity cause, they are not able to understand or willing to listen to the Indigenous communities' ecological practices. In many cases, the interviewees put this conflict into a broader context, where global power structures are seen as a reason for the fundamental lack of understanding of the environment.

One student quoted Inocencio Ramos from the Consejo Regional Indígena del Cauca (CRIC) in Colombia. Ramos sees the economic system as the underlying cause behind the conflicts.

> Capitalism looks at the land from the outside and see a resource, as synonymous with money. For Indigenous Peoples it is different. We see the land as a relative, as "family." That is how deep the differences between the two visions are.

At the same time, he and other interviewees point out that the struggle against the extractive industries has been important to create intercultural alliances between different peoples, between Indigenous and non-Indigenous sectors.

Anti-capitalism is fundamental not only to Indigenous environmentalists such as Inocencio Ramos but also to the Indigenous universities, as becomes clear when reading *The philosophy of the Pluriversity Amwatay Wasi, The Great Road of Learning* (Sarango et al., 2017). Capitalism is presented as the engine driving destructive extraction of natural resources and as the generative mechanism behind individualism threatening to destroy communities.

A large group of interviews tell about collaborations with state agencies and NGOs that fail – despite having the best of intentions – because of the conflicting motives. Julián Caluguillin, leader of the community Florencia-Cayambe in Ecuador, says that the challenge for leftist organizations from the urban areas is to take the fight for the land seriously. "The left needs to take more seriously the critique of "progress" as the only goal of the peoples. Indigenous Peoples and ecologists question the very idea of eternal progress that is destroying the planet."

Many share a concern that political parties, organizations, state agencies, and NGOs mainly serve their own interests when collaborating with Indigenous communities on environmental issues. Adriana Quinto Sánchez from the village Pueblo Bello in the Cesar Department in Colombia says that even some achievements have been made in terms of protecting nature. However, the NGOs exist within the framework of particular interests that make it impossible for them to "escape the logic of the system."

A last category of interviews covers experiences the interviewees see as positive and fruitful, where communities and outsiders have managed to work together despite different perspectives. Community leaders here mention collaborations where NGOs and state agencies have worked as supporting mechanisms for ongoing struggles, providing economic or educational resources such as workshops in media production to spread information and raise awareness.

The municipality Nueva Guinea in the autonomous region on the Caribbean coast of Nicaragua has benefitted from NGOs such as Technoserve and Amlae supporting small women's cooperatives, according to community leader and cooperativist Rosa Idalia Reyes. Reyes holds that the processes of leadership, gender, and agricultural practices that these NGO's promote, have made it easier for women like her to get access to governing spaces. It has strengthened the independence of the women of the cooperatives:

> Women's participation in productive activities in rural areas has been strengthened and has created more consciousness about environmental issues within families. This has been reflected in protection of the trees, sources of water, against land degradation and over exploitation and in cultivation of plants and products that benefit the environment.

While the students have found examples of collaborations based on mutual understanding and respect, these are mostly found in regions with less indigenous influence. This reflects the fact that most Nicaraguan students are Spanish speakers living in regions of Nicaragua where a large section of the population is non-Indigenous. The master students draw different conclusions and emphasize different factors concerning advantageous cooperation on environmental issues. Even though most do not believe that extractive industries are part of the solution, many students see cooperation between Indigenous communities and NGOs as necessary to build a sustainable future. Many point out the importance of educating young people both in urban and rural areas about environmental issues and do feel that NGOs can play a facilitating role in this process. However, as many remark, intercultural cooperation have to be built based on equality or mutuality which often proves to be difficult when Indigenous communities and organizations and the NGOs have conflicting worldviews. Indigenous leaders do.

Master students on nature and society

Building further on the insights of the students, this section will systematize and highlight some of the relevant findings from master theses. The purpose is to deepen the understanding of how Indigenous Peoples imagine the social and the natural.

Almost all indigenous students states to have a "universal commitment" to defend life itself. Dora Estella Muñoz Atillo, for instance, in her thesis explains the Nasa concept of "Puutx We'wnxi Uma Kiwe" (Muñoz, 2016). The concept of "Puutx We'wnxi Uma Kiwe" is of great importance for the Nasa people in Cauca, Colombia. For the Nasa, "communicating from the standpoint of Mother Earth" means to embark on a "journey guided by a natural command" and to commit as "sons and daughters to defending Mother Earth." "Puutx We'Wnxi Uma Kiwe" involves carrying out practical and determined action to defend nature – "it means to walk the spiritual command to free Mother Earth." According to Muñoz Atillo, Nasa elders, based on lifelong learning and practice, teach "spiritual communication" as "a natural form of relationship with all beings."

Another common perspective is to produce knowledge about the world that allows for spirituality to be an integral part of the process. Hover Hernan Majin Melenje seeks to document the Yanacona "circle of word" (Majin, 2016). Like the Nasa, the Yanacona lives in Cauca, Colombia. The circle of word ("círculo de la palabra," in Spanish) is a "de-colonizing process" that supports the "cultivation of traditional knowledge and wisdom" among community members. According to the author, the circle of words, also known as "Chakana" (a symbol representing four life and after-life paths), symbolizes the socio-cultural path taken in order to create order and guide production of knowledge. The process includes the *tullpa* (originally a collective way of preparing fire for cooking food), oral history, traditional semiotics, and "Mother Earth language and spirituality" as the main methodologies to gather information.

The third category I will mention here explicitly connects social and economic activity to preservation of nature. Luz Mary Avirama Calambas, for instance, documents alternative forms of economic activity such as traditional bartering (Avirama Calambas, 2016). Avirama sees bartering activities as very important for the communal sharing of knowledge, wisdoms, and economic benefits. As part of these activities, Avirama explains, a group of elders collects and safeguards seeds with the purpose of preserving traditional agriculture. The thesis documents the close relationship between activities to preserve nature, cultural traditions, and Indigenous forms of social organization.

A number of master students deal with issues related to traditional forms of education and pedagogy. Often, the theses in this fourth category seek to understand how traditional ways of producing knowledge about the world are transmitted from one generation to another. Nidia Isadora Cruz, for instance, investigates education and pedagogy as it has historically been promoted by Nasa elders (Cruz, 2016). The author finds that pedagogy and education is adapted according to the stages of development of the child. Nonetheless, pedagogy and education are always based on the commitment to "defend Mother Earth" and to create "harmonic relationship with plants, animals, stars, water." In addition, Cruz also underlines the importance in Nasa pedagogy of grounding human values in "the standpoint of Mother Earth."

The sixth category seeks to contribute to develop suitable Indigenous and communitarian research methodologies. Nixon Yatacue Collazos, for instance, takes Participatory Action Research in a radical direction (Yatacue, 2016). Yatacue started with a survey of 25 community members in addition to participant observation. However, the research also included what Yatacue calls "minga de pensamiento" or "joint community action."

Yatacue describes it as a "collective space of reflection." This methodology builds on the Indigenous agricultural praxis of organized communal work ("minga"). All members of a community take part and share both work and food, drinks, and music. Traditionally, exchange of knowledge and wisdom is integral parts of a minga. However, the minga is also a place where joint decisions are taken. According to Yatacue, seeing the research as a minga helps transform the community from being an object of study into becoming the real agents of the investigation.

The last category connects the political and the spiritual. Monica Zambrano Campo, for instance, explores what she calls a "duality in the Indigenous movement." By "duality," she refers to the "combination of politics and spirituality" (Zambrano, 2016). According to the author, politics are represented by "organized collective actions to influence local, regional, national and international realities" in order to foster a decent living. Simultaneously, Indigenous rituals and a respectful relationship with nature and the sacred support organized collective work.

These master students ask questions and seek answers that sometimes seem quite far removed from mainstream science in the Global North. Some scientists will perhaps feel estranged by the references to spirits and spirituality. Others might have problems with the vision of the community as the real scientist while the researcher is "limited" to being a "servant" of the community. Nevertheless, it is difficult to imagine that outsiders can produce similarly deep and rich interpretations of Indigenous life and worldviews based on interpretation of observation and empirical evidence. A deep understanding of the diversity of life forms is limited by the fact that most of those who are engaged in the so-called scientific production of knowledge are trained at universities in the Global North (including those that are located at Southern centers of power). Are Northern scholars able to fully interpret and understand indigenous people's worldviews? According to the RUIICAY universities, only indigenous researchers rooted in indigenous communities can be expected to cultivate and nurture truly deep understandings of Indigenous Peoples and indigenous worldviews.

The Network of Intercultural, Indigenous and Communitarian Universities of Abya Yala

Reading the CCRISAC, it becomes clear just how much emphasis the RUIICAY universities put on grounding research and education in a community. The CCRISAC mentions "community" 94 times on 47 pages.

> It is, therefore, essential to RUIICAY, that teaching and community-oriented activities are directly linked to research, in order to fulfill the functions of the universities and respond to the basic needs and demands of the communities.

(p. 6)

CCRISAC "responds to the cosmovisión and practices of the people, highlighting the relevance as well as the personal and collective awareness. It is the ways of community living and the understanding of the inter-relationships of life. It articulates individual life with collective life harmonically. It includes actions and attitudes of appreciation and respect for the social, economic, political and spiritual fabric of the components of the community structure. The practice of CCRISAC necessarily involves the community context."

(p. 9)

We also observe how nature, as noted earlier, is an integral part of the imagined community:

Intercultural communication is perceived as the communication of nature reflected in the chirps of the birds, the howls of the dogs, the movements of the fish, the flutter of the turtles that warns when danger threatens the community. It is the dialogue between the mountains and the lakes, the whispering of the winds in languages that bridge the trans mission of knowledges and ancestral wisdoms from one generation to another. CCRISAC is bound to be the interlocutor and interpreter of the messages, signs, and signals of Mother Earth. The task implies assuming the cultural mandate that commits us as his sons and daughters.

(pp. 10, 11)

One must be inside and feel the territory and the community, in order to possess a knowledge that will help us act, according to the great fabric of life, says the CCRISAC. Researchers must be "sentient thinkers rooted to the territory, as if with an umbilical cord" (p. 12).

Yachay refers to the capacity to dialogue and to see both from inside and from outside. It is the knowledge required to consolidate the community from the pathways of being and feeling the territory. It is to place the experiences learned in the plot of wisdoms and knowledges of the community, in order to achieve cultural and territorial strengthening.

(p. 13)

Autonomy of universities versus autonomy of Indigenous Peoples.

Næss on decentralization

For Næss, an "ecological attitude" meant enhancing local autonomy and decentralization. Næss pointed out that the existence of "exploitation and suppression" called for "extreme caution toward any overall plans for the future, except those consistent with wide and widening classless diversity" (Næss, 1999b, p. 4).[2]

Næss' distrust against "overall plans for the future" was grounded in philosophical skepticism. He did not believe much in planners claiming to be able to look into the future to create a better future. But it also came on the back of the ecological crises caused by the centralized planning economies of then Eastern Europe. In *Ecology, Community and Lifestyle*, *Næss* disapproves of "socialist slogans" (for instance "maximize production," "centralization," and "high consumption") and dedicates a chapter to the censure of "bureaucracy" (Næss and Rothenberg, 1989, pp. 157, 159). "Roughly speaking," he argues, "supporters of the deep ecology movement seem to move more in the direction of nonviolent anarchism than towards communism" (A. Næss and Rothenberg, 1989, p. 156). According to Næss himself, such views were "heavily influenced by Kropotkin's Mutual Aid: A Factor of Evolution" (quoted in Clark, 2010, p. 26). Nevertheless, he became more critical of anarchism after observing that many traditional communities that approximated to Kropotkin's communitarian ideal "no longer took good care of their environments" (Clark, 2010, p. 26).

Næss's concern was not with the *correct* "total" view but with the personal and political "importance of having, and negotiating from, ecologically acceptable ... total views" (Warren, 1999, p. 264). As Warren notes, the critical goal of deep ecology is not *sameness* but the "solidarity achieved by agreement to the values and beliefs expressed through the ... platform" (Warren, 1999, p. 264). Næss's insisted on *pluralism* in the face of "our state of ignorance." Caution towards overall plans provides an important perspective for a libertarian environmentalist movement which seeks to understand and fully allow for the integration of minority and Indigenous Peoples' perspectives (Krøvel, 2013).

Indigenous Pluriverse and anti-capitalism

In *Kapak Ñan Pedagógico: Filosófico de la Pluriversidad "Amawtay Wasi,"* "rector" Luis Fernando Sarango explains the philosophy of the indigenous university (Sarango et al., 2017).[3] The document places the pluriversity firmly as an actor in Ecuador's social and political struggles.

> ... the arrogant, hegemonic and destructive (*avasallador*) system of education of the occident ... has as its prime motive to maintain the world as a market and to extinguish culturally original peoples because we are an obstacle to achieving their goals ... Now, the system lacks the moral authority to push through their goals. It is not a question of becoming more like them. We are already demonstrating that the nature of humanity is to be *distinct* ... we come from a different matrix of civilization. We are only similar in the condition of being *humans*. Nothing more.
>
> (Sarango et al., 2017, p. 16)

Education often contributes to destroy diversity in life forms: "the occidental school is a perfect domesticating space for manipulation. It is where the deceiving death of cultural identity begins, the ethnocide of originary peoples" (Sarango et al., 2017, p. 16). Because the current epoch is dominated by the "globalization of capital" (Sarango et al., 2017, p. 20), science and higher education have become "responsible for producing efficient, effective and competitive products." "Quality" is measured in terms of mercantile parameters. Universities are "capitalism's most cherished creature used to impose its regime of truths" (Sarango et al., 2017, p. 23).

Therefore, the pluriversity must help "recuperate the feeling of belonging to a community." Indigenous Peoples need to "change the system of economic, social and political organization of society" and replace it with an alternative (Sarango et al., 2017, p. 29).

It would be mistaken to believe that the indigenous academics of the pluriversity see capitalism and the market as the sole or major cause behind destruction of diversity of life forms. In *Kapak Ñan Pedagógico*, Sarango et al. probe various mechanisms. States emerging after Spanish and Portuguese colonial rules played an important role in "modernizing" Indigenous Peoples and homogenizing cultures in Latin America. The new elites constructed new forms of identities, such as Mexicans, Nicaraguans, Colombians, and so on. "(T)hey planted a tree without roots" (Sarango et al., 2017, p. 30). The elites used those newly created "imagined communities" to "de-Indianize" Indigenous Peoples. However, as Sarango notes, the elites could not have succeeded without the help of indigenous teachers and other indigenous community leaders (Sarango et al., 2017, p. 54).

Næss and eco-philosophy T

Deep ecology has been criticized for putting too much emphasize on harmony and too little on the need to fight social hierarchies. Murray Bookchin, for instance, opposes deep ecology's preoccupation with human–nature relationship because it is seen as a distraction from the real root cause of ecological degradation. Instead, Bookchin writes, we need "a resolute attempt to fully anchor ecological dislocations in social dislocations; to challenge the vested corporate and political interests we should properly call capitalism; to analyze, explore, and attack hierarchy as a reality …" (Bookchin, 1991, p. 61).

As we have already seen, Næss and other Nordic deep ecologists were keenly aware of exploitation and social unjust around the world. Bookchin was a social ecologist, a former Marxist, who perhaps first and foremost had exploitation of the working class and class struggle in mind when pointing the finger at "social hierarchies." However, Næss was no apologist of capitalism. Bookchin's criticism was misplaced when it comes to Næss but much more precise when it comes to some North American sympathizers with deep ecology.[4]

A more relevant criticism of the role of "harmony" in deep ecology came from a former student of Næss, Sigmund Kvaløy: "(…) although it is important to have strong feelings about nature, we have to concentrate on the human society and the human being, otherwise everything we cherish will be destroyed. We have so little time" (Kvaløy, 1993, p. 148).

> We are reaching a future through conflict – and this is not coinciden-tal, but rather what has always happened at major shifts in the various events building futures in history... we now need to think in a model of conflict, to be prepared at every turn for strife. And what I have been saying here is, all of it, a product of conflict thinking."
>
> (Kvaløy, 1993, pp. 136–137)

The disagreement was not between opposites but, rather, the slightly dif-ferent ordering of priorities. Some believe Næss took a different stance on the role of environmental action to some of the younger generation of deep ecologists. For Kvaløy, action was the teacher, not a university seminar (Orton, 2005). Kvaløy, nevertheless, echoes Næss's activist approach to so-cial change and he reinforced the view that the activist does not need a "picture of the future society because there are a range of possibilities" (Orton, 2005).

In 1970, Næss quit his post as professor at the University of Oslo to be-come an activist, engaging himself in environmental actions and civil disobedience in, for instance, Mardøla and Alta. In particular, the environ-mental actions in Alta resulted in a stronger focus on the exploitation and suppression of the Sámi (indigenous people).

Indigenous harmony and social conflicts

Judging from the RUIICAY documents and master theses, it seems that in-digenous students and researchers not unlike Næss value harmony. Never-theless, echoing Kvaløy, RUIICAY academics and students are constantly involved in social activism and conflict to defend and strengthen indigenous rights and autonomy. A superficial analysis could raise suspicion that such activism leading to social conflict undermines "harmony." A closer inspec-tion of the CCRISAC, however, reveals that autonomy and rights are pre-conditions for "harmony."

According to CCRISAC, a good indigenous research methodology "is the pathway where balance and harmony with existential reality is achieved" (p. 13). Moreover, "human beings make use of all their senses in order to live a life in fullness. They make use of love, intuition, harmony and tenderness" (p. 25). Harmony is essential for hermeneutics: "This is the stage of interpre-tation from within, in harmony with the external events" (p. 27). But also in looking out, seeking knowledge from other cultures and worlds, harmony is goal. CCRISAC defines a "Third Moment" in the research process: "Har-mony Between Knowledges" (p. 30).

As Viveiros de Castro has showed us, in the Amazon, the task of the sha-man is to visit spirits and being to negotiate balance and harmony. Similarly, the researcher is expected to be in harmony in research and to use research help create and maintain harmony between all life forms.

Nevertheless, at the same time, indigenous universities joined indigenous organizations in mass mobilizations in Colombia and Ecuador among other things to defend indigenous education. In fact, the Indigenous Regional Counsel of Cauca (CRIC) that runs the Autonomous Indigenous Intercultural University (UAIIN) has been formed in a context of extreme violence. Reliable sources estimate that more than 400 members of CRIC were killed during the first 30 years of the organization.

Also elsewhere in Latin America, the emerging indigenous and communitarian universities grow out of contexts of violence. Defending community autonomy is seen as the only viable way to create the conditions for Buen Vivir. While most universities in Latin America vehemently defends "autonomy" in the meaning of autonomy for the university to decide university matters, indigenous universities depend on local communities to survive and flourish. Therefore, "autonomy" for indigenous and communitarian universities take on a different meaning. The university is not understood to be autonomous from indigenous society. Instead, it is conceived to be an integral part of indigenous autonomy.

Spirituality

The discussion so far has reflected commonalities between deep ecology and RUIICAY perspectives on nature and science. The role of "spirituality" would appear to be a point of difference. For the RUIICAY universities, *spirituality* is considered as "the forms of relationship that help achieve physical, mental, emotional and spiritual balance and harmony between all persons and communities that make up Mother Earth" (CCRISAC). Spirituality has a role to play in all aspects of academic life and research.

One of the first things a researcher is advised to do when doing research in a community is "to listen, feel and sense" the community (CCRISAC). This includes spirits and a spiritual level. Spirituality is accepted as one way of producing knowledge alongside more conventional methodologies. To understand the importance of spirits and spirituality, Viveiros de Castro is helpful to understand better Amerindian ontologies. Eduardo Viveiros de Castro shows that "(...) modern distinctions between nature and culture, animals and humans, and even descent and marriage ties are effectively inverted" (Skafish, 2013, p. 15).

Arne Næss, meanwhile, was profoundly influenced by Baruch de Spinoza (1632–1677). However, Næss quietly chose to ignore the important aspects of spirituality in Spinozism. Other eco-philosophers have in contrast seen Western de-spiritualization as part of the problem that makes human treat nature as a resource to be consumed.

> Western society has been diverted from the goal of spiritual freedom and autonomy ... modern Western society has arrived at the opposite

pole of anthropocentric "absolute subjectivism" in which the entire
non-human world is seen as a material resource to be consumed in the
satisfaction of our egoistic passive desires.

(Sessions, 1977, p. 481)

No interest in becoming like them

Disagreement and difference, however, is not a problem for the RUIICAY
academics. On the contrary, being different and defending difference is essential to cultivate and nurture diversity.

> It is not a question of becoming more like them. We are already demon-
> strating that the nature of humanity is to be *distinct* (...) we come from
> a different matrix of civilization. We are only similar in the condition of
> being *humans*. Nothing more.

(Sarango et al., 2017, p. 16)

Sarango and his co-authors rejects homogenization of cultures and life
forms. Survival as peoples for them means valuing difference. In a similar vein, Næss warns against diminishing "classless diversity" (Næss, 1973,
p. 97). From both perspectives, maintaining "classless diversity" cannot
be achieved without vibrant communities. The focus on individual rights
must be broadened to encompass collective rights if classless diversity in
languages, etc. is to be widened or protected.

Current political philosophers, such as Will Kymlicka, have argued along
similar sounding lines. Kymlicka understands the identity of individuals as
being "embedded within a social and cultural context that links it to the
identity of communities." Collective indigenous rights are defended on "the
grounds that a secure sense of cultural belonging is of great importance for
individual wellbeing." For Kymlicka, rights to protection and autonomy for
minorities are necessary because of the disadvantages they face in enjoying
secure cultural membership (Braund, 2015). The RUIICAY, however, puts a
much stronger emphasis on community than individual rights as the starting point for the argument. Only communities can be creators of widening
classless diversity.

Maximum classless diversity versus "guided" interactions

The renowned philosopher Paul Feyerabend took a social libertarian approach to education. If parents want their children to learn magic as well
as science at school, then schools should teach magic as well as science, he
argued (Deval, 1999). Næss did not agree. But he agreed with Feyerabend
when it came to the concept "guided" exchange or interaction: According
to Næss, "the outcome of seemingly friendly interactions between nonindustrial and industrial traditions or cultures is largely determined by the

superior power of the latter" (Næss in Witozek, p. 59). The powerful defines the kind of rational debate and the characteristics of the decision-making process. "The weaker party is more or less forced to adopt the ways of the stronger." In the case of the indigenous Sámi, Næss argues, there is scarcely any intention left to dominate or exploit, but because the exchange or inter-action is "guided," the stronger party wins. Lack of intention is no guarantee against destruction of diversity of life forms.

More recently, another instructive debate between two anthropologists studying indigenous and nonindustrial peoples erupted around radical alterity. Viveiros de Castro criticized Graeber for treating magical power among the Merina as a theory or belief and not as a reality (Viveiros de Castro, 2015). Graeber responded that

> (w)e appear to be in the presence of two quite different conceptions of what anthropology is ultimately about. Are we unsettling our categories so as (1) to better understand the "radical alterity" of a specific group of people (whoever "we" are here taken to be); or (2) to show that in certain ways, at least, such alterity was not quite as radical as we thought, and we can put those apparently exotic concepts to work to reexamine our own everyday assumptions and to say something new about human beings in general?
>
> (Graeber, 2015, p. 6)

What can we "bring home" from studying and comparing deep ecology and indigenous people's knowledges to re-examine our everyday assumptions? First, according to Julian Baggini, "By gaining greater knowledge of how others think, we can become less certain of the knowledge we think we have, which is always the first step to greater understanding" (Baggini, 2018, p. 6). In this sense, Indigenous Peoples and indigenous thinking are "others" that can help enrich the understanding "we" (non-indigenous) have of ourselves. Increasingly, environmentalists and Indigenous Peoples are forming global alliances to protect nature and peoples from accelerating exploitation of limited natural resources around the world. A better mutual understanding is necessary if these alliances are to continue to flourish. Additionally, I argue, a deeper understanding of ecology and indigenous people's knowledges can help us examine critically international blueprints such as the Sustainable Development Goals (SDGs).

Both Deep Ecology and organizations representing Indigenous Peoples have had some impact at the international level through for instance processes in the United Nations (UN). However, along the way, core ideas and concepts have been transformed and adopted to the hegemonic discourses employed at the inter-state level. For instance, Deep Ecology had a profound impact on early sustainability thinking. To some extent, the influential Brundtland-report to the UN, *Our Common Future,* was a response to the challenge posed by ecologists such as Næss and Kvaløy

Sætereng (World Commission on Environment and Development, 1987). But in contrast to the Deep Ecologists, the emerging UN sustainability discourse on the inter-state level insisted on the need for economic growth supposedly to make us able to afford ecological sustainability. Similarly, pressure from numerous Indigenous Peoples and organizations led to the adoption of a series of international treaties on the rights of Indigenous Peoples since the late 1980s. Still, as documented by numerous reports from the UN Special Rapporteur on the rights of Indigenous Peoples, most states have so far been reluctant to implement fully international treaties on indigenous rights, especially when these rights have collided with state policies designed to foment economic growth and exploitation of natural resources.

To some degree, Indigenous Peoples were involved in the process leading up to the SDGs. The Indigenous Peoples' Major Group for Sustainable Development, for instance, has become the main mechanism of indigenous engagement and a forum for coordination and planning.[5] To be fair, the Agenda for Sustainable Development does refer to Indigenous Peoples six times: In the political declaration, related to "Zero Hunger" and related to education. In addition, the section on follow-up and review calls for Indigenous Peoples' "participation." Nevertheless, indigenous organizations have been critical of the process.

The Indigenous Peoples Major Group (IPMG) was concerned that many specific references to "Indigenous Peoples" were deleted in the final Outcome Document of the Open-ended Working Group on the SDGs (OWG) (Indigenous Peoples Major Group, 2015). "The near "invisibility" of Indigenous Peoples in the current draft of the SDGs poses a serious risk of repeating their negative experiences with national development processes" (Indigenous Peoples Major Group, 2015). As The IPMG correctly notes, the Millennium Development Goals (MDG) failed to recognize Indigenous Peoples as distinct groups and was unsuccessful in stipulating pertinent targeted measures to address their specific situations.

Indigenous organizations have long been aware of the limitations to state centered approaches to fight hunger and poverty and protect nature and diversity. While Indigenous Peoples have gained some rights and recognition on the international level, most states have been averse to fully implement collective rights concerning Indigenous Peoples and indigenous territories. For that reason, it is no surprise that documents such as the MDGs and SDGs tend to envisage Indigenous Peoples primarily as yet another group in need of being "lifted" out of poverty.

The above discussion of deep ecology and indigenous people's knowledges can help non-indigenous sympathizers understand why indigenous organizations want more meaningful change. In the words of Feyerabend and Næss, the international dialogue on the SDGs is a "guided interaction." States and governments remain in control over the decision-making process through high-level state-to-state negotiations on controversial issues. The SDGs were ultimately formed in negotiations between states and heads of states, even though spaces were created for indigenous participation. In consequence, it took place submerged in the flow of broader global inter-state processes on issues such as global free trade and developed within the growth-oriented sustainability discourse. Following Næss, the outcome of this seemingly friendly interaction between nonindustrial and industrial traditions was ultimately decided by the superior power of the so-called developed nations. While it might seem as if the powerful is "winning," Næss would argue that everyone lose if diversity is lost. Returning to the issue of education, Næss was similarly negative to overall plans reducing diversity. When education is stereotyped through the adoption of "universal" criteria of learning, the path toward monoculture is made smoother, Næss argued.

As world leaders and the UN try to construct global blueprints to achieve a better and more sustainable future for all, the indigenous and intercultural universities of RUIICAY and the deep ecologists represents two alternative perspectives on "buen vivir" and sustainability. They remind us of the pitfalls of "guided dialogues," "world-wide criteria of learning" and loss of diversity. Both agree that only communities can be creators of widening classless diversity. Both would agree that indigenous autonomy is a prerequisite for constructing good lives ("buen vivir").

From both these perspectives, de-colonizing knowledge and academia would be essential in order to cultivate and nurture the greatest classless diversity possible.

Notes

1 All eight points of the platform can be read at The Deep Ecology Platform www.deepecology.org/platform.htm
2 I have discussed these issues more in depth in Krøvel, Roy (2013). "Revisiting social and deep ecology in the light of global warming." *Anarchist Studies* 21.2. p. 28.
3 A more detailed analysis in Halvorsen, Tor, Skare Orgeret, Kristin & Krøvel, Roy (eds). (2019). *Sharing Knowledge, Transforming Societies: The Norhed Programme 2013–2020.* African Minds. Cape Town. Published Date: 19/10/2019.
4 Parts of the argument in this section was put forward in Krøvel (2013).
5 See www.indigenouspeoples-sdg.org/index.php/english/who-we-are/about-the-ipmg

References

Avirama Calambas, L. M. (2016). *The Role of Women in the Practice of Bartering as a Local Communication Process in the Indigenous Territory of Kokonuko, Municipality of Purace, Cauca, Colombia.* Managua: Universidad de las Regiones Autónomas de la Costa Caribe Nicaragüense (URACCAN).
Baggini, J. (2018). *How the World Thinks: A Global History of Philosophy.* London: Granta.

Bookchin, M. (1991). "Ecology and the Left" in M. Bookchin, D. Foreman and S. Chase (Eds.), *Defending the Earth: A Dialogue between Murray Bookchin and Dave Foreman*. Boston, MA: South End Press, p. 61.

Bookchin, M. (1993). *Deep Ecology & Anarchism: A Polemic*. London: Freedom Press.

Braund, M. (2015). "Will Kymlicka" In *The Canadian Encyclopedia*. www. thecanadianencyclopedia.ca/en/article/will-kymlicka Accessed 10 August 2019.

Carson, R. (1962). *Silent Spring*. Boston, MA: Houghton Mifflin Company.

Clark, J. P. (2010). "A Dialogue with Arne Naess on Social Ecology and Deep Ecology (1988–1997)." *The Trumpeter*, 26 (2), 20–39.

Cruz, N. I. (2016). *The Power of the Belly Button: The Nasa Pedagogy of Life, Cauca, Colombia*. Managua: Universidad de las Regiones Autónomas de la Costa Caribe Nicaragüense (URACCAN).

Deval, B. (1999). "Comment: Næss and Feyerabend on Science" in N. Witoszek and A. Brennan (Eds.), *Philosophical Dialogues: Arne Næss and the Progress of Ecophilosophy*. Lanham, MD: Rowman & Littlefield Publishers.

Diálogo de Saberes. Alternativas eco-sociales. *Nuestras premisas*. www. dialogodesaberes.com/ Accessed 20 November 2019.

Drengson, A. "Some Thoughts on the Deep Ecology Movement". Foundation for Deep Ecology. www.deepecology.org/deepecology.htm Accessed 20 November 2019.

Graeber, D. (2015). "Radical Alterity Is Just Another Way of Saying "Reality": A Reply to Eduardo Viveiros de Castro." *Journal of Ethnographic Theory*, 5 (2), 1–41.

Gutiérrez, N., Perera, F., Paiz, G., Flores, C. M., Mejía, M., Treminio, X., Sarango, F., et al. (2019). *Base Document for the Nurture and Cultivation of Wisdoms and Knowledges: CCRISAC*, 2nd edn. Managua: Universidad de las Regiones Autónomas de la Costa Caribe Nicaragüense.

Halvorsen, T., Orgeret, K. S. & Krøvel, R. (eds). (2019). *Sharing Knowledge, Transforming Societies: The Norhed Programme 2013–2020*. Cape Town: African Minds.

Indigenous Peoples Major Group. (2015). "Policy Brief on Sustainable Development Goals and Post-2015 Development Agenda: A Working Draft". https:// sustainabledevelopment.un.org/content/documents/6797IPMG%20Policy%20 Brief%20Working%20Draft%202015.pdf Accessed 20 November 2019.

Krøvel, R. (2013). "Revisiting Social and Deep Ecology in the Light of Global Warming". *Anarchist Studies*, 21 (2), 28.

Kvaløy, S. (1993). "Complexity and Time: Breaking the Pyramid's Reign" in P. Reed and D. Rothenberg (Eds.), *Wisdom in the Open Air: The Norwegian Roots of Deep Ecology*. Minnesota: University of Minnesota Press, pp. 117–145.

Majin Melenje, H. He. (2016). *The Circle of Word. An Indigenous Communication Strategy to Strengthen Spaces of Intercultural Interaction in the Yanacona Community of Popayan*, Cauca, Colombia.

Merriam-Webster, Self-realization. (2019). www.merriam-webster.com/dictionary/ self-realization. Accessed 6 August 2019.

Merton, R. (1942). *The Sociology of Science: Theoretical and Empirical Investigations*. Chicago, IL: University of Chicago Press.

Muñoz Atillo, D. E. (2016). *Puutx We'Wnxi Uma Kiwe". Communication from the Mother Earth: The Road of Wisdom that Invites Us to Liberate Her*. Popayan.

Næss, A. (1990). *Ecology, Community and Lifestyle. Outline of an Ecosophy.* Cambridge: Cambridge University Press.

Næss, A. (1999b). "The Shallow and the Deep, Long-range Ecology Movements: A Summary" in A. Brennan, N. Witoszek and A. Næss (Eds.), *Philosophical Dialogues: Arne Næss and the Progress of Ecophilosophy.* Lanham, MD: Rowman and Littlefield, pp. XIX, 492 s.

Næss, A. (2000). *Gandhi.* Oslo: Universitetsforlaget.

Næss, A. and Sessions, G. (1984). "Deep Ecology Plattform" www.deepecology.org/platform.htm Accessed 20 November 2019.

Orton, D. (2005). Conflict and Marxism in Deep Ecology. http://home.ca.inter.net/~greenweb/Conflict_and_Marxism_in_Deep_Ecology.html. Accessed 11 November 2011.

Sarango, L. F., et al. (2017) Kapak Ñan Pedagógico: Filosófico de la Pluriversidad 'Amawtay Wasi' (The Great Road of Learning: The Philosophy of the Pluriversity 'Amawtay Wasi'). Quito: Pluriversidad Amawtay Wasi.

Sessions, G. (1977). Spinoza and Jeffers on Man in Nature. *Inquiry*, 20 (1–4), 481–528.

Skafish, P. (2013). Introduction. *Radical Philosophy*, 182(Nov/Dec), 14–15.

Viveiros de Castro, E. (2015). "Who's Afraid of the Ontological Wolf: Some Comments on an Ongoing Anthropological Debate." *Cambridge Anthropology*, 33 (1), 2–17.

Warren, K. (1999). "Ecofeminist Philosophy and Deep Ecology" in A. Brennan, N. Witoszek and A. Næss (Eds.), *Philosophical Dialogues: Arne Næss and the Progress of Ecophilosophy.* Lanham, MD: Rowman and Littlefield, pp. XIX, 492 s.

White, A. (February 2018). "Farewell to Development" in *The Great Transition Initiative.* https:// greattransition.org/publication/farewell-to-development Accessed 20 November 2019.

World Commission on Environment and Development (1987). *Our Common Future.* Oxford: Oxford University Press.

Yatacue Collazos, N. (2016). *Development of a Communication Strategy for Promoting Community Ownership of the Indigenous Education System (SEIP)*, Popayan.

Zambrano Campo, M. (2016) *The Way Paved by the "El Andarin" Popular Communication Collective*, Managua: Universidad de las Regiones Autónomas de la Costa Caribe Nicaragüense (URACCAN).

8   Indigenous good sense on climate change

Andreas Ytterstad

Introduction

In the wake of intensified climate change, a broad array of critics, NGOs and social movements have summoned indigenous knowledges, oftentimes specified as traditional ecological knowledge (TEK) (Ridgeway, 2014) as a source of inspiration. Even as the actual existence of indigenous cultures is under siege, indigenous knowledges appear to enjoy something of a renaissance. In his closing plenary statement to COP 24 in Poland on behalf of the Indigenous Peoples forum on climate change, Michael Charles confidently began talking his native language Dine, before saying that "Our indigenous ways of knowing, rooted in the experiences of our ancestors, is the medicine that this sick world needs right now." Indeed, most of the big climate change demonstrations over the last decade, including the largest one so far on Sept 18 2014 in New York, have had indigenous communities in front (Hicks & Fabricant, 2016, p. 99).

This chapter asks *what is indigenous good sense on climate change?* The empirical parts of the answer to this question comes from a reading of expert literature on indigenous knowledges. Most of the scholars cited in this chapter were found by way of literature searches with the keywords "indigenous knowledge" AND "climate change." As a supplement to this literature, I have conducted some original analysis of programmatic statements by indigenous movements, such as the one alluded to above from COP 24, with a particular focus on developments in Bolivia. This choice of emphasis is mostly due to the central role played by indigenous coalitions in Bolivia in the development of joint statements on climate change on a world stage (Bond, 2012). The present author also has a modicum of familiarity with indigenous knowledges in Latin America, having taught and learnt at indigenous universities in Ecuador, Colombia and Nicaragua for more than a decade.

The main novelty of this chapter does not lie in the empirical findings of what indigenous knowledges on climate change *are*. It rather lies – as indicated in the question itself – in the (re)interpretation, and perhaps construction of, indigenous knowledges on climate change *as good sense.*

This concept derives from Antonio Gramsci, who wrote that good sense is the "the healthy nucleus of common sense...which deserves to be made more coherent and unitary" (Gramsci, Hoare, & Smith, 1971, p. 327).

Good sense is much less researched and defined than Gramsci's much more famous concept of hegemony. A fairly established way Western scholars can show their solidarity and willingness to learn from indigenous epistemologies is to present the latter in opposition to Western hegemony (cf Breidlid, 2012).[1] I am a climate activist, with a similar sense of solidarity. As a Western Scholar, however, most of my research has attempted to give (much) more meaning to what Gramsci – yet another western scholar – wrote about good sense (cf esp Ytterstad, 2012, 2014). Gramsci knew nothing of climate change and he probably had Sardinian peasants or workers in Turin in mind – not indigeneous communities – when he wrote of the "healthy nucleus of common sense" in Mussolini's prison. So, by asking and answering a question about indigenous good sense on climate change, I may be vulnerable to the charge of exporting more of the same western epistemology in need of indigenous medicine.

What I hope to present in this chapter is something different, something more akin to a dialogue of knowledges (dialogo de sabers) (Krainer, Aguirre, Guerra, & Meiser, 2017): to open a space for a dialogue between the substance of indigenous knowledges on the one hand and an exploration of the concept of good sense vis-à-vis global warming on the other. In the Anthropocene, any solution to climate change must find ways of reconciling autonomy with universal interest, difference with global solidarity (cf Krøvel, 2018).

I want to stress that my approach is no mere application, but rather a significant revision and expansion, of Gramsci's philosophy of praxis (Freedman, 2012, 2014; cf esp Ytterstad, 2012, 2014). I begin the analysis with the practical knowledge side of good sense, the aspect of good sense that coincides most closely with TEK. Subsequently, indigenous knowledges are placed vis-à-vis the scientific capacity and the moral dimension of good sense. I then move on to consider good sense as an interest in truth, before I delve into climate justice as the most important *relational* dimension of good sense on global warming. Finally, I discuss two strands of recent and empirical manifestations of good sense spearheaded by indigenous movements, anti-extractivism and the public goods approach to universal needs.

As a preamble to the conclusion, some initial clarification of the limits of this analysis is in order. I concur with Sharon Ridgeway and Peter Jacques, both in their goal to pass the "talking stick" to those Indigenous Peoples "who have felt the boot of the Western hegemony most vividly" and in saying that "we are in desperate need of a planetary consciousness that values all our relations" (2014, pp. 117, 139). Although indispensable, indigenous good sense is not sufficient on its own for the ecological revolution necessary to make peace with our planet (Foster, 2009). Indigenous knowledges can help enrich, and become enriched in turn, by climate science and the good sense of other subaltern actors, notably by workers in the cities of Mother Earth. Good sense, however, is only half of the story of common sense. The other half of common sense is deeply influenced by hegemony, which stifles good sense most of the time. All the dimensions of good sense need to be tapped and developed into the most efficient collective climate action project possible, if indigenous planetary consciousness is to matter and supersede the current hegemonic order.

Good sense as local practical knowledge TEK and local adaptation

The first aspect of good sense I want to highlight is the practical and local side of good sense. Alf Nilsen, following Raymond Williams, suggests "that we consider the nature and origins of good sense as a *local rationality.*" (Nilsen, 2009, p. 124). This chimes well with how Raymond Pierotti sees TEK:

> Indigenous knowledge emerges from careful long-term observation of natural phenomena. The "data" collected using this approach are basically an understanding of relationships between specific biological entities…It is only possible to know a limited area in the kind of detail required for true Indigenous knowledge. Thus by definition many of the specific results obtained can only have local application.
>
> (2011, p. 9)

The knowledge accumulated over generations, often orally, bespeaks the authority of ancestors in many indigenous cultures. The traditional element in TEK, however, does not imply "old" or "static" knowledge:

> A vital aspect of TEK, which cannot be stressed enough, is that similarly to other knowledge types it is constantly evolving. The knowledge contained in TEK is fluid, it develops and grows while being transmitted from one generation to the next.
>
> (Royer, 2016, p. 17)

Nor should we interpret the listening and careful observation of natural phenomena as the mythical ability to gauge the exact "balance of nature." Indigenous good sense, seen as the accumulated wisdom of everyday practice, also include stories of how to cope with difficulties and even crisis in the many relationships between humans, animals, Mother Earth and "grandpa wind." It is precisely the longevity of lived relationships with nature that gives Indigenous Peoples in the United States "where home is identified with ecosystems and natural environments, not street addresses" (Wildcat, 2014, p. 510), an awareness of climate change effects and adaptation strategies.

This part of indigenous knowledges is both recognized and summoned, for example, by Alexandra Ocasia-Cortez, in her vision of the Green New Deal.[2]

One thread of inspiration from indigenous knowledges emerges then, quite simply, as a sense of resilience. In the local part of North Norway I come from, we have an expression saying "we have survived a winter day before." The sheer volume of scientific articles on indigenous knowledges and climate change who highlight adaptation in various localities (e.g. Boillat & Berkes, 2013; Makondo & Thomas, 2018; Mugambiwa, 2018) seem to indicate that this may very well be the most powerful inspirational thread from indigenous good sense on climate change.

Good sense as conception of necessity

The scientific capacity

The second aspect of good sense on global warming is more abstract, global and highlights the need for radical mitigation efforts. The closest we get to a definition of good sense by Gramsci himself is that it is a *conception of necessity*. And again partly, as Alex Lofthus points out "Good sense emerges within the already existing practices of subordinate groups" (2013, p. 193). But in the case of global warming, it is the higher, more philosophical and critical version of a conception of necessity that is most relevant. By necessity, Gramsci means *perceived* necessity:

> necessity exists when there exists an effective and active premiss, consciousness of which in people's minds has become operative, proposing concrete goals to the collective consciousness and constituting a complex of convictions and beliefs which act powerfully in the form of "popular beliefs"
>
> (Gramsci et al., 1971, pp. 412–413)

We have, as humans, a species being capacity to understand science (Ytterstad, 2012, p. 46). In the era of climate change, the concrete goals Gramsci alludes to, for reasons climate science alone can explain, must add up as global numbers. That is why there is a climate movement called 350.org and that is why the IPCC in October 2018 launched its 1,5 degrees report – prompted by popular slogans issued by island states like the Maldives "1,5 to stay alive."

To exempt indigenous knowledges from this aspect of good sense would not only be racist but wrong. However we may suffer from prejudice or think through the prism of different religions or cosmologies, we all have the potential to grasp "principles of a more advanced science" (Gramsci et al., 1971, p. 324). Dolphins or wolves do not. And importantly, however you assess the climate sensitivity of more and more greenhouse gases in the atmosphere, the most important "active premise" on global warming remains universal. "Surviving the warming condition requires full alignment with cutting-edge science," writes Malm (2018, p. 132) in his exposition of climate realism.

So, what does this scientific aspect of good sense imply for indigenous knowledges?

The discovery of global warming was a feat of the scientific community (Weart, 2008). It was just as little a product of indigenous knowledges as it was something that sprung out of the minds of oil and gas workers. That does not mean that local indigenous knowledges are devoid of scientific merits. Sometimes, the accumulated local experiences of indigenous communities can become scientific data in its own right, supplementing rather than contradicting climate models. But to strengthen local indigenous good sense on climate change requires learning, not just of the numbers, but of the causal mechanisms that make both mother earth and grandpa wind act so crazy in a warming world.

To stop global warming in time, to facilitate a modicum of adaptation, "science and common sense" must be integrated (Bond, 2012, p. 199). That means climate change mitigation and societal transitions that are "unprecedented," as the latest IPCCC report puts it.

Moving from is to ought: the moral dimension of good sense

If the actual climate science of such reports is mostly exogenous knowledge to Indigenous Peoples, the moral impulse to mitigate – once the science is grasped – is not. The definition of good sense as "conception of necessity" includes morality as well as the capacity to grasp science. Indigenous philosophy, with its principles that all things are both connected and related (Pierotti, 2011, p. 18), is not particularly prone to the Humean schism between facts and values, is and ought. Whereas natural scientists will sometimes be at pains to distinguish between their role as scientists and their role as concerned scientists, most people are evaluative realists:

> Until the *is* of global warming leads to the *ought* of slashing emissions from fossil fuels humanity, to repeat the ending of *Common Sense* by Thomas Paine "will feel itself like a man who continues putting off some unpleasant business from day to day, yet knows it must be done, hates to set about it, wishes it over, and is continually haunted with the thoughts of its necessity".
>
> (Ytterstad, 2014)

Arguably, because of its closer relationship to other species and to the land, there is less of a practical denial of nature (Vetlesen, 2015) in indigenous knowledges than in modern western (adult) societies. So, when record heatwaves reports are coupled with reports of the rapid extinction of animals, these are facts hurting many Indigenous Peoples in their very moral being. Indigenous good sense on climate change comes across with a moral force much less subdued than the one usually on display by climate scientists.

500 years of the wrong model: good sense as an interest in knowing all truths about climate change

In this section, I consider good sense as an *interest in truth*. Before I elaborate, let me spell out the analytical move away from a species being approach to a relational approach to good sense. Evolutionary biologists and climate psychologists alike (Stoknes, 2015; Terje Bongard & Røskaft, 2010) tend to address the species being question: how are homo sapiens cognitively equipped (or not) to understand the truths of climate science? The arrival of Trump on the world stage makes another question more pertinent: which groups of Homo sapiens are interested in the truths of climate science?

This is where one of Gramsci's most interesting formulations of the philosophy of praxis comes to the fore. He writes that the subaltern classes "have an interest in knowing all truths" (in Thomas, 2009, p. 452). If we take acceptance of climate change science as a proxy for interest in truth, there is research available to support this bold claim. On the one hand, studies have found old conservative men both in the US and Norway to be predominant amongst the climate denialists, or "cool dudes" (Claeys & Pugley, 2017; Tramel, 2018). On the other hand, Andreas Malm cites a number of studies on climate change concern and finds that the subalterns of the world are the bearers of the truth: "The demographic segments least invested in the prevailing order and therefore most prone to mistrust it – inhabitants of the Global South, women, people of color, the left – are also most appreciative of climate science: the correlation is crystal clear" (2018, p. 136).

Indigenous Peoples are not alone among the subaltern, indeed, indigenous movements have often allied themselves with other social movements, especially with other groups concerned with land rights (Claeys & Pugley, 2017; Tramel, 2018). But their subaltern position in society has a long and particularly oppressive history and – although some indigenous communities certainly have received more spoils from their oppressors than others – they are among the groups least invested in the prevailing order. A special issue on Indigenous Peoples in the US, highlighted "why awareness of climate change is so high among Indigenous Peoples of the USA when compared to most citizens of the USA." Daniel R. Wildcat explains this as a result of the "practical lifeway experiences and sensitivity to the rhythms of seasons" of American Indians and Alaska natives (Wildcat, 2014, p. 510). Greater climate awareness can also be interpreted as an expression of this interest in truth by the subaltern.

All the truths about climate change, however, must encompass more than the science of the climate itself. "Great blender and trespasser, climate change sweeps back and forth between the two regions traditionally referred to as "nature" and "society"" (Malm, 2018, p. 15). What is noteworthy about the indigenous response to climate change is how they see capitalism as the root causal mechanism of climate change. Consider the second introductory paragraph of the Declaration of the Indigenous Peoples of the World to COP17 in Durban:

> For decades, Indigenous Peoples have warned that climate change confirms that the harmonic relationship between humans and Mother Earth has ruptured, endangering the future of humanity in its entirety. The whole model of civilizations that began 500 years ago with the pillaging of the natural resources for profit and the accumulation of capital, is in crisis.

Sharon Ridgeway catalogues a series of similar statements at international summits, before concluding that "We must focus on sustainable communities based on indigenous knowledge, not on capitalist development" (2014, p. 153).

Indigenous good sense on climate change is thus anti-capitalist, and Bolivia is no doubt the place where the climate justice movement as a whole has most visibly mobilized indigenity on a world stage (Hicks & Fabricant, 2016). The very first Declaración de Quillacolla on February 18th 2009, precursors to the Cochambamba Declaration and the Bolivian Climate Change Platform,[3] moves seamlessly from noting there is enough scientific evidence of climate change, to the vulnerability of the Bolivian people, to noting that "the causes of CC are to be found in the development models that superimpose the interest of capitalist development before human rights in general..."[4] No wonder indigenous communities have spearheaded "system change – not climate change" demonstrations, from Copenhagen to Lima to New York.

Climate justice and the right to atmospheric space: good sense in motion

What we discovered at the Rio Summit in 1992, writes Ramachandra Guha in his magisterial *Global Environmental History* (1999), was that we have two worlds, not one. It was at the Rio Summit that climate justice got its legal reference point, the Climate Convention article 7 on the "common but differentiated responsibilities" to mitigate global warming. Despite the rise and growth rates of China and others, and despite the many linguistic deconstructions of the North-South divide by scholars, inequality between rich and poor along geographical, imperialist lines remains real and perceived ones (Angus, 2009). The history of oppression and exploitation forms the objective backdrop of the interest in truth discussed in the previous section. In this section, I will highlight the more subjective and emotive expression of this interest in truth, what Gramsci called the "spirit of cleavage" against "signore's and bosses" (Robinson, 2005; Thomas, 2009, p. 438;

Ytterstad, 2012, pp. 47–50). The rise of a profound sense of climate injustice has put indigenous good sense on climate change in motion.

Examples of this spirit of cleavage in the case of climate justice abound and is by no means restricted to Indigenous Peoples. Given the dawning realization of a definite carbon budget, countries like India and China did the math. The environmental movement had argued that the rich countries (so called Annex 1) would need to cut 25–40% of its emissions by 2020, numbers drawn from the "Bali-Box" of the IPCC report. But although no fixed targets were formally set for the poor countries (Non-Annex 1), the scientists behind the numbers had to admit that – in order to stay beneath the 450 ppm threshold, – these countries would de facto have to reduce their emissions as well by an estimated 15–30%. Bård Lahn, a Norwegian environmentalist and researcher who took part in the UN negotiations, tells the story of how a spirit of cleavage, already manifest in decades of discussions on "environmental colonialism" and "ecological debt" was sharpened when the numbers behind the carbon budget was broken down this way. A split within the Climate Action Network ensued, leading to the formation of the newer and more radical "Climate Justice Now!" coalition. (Angus, 2009, pp. 154–158; Lahn, 2013, pp. 85, 95–97). These groups went on to organize some of the more militant demonstrations outside (and inside) the Copenhagen Summit (Reitan, 2013).

Prompted by the failure of Copenhagen, Bolivia came to represent the most clear-cut anti-imperialist version of climate justice, voicing the notion of climate debt in ever more radical terms and numbers. In April 2010, the Cochabamba Working Group on Climate Finance provided a document demanding that the Global North must commit at least 6% of their annual GDP, the equivalent amount spent each year on national defense, for climate finance in the countries of the Global South (Bond, 2012, p. 134). This very number also found its way into the Declaration of the Indigenous Peoples of the World the COP17 in Durban, 2011. A brief analysis of the text of this declaration illustrates why the indigenous conception of necessity on climate change may be stronger in its relational than its scientific aspects.

Under the heading Shared Vision, the declaration "propose emission reductions of at least 45% to 1990 levels by 2020 and at least 95% by 2050." These are ambitious numbers but not exceptionally so. The "conception of necessity" expressed in the shape of concrete global targets for emission reductions may even be stronger in scientific reports than in Declarations by Indigenous Peoples. It is also worth noting the use of the word "propose." This is a low modality word (Fairclough, 1992). In 2019, after ever more dire scientific reports, Greta Thunberg and the Extinction Rebellion, it is not hard to find stronger expressions of the demand for emission cuts.

Under the "Financing" part of the Declaration, by contrast, the numbers and the wording of the demands are both much more radical. The Indigenous Peoples of the World demand that "Developed countries must commit new annual funding of at least 6% of its gross national product to face climate change in the developing countries." To put this number in perspective: Norway has lauded itself as a humanitarian superpower, partly with the ambition that 1% of its GDP should go to foreign aid. The final two bullet points under this heading are worth citing in full. There are no low modality words in the phrasing of the relational demands:

- Developed countries, the principal countries that have caused climate change, must assume their historic and current responsibility and honor the climate debt fully, which is the basis for a just, effective, scientific solution to climate change.
- In the framework of climate debt, we demand that the developed countries return to the developing countries the atmospheric space that is occupied by their GHG emissions.

As this chapter is being finalized in October 2019, indigenous communities in Ecuador (successfully, so far) fight against austerity imposed by the International Monetary Fund. This, of course, echoes the traditional way we think of the North-South flow of depth: countries in Latin America and Africa suffer the consequences of "structural adjustment programs" (Harvey, 2005) because they have to pay off their debt to the North. The demand for climate debt is a veritable *volte-face*: the payment should go in the opposite direction. The present authors first encounter with indigenous movements at climate summits was at the Copenhagen Summit in 2009 (Ytterstad, 2010; Ytterstad & Russell, 2012). One of the more memorable moments was a question posed by a spokesperson for an indigenous community in Panama: "How much are you going to pay us for our carbon sequestration in the rainforest for the last 500 years?"

This formulation suggests a leap in indigenous good sense on climate change from the local to the global. The traditional demand for autonomy rights in local territories morphs into a demand for an increased atmospheric space, setting the stage for relational conflict. Chief US climate negotiator in Copenhagen Todd Stern was blunt: "The sense of guilt or culpability or reparations – I just categorically reject that" (Bond, 2012, p. 114). Notwithstanding Stern, the feeling that *you owe us* is an unequivocal aspect of indigenous good sense on climate change.

Emergent good sense: no to extractivism, yes to more public goods

The last aspect of indigenous good sense I will assess in this chapter, I call emergent good sense. Gramsci alludes to this emergence property of good sense when he writes that

> The social group in question may indeed have its own conception of the world, even if only embryonic; a conception which manifests itself in action, but occasionally, and in flashes—when, that is, the group is acting as an organic totality.
>
> (Gramsci et al., 1971, p. 327)

So methodologically speaking, it makes sense to track mass protest movement, to find the last empirical manifestations of good sense. I will limit myself to two recent emergent examples of empirical and concrete indigenous good sense on climate change: anti-extractivism and a public goods approach to universal needs. They both have the potential to feed into broader constituencies.

Anti-extractivism

Autonomy is more than just another demand, writes Roberta Rice in her book on the rise of Indigenous mobilization in Latin Americas Neoliberal Era. "(I)t is the foundational claim of indigenous movements" (2012, p. 144). Combined with the dual experience of colonialism AND capitalism (including its now infamous neoliberal phase), the fight for autonomy is intrinsically linked to *anti-extractivism*. In both North America and Latin America, in Africa and in my own country of Norway, Indigenous Peoples and communities have often been at the forefront of resistance to fossil fuel but also other mining projects, particularly when such extractivist project infringe upon the lands of Indigenous Peoples (Petras & Veltmeyer, 2014; Willow, 2018). "I will chain myself for the Fiord, if I have to" wrote the Sámi singer Ella Marie Hætta Isaksen, about the plans of a mining company to dump 30 million tons of waste into the Repparfjord in North Norwegian Sámi territory.[5]

This mining project is opposed because of the perils of local pollution, not because of climate change.[6] Indeed, extractivism can also include industrial renewable energy projects, like dams or wind mill parks. Another caveat is that even in countries like Bolivia and Ecuador, where indigenous autonomy and political influence have arguably been most successful, political leaders influenced by indigenous good sense against extractivism have *also* embarked upon significant oil and gas projects (Valladares & Boelens, 2017; Villalba-Eguiluz & Etxano, 2017). The Buen Vivir vision of Evo Morales, for instance, includes a vision of "progressive extractivism" – using revenues from oil and gas to redistributive programming (Hicks & Fabricant, 2016). However inconsistent, anti-extractivism remains a central conceptual part of the struggle against climate change for indigenous communities. In the "shared vison" of the Indigenous Peoples of the World declaration to COP17, immediately after their proposed emission reductions, it reads "Gradual elimination of the development of fossil fuels and a moratorium on new fossil fuel exploitation in or near Indigenous Peoples lands and territories, respecting the rights of Indigenous Peoples."

There are many other initiatives directed specifically towards trying to stop the expansion of fossil fuel projects and thus further lock-in effects exacerbating global warming, like the disinvestment campaigns or the legal campaigns to outlaw new drilling projects. But viewed both from the activists of "blockadia" fighting against fracking (Klein, 2014; Willow, 2018) and from theoretical positions of an autonomy of nature (Malm, 2018; Vetlesen, 2008, 2015), there is something particularly heroic about the stance of indigenous communities fighting both for their ancestral rights AND against fossil fuel mega projects.

"El agua no se vende, el agua se defiende": a public goods approach to universal needs

Perhaps the most interesting emergent aspect of indigenous good sense is the convergence of climate change science, social justice movements and the defense of natural resources. Salena Tramel draws attention to the indigenous identity of the Black Mesa Water Coaliton

> as demonstrated by its participation and leadership in the struggle against the Dakota Access Pipeline where more than 280 tribes met on Standing Rock Sioux territory. That water-inspired political battle culminated in the largest gathering of indigenous people in North America since the Battle of Little Bighorn in 1876.

> (2018)

A similar convergence took place at the large demonstration during the 2014 COP in Lima. Indigenous miners had their own contingency, wearing helmets in the demonstration. "You do not sell the water, you defend it" was among the most heard slogans, perhaps because one of the key organizers of the demonstration was FENTAP, the Peruvian water workers union.[7] The fear of losing that most crucial and universal resource of nature – water – also informed the opening statement of the International Indigenous Peoples Forum on Climate Change, at the COP24 in Poland.

In such instances, the global of global warming becomes something local. Defending your local water supply makes perfect Oxford dictionary good sense: "The ability to make sound judgements and sensible decisions, especially about practical matters arising in everyday life." But such indigenous good sense on climate change also illustrates a more general public goods approach. Defending the commons from enclosure and commodification is an old battle. Over 200 years ago, the eighth Earl of Lauderdale contended that "'The common sense of mankind would revolt' at any proposal to augment private riches 'by creating a scarcity of any commodity generally useful and necessary to man'" (Foster, Clark, & York, 2011, p. 55). That rebellion might very well resurface as a species being global demand, as the warming condition intensifies:

> We find commons in the air, on the land and in all water…In defending the key life supports in regional areas, through transnational social networks and movements, we can develop a transnational civil society. Such an alliance with the global Indigenous movements and others can

help us focus on the interconnected needs of all ecologies on the planet Earth, allowing us to insure that the conditions for life on Earth may be preserved in whole.

(Ridgeway, 2014, pp. 148–149)

One illustration of such alliance potential will have to suffice. The Peruvian FENTAP water workers union is part of Trade Unions for Energy Democracy (TUED). TUED is on the radical wing of the international trade union movement and was present at the latest COP, arguing precisely for a public goods approach.[8] As Sean Sweeney and John Treat concludes in a TUED working paper on the public solution to climate change:

Unions and their allies are well positioned to challenge the myth that a transition to renewable energy can only be accomplished by catering to the interests of big companies and private investors. The global labor movement can and should demand and fight for a viable transition pathway—one that is anchored in public financing, social ownership, and democratic control.[9]

If a modern urban society is to flourish in a warming world, energy must be on the list of commons and be seen as a universal need in the cities, just as water is for those who live off the land. Bernie Sanders ambitious and costly version of the Green New Deal in 2019 enthused TUED further, and their bulletin put in bold Sanders commitment that **"renewable energy generated by the Green New Deal will be publicly owned."**[10]

Mixing good sense together and dosing out the medicine to the right people

Just as indigenous knowledges revolve around *practice* (Ridgeway, 2014, p. 138), so does Gramsci's philosophy of practice. In the era of global warming, practical knowledge of both kinds needs to combine the local with the global. The global is largely defined by climate science (but also carries the scars of an unjust human history). Combining the aspects of good sense discussed in this chapter, facilitating further convergence of social forces that can put such emergent themes as anti-extractivism and the public good into practice is mostly a political and strategic task. The hopeful note on which the analysis in this chapter has ended, however, warrants an injection of some pessimism of the intellect.

Indigenous good sense on climate change does not flourish unopposed. Just as climate justice and anti-imperialism most of the time is weaker than Imperialism, good sense has a larger adversary in hegemony, international, regional and national (Budd, 2013). Hegemony combines force and appeals to consent, and incorporate and soften resistance, in myriad ways. Bolivia and Ecuador were punished for their criticism of the Copenhagen Accord, by the millions, through cuts in foreign aid. By contrast, "the Maldives leaders reversed course, apparently because of a $50 million aid package arranged by US deputy envoy Jonathan Pershing" (Ibid., p. 91). The prime minister of Ethiopia played a similar role in softening the edge of Climate Justice emerging from Africa.

The incorporation of resistance and the softening of indigenous good sense on climate change are all signaled by euphemisms like "equity" instead of "justice," "Green Development Mechanisms" or notoriously vague concepts like sustainable development. A market-driven version of the "green economy" may zap the energy of people-driven climate transformations (cf Ytterstad, 2021). Oftentimes, environmental organizations, or leaders of the Global South, partake in this stifling of climate justice from below, as was the case in Cancun, the year after Copenhagen. Jairam Ramesh, the negotiator from India, a country that used to insist on the "equitable access to atmospheric space," proposed a colombi egg reformulation that earned him the reputation as a "deal-maker." With the exception of Bolivia, negotiators in Mexico drew a sigh of relief settling for "equitable access to sustainable development" (Lahn, 2013, pp. 219–220).

If hegemony seldom squashes resistance completely, it tends to succeed in prolonging paralysis, thus enabling business as usual. Indeed, in the last few years, even the beacon of indigenous good sense on climate change in Bolivia has begun to flicker, with tensions appearing between the Bolivian climate change platform and the Morales Government:

> Morales has emphasized that the poor and indigenous are at greater risk and the globe should call upon their wisdom and leadership. Yet Bolivia as a resource-dependent country continues to rely upon extractive industries and the degradation of the environment as a strategy for redistributive governmental programming and national economic development.
>
> (Hicks & Fabricant, 2016, p. 96)

With the "pink tide" in Latin America on a definite ebb, there is perhaps even more reasons to be skeptical of Morales inspirational capacity to maintain the vision of an alternative development model "Buen Vivir" (Claeys & Pugley, 2017).

But the degree of real political autonomy exercised by indigenous communities in Bolivia today should not be neglected. Nor should the aspects of indigenous good sense on climate change depicted in this chapter. As the consequences of climate change pan out, new agencies with a sense of urgency emerge and merge. Greta Thunberg did not win the Nobel Prize but she was honored by tribal leaders of Standing Rock, and she in turned showed her solidarity with the indigenous struggle against the Dakota Access oil pipeline.[11] Some important ingredients of that medicine that the world needs at the moment come from indigenous knowledges; other ingredients – like climate change science – are exogenous knowledge. Mixing the ingredients together in theory is perhaps easier than finding enough doctors in real life, who can dose out the medicine to the right people.

Notes

1 Quite a few Gramcian scholars use the term "counter-hegemonic" to signal their support for opposition to hegemony, although this term is not used by Gramsci himself. I prefer good sense because it invites us to enquire into the *substance* of ideas in opposition to hegemony.
2 www.youtube.com/watch?v=d9uTH0iprVQ The Intercept 17.4.2019
3 There is more information in Spanish than in English, see https://cambioclimatico. org.bo/
4 My translation from Spanish. The document can be read with hand written signatures here https://cambioclimatico.org.bo/wp-content/uploads/2018/10/ declaracion-quillacollo.pdf
5 www.nrk.no/ytring/jeg-lenker-meg-for-fjorden_-om-jeg-ma-1.14295499
6 The leader of the Environmental NGO Bellona in Norway supported the dumping of waste in the Repparfjord, because he believed the production of more copper would be necessary for the grand scale electrification of society, putting him at odds with the more locally orientated parts of the environmental movement. www.vg.no/nyheter/innenriks/i/216rAG/bellona-leder-vil-ikke-stanse-dumping- av-gruveavfall-i-repparfjorden-ser-ingen-bedre-alternativer
7 www.fentap.org.pe/ The present author attended both the demonstration and a meeting hosted by the Fentap union in Lima.
8 http://unionsforenergydemocracy.org/tued-bulletin-81/
9 http://unionsforenergydemocracy.org/wp-content/uploads/2017/10/ TUED-Working-Paper-10.pdf
10 http://unionsforenergydemocracy.org/tued-bulletin-89/
11 www.theguardian.com/environment/2019/oct/09/greta-thunberg-standing-rock- north-south-dakota-nobel-peace-prize

References

Angus, I. (Ed.). (2009). *The global fight for climate justice: Anticapitalist responses to global warning and environmental destruction.* London: Resistance Books.

Boillat, S., & Berkes, F. (2013). Perception and interpretation of climate change among Quechua farmers of Bolivia: Indigenous knowledge as a resource for adaptive capacity. *Ecology and Society, 18*(4), 21.

Bond. (2012). *Politics of climate justice: Paralysis above, movement below.* Scottsville: University of KwaZulu-Natal Press.

Breidlid, A. (2012). *Education, indigenous knowledges, and development in the global south: Contesting knowledges for a sustainable future* (1 ed.). New York: Routledge.

Budd, A. (2013). *Class, states and international relations: A critical appraisal of Robert Cox and neo-Gramscian theory.* Abingdon, Oxon: Routledge.

Claeys, P., & Pugley, D. D. (2017). Peasant and indigenous transnational social movements engaging with climate justice. *Canadian Journal of Development*

Studies / Revue Canadienne d'études Du Développement, *38*(3), 325–340. doi:10.1080/02255189.2016.1235018

Fairclough, N. (1992). *Discourse and social change*. Cambridge: Polity Press.

Foster, J. B. (2009). *The ecological revolution: Making peace with the planet*. New York: New York University Press.

Foster, J. B., Clark, B., & York, R. (2011). *The ecological rift: Capitalism's war on the earth*. New York: Monthly Review Press.

Freedman, D. (2012). Andreas Ytterstad: Norwegian Climate change policy and the media: Between hegemony and good sense. *Norsk medietidsskrift*, *19*(04), 364–366.

Freedman, D. (2014). *The contradictions of media power*. London: Bloomsbury Academic.

Gramsci, A., Hoare, Q., & Smith, G. N. (1971). *Selections from the prison notebooks*. London: Lawrence and Wishart.

Harvey, D. (2005). *A brief history of neoliberalism*. New York: Oxford University Press.

Hicks, K., & Fabricant, N. (2016). The Bolivian climate justice movement: Mobilizing indigeneity in climate change negotiations. *Latin American Perspectives*, *43*(4), 87–104. doi:10.1177/0094582X16630308

Klein, N. (2014). *This changes everything: Capitalism vs. the climate*. New York: Simon & Schuster.

Krainer, A., Aguirre, D., Guerra, M., & Meiser, A. (2017). Educación superior intercultural y diálogo de saberes: El caso de la Amawtay Wasi en Ecuador. *Revista de La Educación Superior*, *46*(184), 55–76. doi:10.1016/j.resu.2017.11.002

Krøvel, R. (2018). Indigenous perspectives on researching Indigenous Peoples. *Social Identities*, *24*(1), 58–65. doi:10.1080/13504630.2017.1314417

Lahn, B. 1983. (2013). *Klimaspillet: En fortelling fra innsiden av FNs klimatoppmøter*. Oslo: Flamme.

Lofthus, A. (2013). Gramsci, nature and the philosophy of praxis. In M. Ekers (Ed.), *Gramsci: Space, nature, politics* (pp. 178–197). Chichester: John Wiley & Sons.

Makondo, C. C., & Thomas, D. S. G. (2018). Climate change adaptation: Linking indigenous knowledge with western science for effective adaptation. *Environmental Science & Policy*, *88*, 83–91. doi:10.1016/j.envsci.2018.06.014

Malm, A. (2018). *The progress of this storm: Nature and society in a warming world*. London; New York: Verso.

Mugambiwa, S. S. (2018). Adaptation measures to sustain indigenous practices and the use of indigenous knowledge systems to adapt to climate change in Mutoko rural district of Zimbabwe. *Jàmbá; Potchefstroom*, *10*(1). doi:10.4102/jamba.v10i1.388

Nilsen, A. G. (2009). 'The authors and the actors of their own drama': Towards a Marxist theory of social movements. *Capital & Class*, *33*(3), 109–139. doi:10.1177/0309816809033003050*1

Petras, J., & Veltmeyer, H. (2014). *The new extractivism: A post-neoliberal development model or imperialism of the twenty-first century?* Retrieved from http://ebookcentral.proquest.com/lib/ucb/detail.action?docID=1696472

Pierotti, R. J. (2011). *Indigenous knowledge, ecology, and evolutionary biology*. New York: Routledge.

Reitan, R. (2013). *Global movement*. London; New York: Routledge.

Rice, R. (2012). *The new politics of protest: Indigenous mobilization in Latin America's neoliberal era*. Retrieved from http://ebookcentral.proquest.com/lib/ucb/detail.action?docID=3411845

Ridgeway, S. J. (2014). *The power of the talking stick: Indigenous politics and the world ecological crisis*. Boulder: Paradigm Publishers.

Robinson, A. (2005). Towards an intellectual reformation: The critique of common sense and the forgotten revolutionary project of Gramscian theory. *Critical Review of International Social and Political Philosophy, 8*(4), 469. doi:10.1080/13698230500205045

Royer, M. J. S. (2016). Climate change and traditional ecological knowledge. In M. J. S. Royer (Ed.), *Climate, environment and cree observations: James Bay Territory, Canada* (pp. 7–33). doi:10.1007/978-3-319-25181-3_2

Stoknes, P. E. (2015). *What we think about when we try not to think about global warming: Toward a new psychology of climate action*. White River Junction, Vermont: Chelsea Green Publishing.

Terje Bongard, & Røskaft, E. (2010). *Det biologiske mennesket: Individer og samfunn i lys av evolusjon*. Trondheim: Tapir akademisk.

Thomas, P. D. (2009). *The Gramscian moment: Philosophy, hegemony and Marxism*. Leiden: Brill.

Tramel, S. (2018). Convergence as political strategy: Social justice movements, natural resources and climate change. *Third World Quarterly, 39*(7), 1290–1307. doi: 10.1080/01436597.2018.1460196

Valladares, C., & Boelens, R. (2017). Extractivism and the rights of nature: Governmentality, 'convenient communities' and epistemic pacts in Ecuador. *Environmental Politics, 26*(6), 1015–1034. doi:10.1080/09644016.2017.1338384

Vetlesen, A. J. (2008). *Nytt klima: Miljøkrisen i samfunnskritisk lys*. Oslo: Gyldendal.

Vetlesen, A. J. (2015). *The denial of nature: Environmental philosophy in the era of global capitalism* (1st ed.). London; New York: Routledge.

Villalba-Eguiluz, C. U., & Etxano, I. (2017). Buen Vivir vs development (II): The limits of (neo-)Extractivism. *Ecological Economics, 138*, 1–11. doi:10.1016/j.ecolecon.2017.03.010

Weart, S. R. (2008). *The discovery of global warming: Revised and expanded edition*. Retrieved from http://ebookcentral.proquest.com/lib/ucb/detail.action?docID=3301406

Wildcat, D. R. (2014). Introduction: Climate change and Indigenous Peoples of the USA. In J. K. Maldonado, B. Colombi, & R. Pandya (Eds.), *Climate change and Indigenous Peoples in the United States: Impacts, experiences and actions* (pp. 1–7). doi:10.1007/978-3-319-05266-3_1

Willow, A. J. (2018). *Understanding ExtrACTIVISM: Culture and power in nature resource disputes*. Retrieved from http://ebookcentral.proquest.com/lib/ucb/detail.action?docID=5481489

Ytterstad, A. (2010). Alle i samme båt? In K. S. Orgeret & A. H. Simonsen (Eds.), *Elisabeth Eide: Det utålmodige mennesket* (pp. 49–71). Oslo: Unipub.

Ytterstad, A. (2012). *Norwegian climate change policy in the media: Between hegemony and good sense* (Phd dissertation). Oslo University.

Ytterstad, A. (2014). Good sense on global warming. *International Socialism, 144*, 141–165.

Ytterstad, A. (2021). The climate jobs mobilization strategy. In N. Räthzel, D. Stevis & D. Uzzell (Eds.), *The Environmental Labour Studies Handbook*. Springer Palgrave.

Ytterstad, A., & Russell, A. (2012). Pessimism of the intellect and optimism of the will. A Gramscian analysis of climate justice in summit coverage. In E. Eide & R. Kunelius (Eds.), *Media meets climate: The global challenge for journalism* (pp. 247–262). Göteborg: Nordicom.

9 Indigenous knowledges and academic understandings of pastoral mobility

Hanne Kirstine Adriansen

Introduction

By using pastoralists and their use of mobility as an example, I explore the paradoxes and dilemmas involved in applying indigenous knowledges for sustainable development as it relates to Sustainable Development Goal 2 (SDG 2) (promote sustainable agriculture), SDG 13 (combat climate change) and SDG 15 life on land (combatting desertification and land degradation). 'Livestock mobility is a complex concept holding many different meanings for observers of pastoralism. The movement of African pastoralists with their livestock has historically been seen by outsiders as working against both environmental and development goals' (Turner and Schlecht, 2019: 1). While pastoralism has been acknowledged as 'a viable and sustainable livelihood and that pastoralists play a role in attaining the United Nations Sustainable Development Goals' (Zinsstag et al., 2016: 693), there are also concerns that precisely the mobile livelihood makes it difficult to obtain SDG 4, to 'Ensure inclusive and equitable quality education and promote lifelong learning opportunities for all' (Dyer, 2018), and even when education is available, the formal curriculum fails to accommodate the needs of pastoralist communities (Ng'asike, 2019), thereby also missing SDG 4. Despite the increasing recognition in (Western) academia of pastoral mobility as an environmental adaptation and sustainable management practice (Rasmussen et al., 2018; Turner and Schlecht, 2019), pastoralists in Africa are still perceived as being archaic, backward and antidevelopment by their governments and their urban compatriots (Tonah, 2019). Hence, pastoralists and their way of life hold interesting perspectives for studies of environment, development, sustainability and knowledge systems.

When concerned with sustainable development and reaching the SDGs, my fieldwork amongst Senegalese pastoralists made me ponder, how we understand and use indigenous knowledges and use them for sustainable development. I[1] was often asked what my country looked like, if we had cattle and green grass. The typical reaction towards my reply about fat cows and a green country side was 'You must be good people'. When I did not understand that comment, my friend Seydi explained 'If God sends you much rain, it is proof you must be good people'. For me, the only proof was our different cosmologies and the challenges in using indigenous knowledges together with scientific knowledges for sustainable development. Later, this incident made me ponder whose knowledge counts the most and the dilemma when working with different epistemologies and knowledges systems – how can this be done in a meaningful manner?

In the 1950s and 1960s, the academic and development community saw indigenous knowledges as an obstacle to development (Agrawal, 1995a). Over the past 30 years, however, it has become in vogue to combine scientific environmental knowledges with indigenous knowledges for sustainable development (Bollig and Schulte, 1999; Eriksen, 2007; Oba and Kotile, 2001). With recent calls for Africanisation and decolonisation of African education and academy, the importance of indigenous research methods and non-Western epistemologies and knowledges have been emphasised (Chalmers, 2017; Msila, 2009). Yet, as noted by Thomas and Twyman (2004, 215): 'scientific and indigenous land-user views of change do not always tally, leading to conflicts in aid agendas and policy recommendation'. The lack of agreement between scientific and indigenous knowledges can also be seen as a consequence of the purpose of the two types of knowledge. While some scientific knowledges claim to be decontextualized and even universal, indigenous is derived from a physical and sociocultural context and often focuses on its practical usefulness (Briggs, 2005). Hence, the different knowledges can both overlap and contradict each other, because they are the outcome of different knowledge systems and epistemologies (Adriansen, 2008).

In this chapter,[2] I want to explore how different knowledge systems such as scientific or academic knowledges and indigenous knowledges sometimes clash and sometimes go hand-in-hand. I use the concepts indigenous/local knowledges and scientific/academic/Western knowledges with reluctance bearing in mind the critique made (among others) by Agrawal (1995b: 3):

> The classification into indigenous and Western knowledge fails not only because there are similarities across those categories and differences within them. The attempt founders at another, more fundamental, level as well. It seeks to separate and fix in time and space (i.e. separate as independent and fix as stationary and unchanging) knowledge systems that can never be so separated or fixed. In the face of evidence that suggests contact, diversity, exchange, communication, learning and transformation among different systems of knowledge and beliefs.

Pastoral mobility in Africa has been discussed by rangeland ecologists as part of the 'new rangeland paradigm' for dryland ecosystems and pastoral production systems.[3] Within this paradigm, mobility is perceived as ecologically rational in an environment characterised by high variability of natural resources (Sayre et al., 2013). While the positive perception of mobility only emerged amongst dryland ecologists in the 1990s, this is not a new line of thought among anthropologists studying pastoralists (e.g. Dyson-Hudson and Dyson-Hudson, 1980; Stenning, 1957). This shows the importance of thinking about scientific knowledges in plural; within the research communities, there are multiple, competing epistemologies and different knowledge systems. And, as Agrawal (1995b) pointed out, academic knowledges change over time through its interaction with other knowledges.

My arguments are unfolded through three main sections. The first section outlines the 'new rangeland paradigm' and shows how academic understandings of pastoral mobility have changed. The second section is a case study of the use of mobility amongst Fulani pastoralists in Senegal and analyses indigenous knowledges and pastoral mobility. The third section uses the first two sections to discuss the paradoxes and dilemmas entailed in applying knowledges based on different epistemologies for sustainable development.

Pastoral mobility according to Western sciences

For decades, parts of the research community especially anthropologists argued that the pastoral way of life was rational (e.g. Dyson-Hudson and Dyson-Hudson, 1980; Stenning, 1957). However, amongst other parts of the scientific community and noteworthy among policy and development planners, pastoralism was perceived as an irrational and destructive production system (Brown, 1971; Picardi, 1974). In the 1990s, a so-called 'new rangeland paradigm' emerged, which was argued to provide coherent theory linking the dynamics of drylands with pastoral strategies not least understanding these in the context of climate variability. In my article *Pastoral mobility as a response to climate variability in African drylands* (Adriansen, 1999), I have analysed how this new paradigm emerged and how different academic knowledges competed and influenced one another. It is a good example that academic knowledges are neither singular nor static. In the following, I will provide a shorter outline.

The West African droughts in the 1970s and the subsequent development aid caused much new policy and development research concerning dryland pastoralism. The focus was often the so-called failure of pastoral production systems; the impact of drought seemed devastating, and development projects seemed to fail (Scoones, 1995). Pastoralism was unpopular with most Africa Governments because of the mobile nature of pastoralists which made administration and development work difficult. Desertification and degradation became commonplace terms in the discussion of pastoral production systems, and pastoralist behaviour was often claimed to be destructive as well as irrational. The pastoral production systems were accused of causing land degradation, because it appeared that livestock grazing altered the vegetation composition and changed the ability of the land to sustain the livestock and thus the human population (Adriansen, 1999). Mobility was an issue of concern for pastoralists, because they required open access to pastures for their livestock. After the biologist Hardin's (1968) article *The Tragedy of the Commons*, this concept was very often applied to pastoral production systems. The herder, Hardin claimed, was likely to extend his herd beyond the point of overgrazing, because the profit of extra animals went to the herder, while the costs of over-exploitation were held in common by all users and thus, only a fraction was paid by the herder. Hardin concluded therefore that common property would lead to common ruin (Hardin, 1968). According to this idea, customary tenure systems were assumed destructive, because they gave open access to resources which lead to over-exploitation. Therefore, privatisation appeared to be the solution, subsequently ending pastoral mobility.

In the 1980s and the early 1990s, the picture changed: the idea of nomadic pastoralism as maladaptive was questioned and the environmental problems were seen in a new light. Some of the first researchers, who drew attention to the need for a complete paradigm shift, were the biologists Ellis and Swift in 1988. Their background and thus starting point was the functioning of dryland ecosystems: 'African pastoral systems have been studied with the assumptions that these ecosystems are potentially stable (equilibrial) systems which become destabilized by overstocking and overgrazing' (Ellis and Swift, 1988: 450). In other words, biologists had perceived African dryland ecosystems to be similar in their functioning to humid ecosystems found in Europe. However, when African dryland ecosystems were recognised as highly variable and unpredictable, pastoral strategies appeared well adapted to the environment. These strategies include moving herds to make best use of the variable and heterogeneous landscape. Hence, instead of seeing the ecosystems as equilibrium systems, dryland or rangelands should be perceived as disequilibrium systems with large variability of natural resources both spatially and temporally (Adriansen, 1999). Subsequently, pastoral mobility was praised in a number of academic articles and books, notably *Managing mobility in African rangelands: the legitimization of transhumance* (Niamir-Fuller, 1999a), which as the title suggests lends scientific legitimization of pastoral mobility practices.

Last but not least, it has been argued that pastoralism is a viable and sustainable livelihood and that pastoralists play a role in attaining SDGs, in particular pastoralism can contribute towards SDG 1 (end poverty), SDG 2 (Sustainable agriculture), SDG 3 (healthy lives and well-being), SDG 8 (inclusive and sustainable economic growth), SDG 10 (reduce inequality), SDG 15 (combat desertification) and SDG 16 (inclusive societies for sustainable development) (Zinsstag et al., 2016).

This could be seen as a 'happy ending' where the scientific community had understood indigenous knowledges, and the path towards sustainable development was cleared. Unfortunately, this is not the case. By providing a case study of pastoral mobility, I will argue that the paradigm shift in scientific knowledges did change the scientific understanding of dryland ecosystems, but it did not include an understanding of pastoralists' epistemologies and cosmologies when it comes to their use of nature, environment and mobility in these drylands.

Pastoralists in Ferlo: their perception and use of mobility[4]

Before the establishment of boreholes in the 1950s, the rangelands of northern Senegal, a region called Ferlo, were utilised as a pastoral area due to the low and variable precipitation and lack of permanent water supplies, which made cultivation and permanent settlement difficult. In the rainy season, when pasture in the area was abundant, Ferlo served as a grazing reserve for mobile pastoralists pursuing large-scale migrations. As temporary water holes (ponds) dried out during the dry season, pastoralists moved north to the Senegalese River valley or south and west to the so-called peanut basin (Weicker, 1993). In the 1950s, the French colonial administration made the first boreholes in Ferlo, which meant that the area could be used on a permanent basis. The possibility of staying in the area during the dry season meant that pastoralists became semi-sedentary (Ba, 1986). They took up rainfed agriculture, especially in the southern part of the area, and more boreholes were established (Touré, 1988). Villages have grown around the boreholes. However, the pastoralists live in the bush where they have permanent rainy season camps. During the dry season, they may go on migration in search of pasture and water. Parts of Ferlo have been divided into resource management units following the boreholes; these are called pastoral units (*unité pastorales*). Before the drought in 1973, the majority of the pastoralists were subsistence-oriented relying on a combination of herding and rainfed agriculture. The herd mainly consisted of milking cattle and a few sheep and goats (Sutter, 1987). The drought years in the mid-1970s and mid-1980s profoundly influenced the pastoralists, who had to adapt their knowledges and livelihood strategies to the changes in life conditions. Moreover, since the 1970s and the desiccation of the climate, many pastoralists do not find cultivation worthwhile anymore. This has also redirected the strategies towards more livestock rearing, especially with a greater reliance on sheep and an increased commercialisation. Evidently, this also changed the use of mobility, which was the focus of my fieldwork, this was carried out in the pastoral unit Tessekre, located in the middle of Ferlo. The village of Tessekre spreads around a borehole established in 1954. In the pastoral unit of Tessekre, the majority of the inhabitants are Fulani (92%); the rest are Wolof (5%) and Moor (3%). The people living in the village itself are Moor and Wolof; they are merchants and some have animals as well. Some of the Fulani have shops and houses in the village even though they live in the bush. The fieldwork was based on the Fulani pastoralists living in the bush.

Besides interviews with key persons of the area and questionnaire interviews with all Fulani households present at the time,[5] nine pastoralists were selected to participate in a GPS study for the purpose of studying mobility in practice. Besides the GPS measurements, which went on for a year, I made participatory herding and spent time at the camps. Further, qualitative, in-depth interviews were made applying the timeline, life history method (Adriansen, 2012). The interviews were quite different, but they all evolved around issues related to livelihood strategies in general and mobility in particular (see Adriansen, 2006). Further, participatory observations were made in the village of Tessekre; I was often at the borehole or sitting outside the shops chatting. The participatory observations provided insight into the socio-cultural fabric of daily life in the village and the camps.

The changes that Ferlo has experienced over the past 70 years, both in terms of droughts and climate change and in terms of politics, infrastructure and management changes mean that the pastoralists have had to adapt and change their knowledges to these new realities. Hence, their knowledges are far from static and independent either.

Indigenous knowledges and perceptions of mobility

On basis of the fieldwork, different issues were found to be of relevance for understanding mobility. Although the use of mobility varied, the pastoralists usually agreed on the perception of mobility. This means the answers concerning the types of mobility, the reasons for going, etc. were more or less the same. Among the pastoralists, there was a common understanding of the changes in the use of mobility and importance of mobility in the area, despite the different practice I observed.

In order to understand the pastoralists' use of mobility, I analysed their perception of mobility and their reasons for going on migration and related it to their practices. The pastoralists all gave the same reasons for going on migration, namely, to search for pasture and water. There were some variations in the answers when it came to pasture, some go because they want to find better quality (pull effect) and others because the quantity is lacking (push effect).

From an ecological perspective, the answers could be interpreted as illustrating the pastoralists' attempt to balance the variability of natural resources and thus to practice sustainable development. However, there are no indications that the pastoralists had sustainability or even the environment as the point of departure for their considerations on mobility. On the contrary, they talked about mobility from the point of view of livestock needs. There is a difference between these two perspectives. The pastoralists of Ferlo are not using mobility because it is ecologically rational. To them, mobility is a means to ensure the survival of the livestock.

The question is: how do the pastoralists perceive the environment? What is their environmental epistemology? First of all, there is no word in their language *Pulaar* that translates into environment, which is a rather abstract concept. Instead, my interpreter used the word *ladde*, which in *Pulaar* means bush or everything outside the camp. The indigenous perception of 'the environment' can be illustrated by the response to two questions concerning herding. The first was: 'Do you think it is better for the cattle not to be herded?' The pastoralists understood this question and did not find it strange. Although the answers varied, it was not difficult for the pastoralists to answer. For example, Ali replied: 'It is best to herd the cattle so they eat well and breed every year'. The other question was: 'Do you think it is better for the environment not to herd?' It was very difficult for them to comprehend and thus to answer. While the pastoralists acknowledged the relationship between herding and animals' performance, it did not seem straightforward for them that their herding practice might affect the environment. For example: 'I have no idea. For me the best thing for the environment is rain' or 'I know rain is good for the environment and bush fire is bad for me'. I heard no indication of pastoralists using mobility out of concern for the environment. This was not part of their epistemology, but an example of the research problem being determined by the researcher (me) and not necessarily resonating with the interviewees, as Smith (2012) has written about in her *Decolonising methodologies*.

Types of mobility

The pastoralists in Tessekre distinguish between the following seasons that are related to different types of mobility:

- Rainy season ~ *Ndungu* (June-August)
- Dry season (September-May)
- Cold dry season ~ *Dabudé* (September-January)
- Hot dry season ~ *Thiédu* (February-April)
- Near rainy season ~ *Cen sedlé / Deminaré* (May)

The different types of mobility can be divided into two main types based on the indigenous perception of mobility: mobility outside the pastoral unit (transhumance) and mobility within the pastoral unit.

Concerning mobility outside the pastoral unit (hereafter called transhumance), the pastoralists identified on the following types (Table 9.1):

Table 9.1 The Fulani's description of different types of mobility

Type	Season	Direction	Duration
Meeting-the-rain (pull)	Near rainy season, *cen seldé*	South, where the first rain falls	Until the rain begins
Better-pasture-elsewhere (pull)	Usually dry season, *dabaude + thiédu*	Anywhere	Anytime
Lack-of-pasture (push)	Any season, but usually dry season, *thiédu*	Anywhere	Until the rainy season
Disease (push)	Any season	Anywhere	Anytime
Lack-of-water (push)	Any season	To nearest borehole in function	Until the borehole functions

Depending on the reason for going on transhumance, it can include all or some of the animals. If there is a lack of water or pasture, it is necessary to bring along all the livestock. In case of 'better-pasture-elsewhere' or 'meeting-the-rain', it is common only to take the cattle or the small ruminants or even only the sheep. Which type is taken depends on the need of the livestock and the livelihood strategy of the household.

An interesting case is pastoralists who raise sheep for the Tabaski.[6] For these 'Tabaski pastoralists', sheep are the real capital, hence most work concern making this capital grow. Tabaski pastoralists will make sure that the sheep are well fed before sale and therefore want them to benefit from the best pastures either by going on transhumance themselves or by paying a herder to take the sheep with him. An interesting point concerning Tabaski sheep mobility is the changing of the time of the *id-al-adha*. In the late 1990s, when I conducted fieldwork, Tabaski was in the hot dry season where the pasture availability was limited and the quality had declined. Therefore, quite a few Tabaski pastoralists went on transhumance (or used a paid herder) in this season and explained that they were in search of better pastures for their Tabaski sheep. This is also when it would be rational to go on transhumance from a range-ecology perspective. However, the Muslim calendar is a lunar calendar and does not follow the solar calendar. This means that the timing of the *id-al-adha* changes by 10–11 days every year. Thus, the Tabaski pastoralists' use of mobility was not guided by environmental concerns but was steered by religious events and thus commercial demand for sheep.

Mobility, herding, and cultural construction of identity

Pastoral nomads have been depicted in several coffee table books, many of which have been written by researchers in the Global North.[7] In this literature, the image of the 'freedom loving', independent and mobile pastoralist is so well established that the importance of mobility for the cultural construction of identity is rarely questioned, even in the academic literature. My preconceived idea of the ethnic identity of the Fulani included this image of mobility as a key aspect. Further, one of the lessons of the 'new rangeland paradigm' is the ecological rationale of mobility. Therefore, I did not question the importance of mobility for the cultural construction of identity, at least not initially. However, among the pastoralists of Ferlo, mobility does not seem to relate to their (ethnic) identity. Nothing in the answers could be interpreted in this way. Further, the practice indicated the same. This can be illustrated by the widespread use of hired herders for going on transhumance.

Small ruminants are herded all year, because these can get lost, stolen or eaten by jackals. Depending upon the strategy of the household, the small ruminants are herded by the children, young men or a paid herder

The semi-sedentary lifestyle and the lack of predators mean that the cattle can be left to roam freely. When they are in the pastoral unit, which the cattle know, many pastoralists choose not to herd their cattle; instead, they spend the time on other activities. Herding of cattle depends on the preferences of the household. It is mainly a question of generation whether the cattle are herded or not; the elders prefer to herd, while the younger generation finds it unnecessary.

For those who do not herd all year, herding is mainly related to transhumance, because it is necessary to herd while on transhumance. Also, many go on transhumance just before the rainy season in order to meet the rain in the southern regions, where the rain starts. Those staying at home have to herd anyway, because the cattle can smell that it has been raining and therefore start to walk south if they are not herded. Interestingly, the use of hired herders had become more common and was an indication of the lack of importance of mobility for the cultural construction of identity amongst the Fulani in Ferlo. Instead, the identity was strongly linked to the livestock, especially the cattle: 'My father had cattle and it is to be Fulani' and 'I have cattle because I'm Fulani – a Fulani without cattle is like a woman without jewels'. While the majority of the pastoralists explained that cattle were necessary for the Fulani identity, nobody expressed mobility as a necessity for their identity. I asked the pastoralists why they had decided to stay where they stayed at the moment (this being the *rumaano* or a temporary camp). If they did not stay in the *rumaano*, this was because the needs of the livestock had forced them to move. They explained that they had to be where the pasture was right for their livestock: 'to look after the livestock is the work of the Fulani'. The women expressed a dislike for transhumance, because this gave them extra work making huts, etc. Also, herding is necessary during transhumance, and because many of the pastoralists have decreased the amount of time they spend on herding, this means that transhumance also increases the workload of men. With regard to the pastoralists of Ferlo, Touré has pointed out that the Fulani 'do not so much choose mobility as submit to it' (1988: 36). Instead, it was clear that the ethnic identity of the Fulani in Ferlo was closely linked to being cattle rearing, as Müller (1993) has also shown.

To sum up this brief overview of perception and use of mobility amongst the pastoralists in Ferlo, there is no doubt that they process a profound understanding of their environment (although this concept is not part of their epistemology) and how mobility can be used to make the most of the variable resources. Interestingly, the Fulani would not frame the use of mobility that way, instead their point of departure is the nutrition need of their livestock (as Turner and Schlecht (2019) have also pointed out). While academic knowledges have legitimised pastoral mobility and shown that the pastoral way of life is sustainable, it has done so from an ecosystem perspective. As the case study shows, the Fulani epistemology is quite different. The question is how we can use indigenous knowledges for sustainable development?

Different knowledge systems – paradoxes and dilemmas

After I have outlined changes in academic understandings of pastoral mobility and presented a case study with a focus on indigenous knowledges about and use of pastoral mobility, I will address some of the paradoxes and dilemmas involved in applying indigenous knowledges for sustainable development and for reaching SDG 2 (promote sustainable agriculture), SDG 13 (combat climate change) and SDG 15 life on land (combatting desertification and land degradation) in relation to nomadic pastoralists.

A number of scholars (also in this book) have shown that indigenous knowledges are important for obtaining sustainable development (e.g. Abate, 2016; Berkes et al., 2000; Ziervogel and Opere, 2010). As Nyong et al. explain: 'Incorporating indigenous knowledge can add value to the development of sustainable climate change mitigation and adaptation strategies that are rich in local content, and planned in conjunction with local people' (2007: 787). Briggs and Sharp (2004) have noted that the increasing interest in indigenous knowledges should be understood in the context of the failure of top-down development after which indigenous knowledges were accredited increasing importance and wisdom. This is also the case with nomadic pastoralists; however, in this case, the increased interest in indigenous knowledges coincided with the advent of the 'new rangeland paradigm'. As shown above, pastoral mobility was seen as rational within the 'new rangeland paradigm'. The paradox remains that while pastoralist practices were perceived as rational, this new understanding was not based on indigenous knowledges. This positive perception of pastoral mobility was a result of the paradigm shift within the scientific understanding of dryland ecosystems.

Based on my study presented above, I argue that even though the 'new rangeland paradigm' seem to have given voice to pastoralists by legitimising their practices, this is not the case. My concerns are the 'ethno-centric' and the 'eco-centric' or environmentalist[8] perspectives on which this new understanding is based, and I will elaborate on these in the following.

The ethno-centric approach can be illustrated by the definition of 'a pastoralist' used by Niamir-Fuller: 'The term "pastoralist" is defined as a mode of production where livestock make up 50 per cent or more of the economic portfolio of a small holder' (1999b: 1). Not only does it seem strange to define 'a person' as 'a mode of production', but I have not found this definition operational for my own fieldwork. Furthermore, it is doubtful that it would make sense to most pastoralists as it is based on Western concepts and epistemology. This ethno-centric perspective means that we run the risk of misinterpreting when we try to understand the pastoralists' actions, practice, motives, values, and culture without taking their epistemology as the point of departure. In my study, I used a constructionist approach for defining concepts. A 'pastoralist' was defined as someone who defines himself or herself as being a pastoralist. According to the indigenous perceptions in Ferlo, a pastoralist is somebody who owns and breeds animals.

Hence, a pastoralist cannot be measured by the amount of time spent on livestock breading, or the percentage of the income or nutrition coming from animals. Further, the pastoralists in Ferlo explain that for the ethnic group Fulani, to which they belong, cattle are the most important animals.

The eco-centric or environmentalist approach is somewhat similar. A thorough understanding of dryland functioning forms the basis of the 'new rangeland paradigm'; unfortunately, the environment remains the point of departure when the analysis concerns the pastoralists and their use of mobility. In some ways, this could be considered ethno-centric. After all, concepts such as 'environment' and 'ecosystem' are social constructions from a western (ecology) discourse. However, the emphasis on 'environment' can be seen as part of the wider discussion of 'environmentalism'. According to Milton (1996), there is a belief of 'primitive ecological wisdom' within the environmentalist discourse. This means that non-industrial people, including pastoralists, supposedly have an environmental understanding that renders them capable of living in a fine adaptation to the environment. Milton explains that this notion of 'primitive ecological wisdom' is not true:

> Some of them may live their lives in ways that are environmentally sound, but ecological balance, where it exists, is an incidental consequence of human activities and other factors, rather than being an ideal or a goal that is actively pursued.
>
> (Milton, 1996: 113)

Still, it is important to acknowledge the indigenous knowledges, which pastoralists have accumulated over generations. These knowledges are built on a conceptualisation that is unlikely to correspond with ours, e.g. how is 'nature' perceived? Can humans affect 'nature' by employing a certain practice? Hence, the key to understanding the indigenous knowledges is to deconstruct the pastoralists' worldview. When discussing (sustainable) resource management, the cultural constructions of 'nature' and 'environment' are very important.

An example is pastoralist behaviour in case of drought. In an arid, highly variable and unpredictable environment, a large number of animals cannot be sustained on a permanent basis. In case of drought, livestock can be moved out of the drought prone area either through mobility (people move with their herd) or through destocking (sale of stock), or livestock can be maintained in the area by fodder. According to the 'new rangeland paradigm', the best response is mobility. This has been the response of pastoralists. They are attributed a 'primitive ecological wisdom' because they behave in a way that is ecologically rational according to the contemporary understanding of dryland functioning. However, this behaviour may not be the preference of all pastoralists. With increased commercialisation, import of fodder becomes an attractive possibility while mobility is considered a burden – at least among the pastoralists of Ferlo, as the case study showed.

It is important to distinguish between the practices of pastoralists and the underlying motives and ideas. Previously, pastoralists have been accused of having a 'cattle complex,'[9] i.e. an irrational attachment to cattle demonstrated by their desire for acquiring large herds, which would lead to overgrazing due to common ownership of land (Hardin, 1968). Within the 'new rangeland paradigm', this desire for high stocking number is explained as opportunistic management and considered an adaptive strategy in dryland environments. The large number of livestock means that pastoralists can make the most of natural resources in good years or create high reliability systems (Roe et al., 1998). In disequilibrium environments, a high stocking density will not cause overgrazing because droughts and diseases occur frequently, thus ensuring that the system is regulated in a density independent manner (Adriansen, 1999). Even though pastoralists have developed opportunistic management, this may not imply that they acknowledge opportunistic management as optimal. The death of livestock caused by drought and diseases is a fact built into the life experience of the pastoralists. However, this does not mean that they will not try to avoid these deaths. In relation to people's experience of famine and life-threatening challenges, Davis explains that these are 'things which may be part of life but which they wish did not occur' (Davis, 1992: 150). Hence, pastoralists have developed opportunistic management to survive in drought prone areas, not to accommodate the environment. Likewise, within the 'new rangeland paradigm', mobility is seen as a highly rational adaptation to climate variability. However, my case study showed that many pastoralists were not particularly eager to be mobile as this involved a lot of work and often split-up of the family. Those who did prioritise mobility, the Tabaski pastoralists, did so because they had adapted to the commercial demand for sheep for a religious feast, they had adapted to the Muslim calendar, not to the 'needs of nature'.

The paradox is that with the 'new rangeland paradigm', pastoralists' mobility practices have been legitimised (Niamir-Fuller, 1999a), but the 'new rangeland paradigm' is based on a scientific understanding of dryland ecosystems and not on indigenous pastoral knowledges. The failure of past development projects is explained by the failure in scientific understanding of climate variability in dryland ecosystems. Further pastoralists' actions and mobility practice are explained using the scientific understanding of drylands and not the pastoralist's explanations or epistemologies relation to 'nature' and 'environment'. It can be argued that with the 'new rangeland paradigm', anthropological knowledge about pastoralists and their life worlds were included in an ecosystems approach, which has been described this way: 'In focusing on the material consequences of human activities, it marginalized people's own cultural understandings of the world, and took ecological anthropology out of the realm of social science and into the sphere of scientific ecology' (Milton, 1997: 483). This shows that multiple types of academic knowledges exist and that these knowledges not necessarily tally.

The dilemma is that using pastoral epistemologies may not lead to what is considered sustainable development in current SDG discourses. As Briggs (2005: 100) argues: 'indigenous knowledge becomes central to later debates about sustainable development because of the way in which such knowledge has apparently allowed people to live in harmony with nature for generations'. This does not mean that indigenous knowledges, accumulated over generations, are not important, but rather to underline the existence of different, and sometimes competing, epistemologies and understandings of nature, environment and sustainability. While my study of the Fulani pastoralists have highlighted some of the dilemmas in using these knowledges for sustainable development, Glasson et al. (2010) have shown how indigenous agricultural practices in Malawi can contribute to the sustainability of both environment and culture along the Shire river in Malawi.

Ziervogel and Opere (2010) have provided an interesting study of how to integrate meteorological and indigenous knowledge-based seasonal climate forecasts for pastoralists and the agricultural sector. They argue:

> *It is clear that IKFs* [indigenous knowledge-based seasonal forecasts] *and SCFs* [seasonal climate forecasts developed by national meteorological services] *both have strengths and weaknesses. A major challenge is how to bring them together in a way that respects their different values and builds on their strengths. This is set against a backdrop of a changing climate, which means that indigenous knowledge indicators might not be as reliable as they were in the past. Some projects have noted that increasing variability in climate has reduced farmers' confidence in traditional knowledge*
>
> (Ziervogel and Opere, 2010: 8)

Ziervogel and Opere also point out the difficulty of getting indigenous knowledges accepted in the scientific community and suggest that indigenous knowledges forecasts should be validated by comparing them to the scientific ones. This illustrates the dilemma when working with different epistemologies and knowledges systems – how can this be done in a meaningful manner? Whose knowledge counts (the most) in relation to sustainable development?

There is a wealth of studies of indigenous pastoral knowledges, combining or comparing with scientific knowledges (e.g. Abate, 2016; Balehegn et al., 2019; Bollig and Schulte, 1999; Eriksen, 2007; Nyong et al., 2007; Oba, 2012). The majority of these studies focus on indigenous knowledges and practices, not on the pastoralists' epistemologies and cosmologies (an exception being Goldman et al., 2018). As my fieldwork showed, the Senegalese pastoralist cosmology tied rain and grazing quality to God and 'being good', this raises some dilemmas in relation to promotion of sustainable development. How can we combat climate change (SDG 13) and desertification and degradation (SDG 15) based on the Fulani epistemology where these concepts do not exist? Which sense do these SDGs make in a cosmology where God is in charge of the weather even if the indigenous knowledges can be used to predict the weather? Moreover, as Balehegn et al. point out, 'apart from showing similarity and correlation between the two knowledge systems and giving the inevitable recommendations of integrating indigenous and modern systems, many researchers failed to show a practical approach for the synergetic use of the two knowledge systems' (2019: 1). Hence, the use of indigenous knowledges for reaching the SDGs is not without its dilemmas and paradoxes. However, as other chapters in this book show, it is important to try.

Concluding remarks

Using pastoralists and their use of mobility as an example, I have attempted to explore the dilemmas and paradoxes involved when trying to understand and use indigenous knowledges and use them together with scientific knowledges for sustainable development as it relates to promoting sustainable agriculture (SDG 2), combatting climate change (SDG 13) and desertification and land degradation (SDG 15). Paradigm shifts in academic understanding of dryland ecosystems and pastoralists' land use illustrate that academic or scientific knowledges are neither singular nor static. Changes in these knowledges and their hierarchies have had implications for pastoralists and how we interpret their knowledges and land use in a context of sustainable development. Until the 1990s and the 'new rangeland paradigm', the international donor community often accused pastoralists of causing land degradation. While this has changed and pastoral mobility today is recognised as a flexible strategy that balances the variability in natural resources, the pastoralists' own perceptions of mobility still need to be understood. While authors such as Niamir-Fuller and Turner (1999) have shown that mobility is necessary for arid lands and hence that pastoral mobility is a rational management strategy, this does not explain how pastoralists themselves perceive mobility, nature, and the environment. The case study from Ferlo showed that the Fulani pastoralists there had quite different epistemologies. Consequently, the question remains how we can use indigenous knowledges for sustainable development without reducing indigenous knowledges to something to be validated against scientific knowledge or integrated into academic knowledge systems, as it is commonly seen with indigenous pastoral knowledges. In his *Reflections on the cultural spaces of climate*, Livingstone (2012: 93) has the following recommendations which seems valuable in relation to indigenous knowledges and academic understandings of pastoral mobility: 'Problematize knowledge claims. Particularise experience. Pluralise meaning'.

Notes

1 I am a Danish woman, trained as a human geographer. I write from a position in Western Academia; hence, when I write 'we', it usually refers to Western Academia and to some extent also the international donor community.

However, it is important to bear in mind (as I also show in this chapter) the importance of thinking about scientific knowledges in plural; within the Western Academy,
there are multiple, competing epistemologies and different knowledge systems.

2 The first thoughts for this paper were presented in a working paper entitled *The
Use and Perception of Mobility among Senegalese Fulani* (Adriansen, 2003).

3 The 'new rangeland paradigm' first emerged in the late 1980s. It has been discussed in a number of papers; some concern dryland ecosystem functioning
only, but most include aspects of pastoral management (e.g. Ellis & Swift, 1988,
Warren, 1995, Westoby et al., 1989).

4 This outline of the ethnographic study of Fulani pastoralists in the Ferlo region
of Senegal is based on Adriansen (2002).

5 A total of 62 Fulani heads (*jomoro*) of households (*galle*) were interviewed using
a structured questionnaire with a combination of qualitative and quantitative,
open-ended questions.

6 Tabaski is the word commonly used in Senegal for the Muslim feast called *id-al-
adha* in Arabic. It takes place the tenth day of the Muslim pilgrimage month and
is a sacrificial feast in remembrance of Ibrahim, who was told by God to sacrifice
his son. This day, Muslims bring an offering, usually a sheep. This means that
the demand for rams all over Muslim Africa and the Middle East is high at this
time of the year.

7 The Carlsberg Foundation's nomad research project, for instance, has published
12 such books (e.g. Nicolaisen and Nicolaisen, 1997).

8 My notion of environmentalism is derived from Milton (1996).

9 Herskovits (1926) originally described the 'cattle complex'. This denotes the 'cultural area' of East Africa where the importance of cattle shapes the everyday life
of people. However, the concept has been abused and has come to represent an
'irrational attachment' to cattle (e.g. Barfield, 1993).

References

Abate, T. (2016). Indigenous ecological knowledge and pastoralist perception on
rangeland management and degradation in Guji Zone of south Ethiopia. *Consil-
ience: The Journal of Sustainable Development*, *15*(1), 192–218.

Adriansen, H. K. (2012). Timeline interviews: A tool for conducting life history research. *Qualitative Studies*, *3*(1), 40–55.

Adriansen, H. K. (2008). Understanding pastoral mobility: The case of Senegalese
Fulani. *Geographical Journal*, *174*(3), 207–222.

Adriansen, H. K. (2006). Continuity and change in pastoral livelihoods of Senegalese Fulani. *Agriculture and Human Values*, *23*(2), 215–229.

Adriansen, H. K. (2003). The use and perception of mobility among Senegalese
Fulani: New approaches to pastoral mobility. *IIS Working Paper* 03.1 Copen-
hagen. Retrieved 08/08/2019 from https://pure.au.dk/portal/files/100397361/WP_
The_use_and_perception_of_mobility.pdf

Adriansen, H. K. (2002) *A Fulani without cattle is like a woman without jewellery.*
Geographica Hafniensia A11, Copenhagen. Retrieved 08/08/2019 from https://
pure.au.dk/portal/files/54213180/A_fulani_without_cattle_is_like_a_woman_
without_jewellery.pdf

Adriansen, H. K. (1999) Pastoral mobility as a response to climate variability in
African drylands. *Danish Journal of Geography*, *99*(1), 1–10.

Agrawal, A. (1995a). Dismantling the divide between indigenous and scientific
knowledge. *Development and Change*, *26*(3), 413–439.

Agrawal, A. (1995b). Indigenous and scientific knowledge: Some critical comments. *Indigenous Knowledge and Development Monitor* [electronic journal], 3 (3–4). Retrieved 08/08/2019 from https://pdfs.semanticscholar.org/29ad/4c49e7c18e100b48302bd2c2367355daab4a.pdf

Ba, C. (1986). *Les Peuls du Senegal.* Etude geographique. Les Nouvelles Editions Africaines, Dakar.

Balehegn, M., Balehey, S., Fu, C., & Liang, W. (2019). Indigenous weather and climate forecasting knowledge among Afar pastoralists of north eastern Ethiopia: Role in adaptation to weather and climate variability. *Pastoralism, 9*(1), 8–23.

Barfield, T. (1993). *The Nomadic alternative.* Prentice Hall, New Jersey.

Berkes, F., Colding, J., & Folke, C. (2000). Rediscovery of traditional ecological knowledge as adaptive management. *Ecological Applications, 10*(5), 1251–1262.

Bollig, M., & Schulte, A. (1999). Environmental change and pastoral perceptions: Degradation and indigenous knowledge in two African pastoral communities. *Human Ecology, 27*(3), 493–514.

Briggs, J. (2005). The use of indigenous knowledge in development: Problems and challenges. *Progress in Development Studies, 5*(2), 99–114.

Briggs, J., & Sharp, J. (2004). Indigenous knowledges and development: A postcolonial caution. *Third World Quarterly, 25*(4), 661–676.

Brown, L. H. (1971). The biology of pastoral man as a factor in conservation. *Biological Conservation, 3*, 93–100.

Chalmers, J. (2017). The transformation of academic knowledges: Understanding the relationship between decolonising and indigenous research methodologies. *Socialist Studies/Études Socialistes, 12*(1), 97–116.

Davis, J. (1992). The anthropology of suffering. *Journal of Refugee Studies, 5*, 149–161.

Dyer, C. (2018). Education inclusion as a border regime: Implications for mobile pastoralists in Ethiopia's Afar region. *International Studies in Sociology of Education, 27*(2–3), 145–165.

Dyson-Hudson, R., & Dyson-Hudson, N. (1980). Nomadic pastoralism. *Annual Review of Anthropology, 9*, 15–61.

Ellis, J. E., & Swift, D. M. (1988). Stability of African pastoral ecosystems: Alternate paradigms and implications for development. *Journal of Range Management, 41*, 450–459.

Eriksen, C. (2007). Why do they burn the 'bush'? Fire, rural livelihoods, and conservation in Zambia. *Geographical Journal, 173*(3), 242–256.

Glasson, G. E., Mhango, N., Phiri, A., & Lanier, M. (2010). Sustainability science education in Africa: Negotiating indigenous ways of living with nature in the third space. *International Journal of Science Education, 32*(1), 125–141.

Goldman, M. J., Turner, M. D., & Daly, M. (2018). A critical political ecology of human dimensions of climate change: Epistemology, ontology, and ethics. *WIRE's Climate Change, 9*(4), 1–15.

Hardin, G. (1968). The tragedy of the commons. *Science, 162*, 1243–1248.

Herskovits, M. J. (1926). The cattle complex in East Africa. *American Anthropologist, 28*, 230–272, 361–388, 494–528, 633–644.

Livingstone, D.N. (2012). Reflections on the cultural spaces of climate. *Climatic Change, 113*(1), 91–93

Milton, K. (1997). Ecologies: Anthropology, culture and the environment. *International Social Science Journal, 49*, 477–495.

Milton, K. (1996). *Environmentalism and cultural theory: Exploring the role of anthropology in environmental discourses*. Routledge, St. Ives.

Msila, V. (2009). Africanisation of education and the search for relevance and context. *Educational Research and Review*, 4(6), 310–315.

Müller, J. O. (1993). Nomadenkultur und ökonomische Rationalität: zum Problem ökonomischer and bio-technologischer Modernisierung unter Peul-Nomaden im Senegal. *Afrika Spectrum*, 28(3), 341–357.

Ng'asike, J. T. (2019). Indigenous knowledge practices for sustainable lifelong education in pastoralist communities of Kenya. *International Review of Education*, 65(1), 19–46.

Niamir-Fuller, M. (ed.) (1999a). *Managing mobility in African rangelands: The legitimization of transhumance*. IT Publications, Exeter.

Niamir-Fuller, M. (1999b). Introduction. In Niamir-Fuller, M. (ed.) *Managing mobility in African rangelands: The legitimization of transhumance*, pp. 1–17. IT Publications, Exeter.

Niamir-Fuller, M., & Turner, M. D. (1999). A review of recent literature on pastoralism and transhumance in Africa. In Niamir-Fuller, M. (ed.) *Managing mobility in African rangelands: The legitimization of transhumance*, pp. 18–46. IT Publications, Exeter.

Nicolaisen, J., & Nicolaisen, I. (1997). *The pastoral Tuareg: Ecology, culture and society*. Thames and Hudson Limited, London.

Nyong, A., Adesina, F., & Elasha, B. O. (2007). The value of indigenous knowledge in climate change mitigation and adaptation strategies in the African Sahel. *Mitigation and Adaptation Strategies for Global Change*, 12(5), 787–797.

Oba, G. (2012). Harnessing pastoralists' indigenous knowledge for rangeland management: Three African case studies. *Pastoralism: Research, Policy and Practice*, 2(1), 1–25.

Oba, G., & Kotile, D. G. (2001). Assessments of landscape level degradation in southern Ethiopia: Pastoralists versus ecologists. *Land Degradation & Development*, 12(5), 461–475.

Picardi, A. C. (1974). *A framework for evaluating long-term strategies for the development of the Sahel-Sudan region, Annex 5: A systems analysis of pastoralism in the West African Sahel*. Centre for Policy Alternatives, Massachusetts Institute of Technology, Cambridge.

Rasmussen, K., Brandt, M., Tong, X., Hiernaux, P., Diouf, A. A., Assouma, M. H., Tucker, C. J. & Fensholt, R. (2018). Does grazing cause land degradation? Evidence from the sandy Ferlo in Northern Senegal. *Land Degradation & Development*, 29(12), 4337–4347.

Roe, E., Huntsinger, L., & Labnow, K. (1998). High reliability pastoralism. *Journal of Arid Environments*, 39, 39–55.

Sayre, N. F., McAllister, R. R., Bestelmeyer, B. T., Moritz, M., & Turner, M. D. (2013). Earth stewardship of rangelands: Coping with ecological, economic, and political marginality. *Frontiers in Ecology and the Environment*, 11(7), 348–354.

Scoones, I. (1995). New directions in pastoral development in Africa. In Scoones, I. (ed.) *Living with uncertainty: New directions in pastoral development in Africa*, pp. 1–36. Intermediate Technology Publications, Exeter.

Smith, L. T. (2012). *Decolonizing methodologies: Research and Indigenous Peoples*. Zed Books, Croydon.

Stenning, D. J. (1957). Transhumance, migratory drift, migration patterns of pastoral Fulani nomadism. *Journal of the Royal Anthropological Institute of Great Britain and Ireland, 87*(1), 57–73.

Sutter, J. W. (1987). Cattle and inequality: Herd size differences and pastoral production among the Fulani of north-eastern Senegal. *Africa, 57*, 196–218.

Thomas, D. S. G., & Twyman, C. (2004). Good or bad rangeland? Hybrid knowledge, science, and local understandings of vegetation dynamics in the Kalahari. *Land Degradation & Development, 15*(3), 215–231.

Tonah, S. (2019). Knowledge sovereignty among African cattle herders, Zeremariam Fre. *African Review of Economics and Finance, 11*(1), 257–260.

Touré, O. (1988). The pastoral environment of northern Senegal. *Review of African Political Economy, 42*, 32–39.

Turner, M. D., & Schlecht, E. (2019). Livestock mobility in sub-Saharan Africa: A critical review. *Pastoralism, 9*(1), 1–15.

Warren, A. (1995). Changing understandings of African pastoralism and the nature of environmental paradigms. *Transactions of the Institute of British Geographers, NS, 20*, 193–203.

Weicker, M. (1993). *Nomades et sedentaires au Sénégal.* Enda- Editions, Dakar.

Westoby, M., Walker, B., & Noy-Meir, I. (1989). Opportunistic management for rangelands not at equilibrium. *Journal of Range Management, 42*, 266–274.

Ziervogel, G., & Opere, A. (eds.). (2010). *Integrating meteorological and indigenous knowledge-based seasonal climate forecasts in the agricultural sector.* International Development Research Centre, Ottawa, Canada. Climate Change Adaptation in Africa learning paper series.

Zinsstag, J., Bonfoh, B., Zinsstag, G., Crump, L., Alfaroukh, I. O., Abakar, M. F., Kasymbekov, J., Baljinnyam, Z., Liechti, K., Seid, M.A. & Schelling, E. (2016). A vision for the future of pastoralism. *Revue scientifique et technique (International Office of Epizootics), 35*(2), 693–699.

10 Struggling with 'clear zoning'

Dilemmas of carnivore-pastoral coexistence in Nordland, northern Norway

Camilla Risvoll and Randi Kaarhus

Introduction

Managing wildlife–people coexistence is often deemed extremely challenging since the parties involved commonly hold different identities, worldviews and knowledges (Redpath et al., 2013; Sjölander-Lindqvist et al., 2015). When we focus on carnivore–pastoralist coexistence, we also see that different knowledges work with different assumptions and rules on evidence concerning large carnivores' behaviour and movement patterns. Norway has changed its governance of large carnivores (wolverines, lynx, brown bear, wolf, golden eagle) considerably over the past decades, whereby international conventions on biodiversity protection have gained increasing influence (Hansson-Forman et al., 2018; Risvoll et al., 2016). While Norway is committed to these conventions, the country has also established explicit policy goals to protect the rights and livelihoods of local and indigenous people, such as sheep farmers and Sámi reindeer herders in rural areas (Krange et al., 2016; Risvoll, 2015). This double objective is stated in the 2011 Carnivore Agreement (*Rovdyrforliket*). Based on a political compromise in the Norwegian parliament, it constitutes the main policy arrangement for ensuring sustainable carnivore populations concurrently with viable pastoral livelihoods in Norway (Fangel & Gundersen, 2012; Strand et al., 2016).

'Clear zoning' has been a basic management instrument in implementing the Carnivore Agreement. Zoning provides a form of land-use differentiation and has been widely used in conservation measures such as the creation of national parks and other protected areas (Linnell et al., 2005).[1] The objective of zoning in carnivore management is to reduce the spatial overlap between large carnivores and domestic livestock such as reindeer and sheep. Large carnivores, such as bear, lynx or wolverine, are given preference in certain defined areas, and grazing animals are prioritized in other areas. While there is no differentiation between different types of domestic livestock in terms of zoning, the different carnivores have their own specific prioritized zone in each region, and carnivore zones may overlap. With *zoning* as a basic instrument, local authorities are expected to deliver on nationally defined population goals for carnivores.

The 2011 Carnivore Agreement further involved a decision on evaluating both the regional carnivore management and the regional carnivore population goals within five years. Here, we present a study of how the revision of the regional management plan for carnivores developed in the Nordland Region, northern Norway, during the period 2015–2018, focusing on the controversies associated with the centrally defined principle of 'clear zoning' as a management instrument. The context of our study is the larger social-ecological structure of the local husbandry systems of reindeer, and we examine how different knowledge systems meet and interact in the co-management around carnivore governance during this revision process.

The national government has expected the revised plan to harmonize conflicting interests, expressed in the 'double objective' of safeguarding sustainable carnivore populations, while at the same time maintaining local pastoralist livelihoods. In our analysis, we show how the double objective at the national level translates into real dilemmas at local levels, and how these are being played out in the revision process in Nordland. The management plan is expected to present an authoritative discourse drawing upon science-based biological knowledge and translate the centrally defined policy objectives into specific management measures at the regional and local levels. We show how locally situated knowledge – in our account represented primarily through Sámi reindeer herders' statements – experiences real barriers to being counted as evidence in the management of large carnivores, and thus to be included in a management plan authorized at the national level.

'Traditional knowledge' is acknowledged in several national and international Conventions (e.g. the Norwegian Nature Diversity Act, the Convention on Biological Diversity) as important for conserving biodiversity and achieving sustainability. Various scholars point to the need for understanding indigenous and local knowledge systems as dynamic and relational, within holistic contexts involving networks, values and practices (e.g. Huntington et al., 2011; Nadasdy, 1999; Scott, 1998; Veland et al., 2014). Current debates on the role of indigenous knowledge in natural resource management, in a Norwegian context furthermore takes place on a backdrop of Sámi people over the centuries being subject to different forms of discrimination, and from the late 19th century onwards to forced assimilation policies. In the late 1970s, however, their situation became an issue of social mobilization at the national level,[2] and in 1989, a Sámi Parliament was established in Norway. In 1990, the Sámi were recognised as an indigenous people according to ILO Convention 169.[3] Today, Sámi pastoralists have an established role through Sámi Parliament representatives in Regional decision-making on carnivore management in Nordland.

In the process analysed here, the Sámi Parliament representatives were, together with the political-party representative voicing pastoral interests (sheep farming and reindeer husbandry), able to constitute a majority in the Regional Carnivore Committee (Nordland RCC). The resulting revision of the Carnivore Plan was in early 2017 submitted to the central authorities, but later the same year returned to the regional level with instructions to make an improved plan complying with the basic principle of 'clear zoning'. A second revision resulted in few changes, and Nordland RCC resubmitted their revised management plan to the central authorities in spring 2018. The Ministry then decided to overrun the plan, withholding it at the central level to make the necessary amendments.

In northern Norway, reindeer husbandry practiced by Sámi people and sheep farming practiced by people with an ethnic identity commonly as Norwegians but also Sámi have traditionally been important in rural districts. Since the 1970s, the Norwegian government has been explicitly committed to protect rural livelihoods and maintain human settlements in marginal rural areas (Vatn, 1984). In 1986, when Norway ratified the Bern Convention on the Conservation of European Wildlife and Natural Habitats, the Norwegian governments also took on a clear commitment towards protecting biodiversity. As a party to the Bern Convention, the country accepts to employ the necessary conservation tools for wild species in need of 'special protection' (Díaz, 2010). This implies safeguarding sustainable carnivore populations on Norwegian territory – of bear, wolf, lynx and wolverine (Norwegian Environment Agency, 2014). In Europe, the implementation of national conservation policies supporting the natural expansion of these large carnivores has contributed to a notable success of wildlife conservation (Chapron et al., 2014; Linnell, 2015). At the same time, this development has led to real dilemmas at the local level, and over the last years, conflicts related to large carnivores in the Nordic countries have increased dramatically (Dressel et al., 2015). A substantial part of the conflict potential manifests itself in carnivore-pastoral conflicts (Risvoll, 2015; Rønningen & Flemsæter, 2016). On the one hand, these conflicts display general traits pertaining to the changing relationship between humans, animals, environment, and the modern state across regions and localities (Nustad, 2011). On the other hand, the dilemmas and conflicts of carnivore–pastoral coexistence are characterized by their site- and habitat-specific dimensions and their locally situated complexity (cf. Benjaminsen et al., 2015).

Methodology and analytic framework

What we present here is a case study of the process of revising the Carnivore Management Plan (CMP) for the Nordland Region in northern Norway, during the period 2015–2018. It is a case of decision-making on a highly controversial issue: carnivore–pastoral coexistence in herding districts, involving struggles to articulate indigenous knowledge and local experience-based evidence in ways that central government authorities can accept. As a case, it is set in a specific time and place (Ragin, 1992: 2) but also in a specific institutional context, at the intersection of regional governance and national carnivore management in Norway. The regional setting is basically

constituted by the geographical area of Nordland County (Figure 10.1);
while our data representing local husbandry practices and local knowledge
mainly rely on material collected in the sub-region of Salten, which constitute the northern part of Nordland (see Figure 10.1). In our inquiry we do,
however, draw upon a broad range of sources, including observations in
meetings, public documents, reports and interviews, in addition to local and
national newspaper clippings and internet sites. As observers, we were able
to attend nine RCC meetings during 2016–2018. Interviews with relevant
actors and agencies at the local, regional and national levels were conducted
during autumn 2016, winter 2017 and winter 2018. Interviewees included
representatives from the RCC, the Norwegian Nature Inspectorate (NNI),
the County Governor, one municipality, farming and herding associations

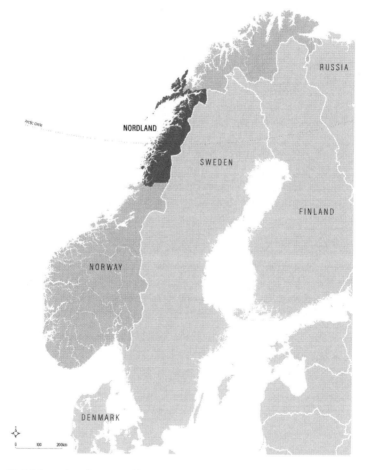

Figure 10.1 Map showing Nordland County in Norway and the Salten region
zoomed in.

Source: Håvard Lundberg/ Analyse&Tal.

and one environmental organization. We were also observers at relevant meetings and seminars with pastoralists, pastoralists' organizations and local government's representatives.

The case was identified through what is often called 'purposeful selection' (Maxwell, 2013: 97). Already at an early stage in the process, we believed the revision of the regional CMP in Nordland could give important insights into decentralized decision-making on a controversial issue, and the role of indigenous knowledge in this type of case. We have taken a process-oriented approach to the case, describing the 'sequence of steps involved in the process under study' (Becker, 1992: 207). However, it was only through following the process itself that our inquiry led to a clear vision of what our case is a 'case of' (Becker, 1992). In this process-oriented approach to studying the carnivore-management plan revision in Nordland, we have further been inspired by elements in Bartlett & Vavrus' (2017) approach to case studies.

We have chosen to analyse our case as a *discursive field* (cf. Kaarhus, 1999: 63). In this discursive field, we find partly diverging understandings of the nature of the problem to be addressed, with local actors struggling to articulate relevant knowledge in ways that comply with governance principles and objectives defined at the state level. These principles and objectives structure the – contested – 'order of discourse' in this field (Foucault, 1971). We see the discursive field of CMP revision in Nordland as located in a context of pastoralist practices, together with the changing agricultural policies shaping these practices, a context involving environmentalist concerns focusing on species conservation and existing legal regulations on carnivore–pastoral coexistence in Norway, but also expanding carnivore populations, especially in Norwegian-Swedish border regions. Discourse analysis provides an intake to examining relations between knowledge and politics in the revision of the Management Plan. Drawing on Foucault's conception of *discourse* as a practice we impose on things (Foucault, 1971: 22), we are concerned with the production of the revised plan as an *authoritative discourse* (Dreyfus & Rabinow, 1983: 48). In the established Norwegian governance structure, it will in principle also be *materialized* in (new) ways of organizing space (Fairclough, 2013: 180). We further relate the authorized discourse of the official CMP revision to elements of unofficial – and in this context mostly subdued – discourses; in particular that of local pastoralists seeking to articulate their knowledge and experience with carnivores in order to influence the authoritative management discourse.

In this approach to analysing discourse, we draw upon the 'early' Foucault (1971, 1972), as interpreted by Dreyfus and Rabinow (1983) and Kaarhus (1999), and the 'argumentative turn' in policy studies (cf. Fischer & Forester, 1993), incorporated into the later versions of Fairclough's (2003, 2013) 'critical discourse analysis'. As an analytic approach, it enables us to examine the relations between the 'discursive field' of the planning process and the material–biological elements of the social life and natural habitats of the indigenous population/Sámi reindeer herders, showing how certain 'rules of formation' (Dreyfus & Rabinow 1983: 66) order the discourse to be taken seriously, and established as authoritative in this field.

Any discourse will be based on *assumptions* in the form of unquestioned 'facts' or notions taken for granted. At certain moments, however, such assumptions become subject to questioning, thus constituting spaces for contestation, argument and competing discourses (Bourdieu, 1977: 168). In our analysis of the CMP revision, we show how 'zoning' as a dominant management instrument is challenged and become contested during the process of revising the management plan, while different versions of 'nature' and carnivore–pastoral coexistence are articulated seeking to shape the outcome of the revision. We further demonstrate how reference to science-based *evidence* becomes a crucial resource in representing reality and in justifying priorities and instruments. Thus, we see how evidence produced through specific standardized procedures constitutes 'current best evidence' on carnivores and is what counts as valid knowledge in the conflictive discursive field of carnivore management planning.

Background and contexts

Pastoralism and agricultural policies

Most of the pastures for reindeer and free-ranging sheep in Norway consist of harsh mountain ranges, which in northern Norway also stretch down to sea level. The pastures are mostly common lands, often called *utmark* (outfields). Access to the outfields has differed in different parts of Norway over time (see e.g. Berg, 2000). The conditions for Sámi pastoralist practices have historically been connected to the development of nation states in the northern regions, and various conventions and regulations have regulated herding for the past 250 years. Reindeer husbandry in Norway is not connected to land ownership; however, access to pastures has been institutionalized since 1751, when the Lapp Codicil was enacted to regulate cross-border migration between Norway and Sweden, while Norwegian Sámi reindeer herding further builds on the doctrine of 'immemorial usage' (Allard, 2015). Since the 18th century, reindeer herders have maintained official user rights to the herding districts. These rights are regulated through a license system referred to as '*siida* shares' (*siida-andeler*). A reindeer owner in northern Norway must be Sámi, and husbandry practices are regulated through the Reindeer Husbandry Act (LOV-2014-03-28–9). Nordland County includes 42 siida shares dispersed across 12 reindeer herding districts with approximately 18,200 domesticated reindeer (Nordland County web site 21.12.2018).

Since the late 1940s, at the national level there have been periodic revisions of agricultural policies. These have been performed within the framework of a dominant 'production discourse', shaped by a continuous modernization and rationalization trend. Effective policy implementation has resulted in increased mechanization, which also made more extensive grazing possible (Jaren & Løvstad, 2001). Since the 1970s, these policy trends primarily informed by Western science-based perspectives on meat production, have also affected reindeer pastoralism, resulting in an increasing market-orientation (Johnsen et al., 2017). The goal has been maximizing meat production through optimal herd structure and a more 'rational' and 'efficient' production, as established in the Reindeer Husbandry Act (1978) and the Reindeer Herding Agreement (1976) (cf. Benjaminsen et al., 2015; Johnsen et al., 2017).

The rationalization and mechanization of herding practices and the associated 'production discourse' is closely linked to the ideal of '[m]odern, industrial, scientific farming characterized by monocropping, mechanization, hybrids, the use of fertilizers and pesticides, and capital intensiveness' described by James Scott (1998: 266). However, the local resource base and often harsh and marginal conditions characterizing the pastoralist practices of reindeer herding and sheep farming in northern Norway are often at odds with 'high-modernist agriculture' (Scott, 1998: 262). Still, the push towards simplification and standardization of herding landscapes and practices have been strong and persistent, and continues today.

We can also identify a more long-term 'rationalization' in the relationship between humans, animals and the state. According to Sandberg (1999), persistent policies from the early 1700s stated the need for 'the eradication of all useless and harmful' wildlife in order to increase and optimize domestic livestock production. As a consequence, there have been long periods with very few wild carnivores in Norway. The large carnivores that historically inhabited mountain regions and forests were almost eradicated by the end of the 19th and beginning of the 20th century. This has been the ecological context in which both reindeer herders and sheep farmers have sought to optimize their production.

Environmentalism and conservation

In a historical perspective, a first wave of modern environmentalism peaked in the early 1970s – including the first United Nations Conference on the Human Environment in Stockholm in 1972. This was the context of the making of the Bern Convention on species and habitat conservation in Europe, which entered into force in 1982. A second wave of environmentalism gained force in the 1980s, with the publication of the World Commission on Environment and Development's (WCED) report *Our Common Future* in 1987 (WCED, 1987). Promoting the concept of 'sustainable development', the WCED report presented the discursive basis for the Rio Conference on Environment and Development in 1992, where also the Convention on Biological Diversity was first opened for signature. This Convention covers the protection and sustainable use of ecosystems and genetic resources globally, in addition to individual-species protection. Norway ratified the Biodiversity Convention in 1993.

In the 1990s, the concept 'rewilding' appeared, connected to conservation biology more generally. Rewilding is associated with a concept of 'wilderness' as a natural environment not significantly modified by human activity. It may be used as a descriptive term with reference to the 'de-agrarianisation' of rural areas (e.g. Krauss & Olwig, 2018) but also refers to the objective of reducing biodiversity loss. Among the organized initiatives under the heading 'rewilding', there is often a focus on large carnivores, and on securing suitable habitats for them in the 'wilderness'.[4] The focus on large predators is associated with the conception of these animals as having a particularly important function in maintaining the 'ecological balance' of natural habitats. The theoretical underpinnings of this view are, however, also questioned with regard to the ecology of Artic landscapes (Benjaminsen et al., 2015). In the Norwegian context, the concept of rewilding is so far not part of public debate, but elements of rewilding narratives and conceptions no doubt influence national efforts to protect large carnivores, while in official discourse, these efforts will be justified with reference to international obligations to comply with biodiversity commitments, and the Bern Convention in particular.

In order to reduce the carnivore–pastoral conflict level, the Norwegian government has delegated management authority to representative RCCs. These are formally appointed by the Ministry of Climate and Environment. In total, eight regional committees have been established; one of these, Region 7, covers Nordland County. The Nordland RCC consists of four political-party representatives and two members appointed by the Sámi Parliament.[5] An important task for the RCC is to develop and adopt a management plan for large carnivores in Region 7. The plan has to comply with overall 'population goals', which are set at the national level with reference to the Bern Convention and defined in terms of reproductive family groups (Parliament's Document Nr. 8:163 S (2010–2011)); in Norwegian *ynglinger*. The population goals for large carnivores in Nordland are: one reproducing bear family group, ten reproducing lynx family groups and ten reproducing wolverine family groups.[6] While *clear zoning* is the management instrument, a spatial separation of carnivores and grazing animals is conceived as an end, since it is 'the only thing that works' to achieve the population goals for large carnivores.[7]

Legal regulations of predator–pastoral coexistence

The Carnivore Agreement of 2011 was supported by all political parties in the Norwegian Parliament (*Stortinget*). It emphasizes biological and ecological knowledge as a major basis for carnivore governance towards achieving desired population goals, while it also aims to diminish the conflict level around carnivores. The Agreement clarifies regulations around population goals and hunting licenses for the different carnivore species. It states that local actors, particularly from the pastoral sectors, should be involved in population registration and represented in local hunting teams, and it further emphasizes the importance of knowledge transfer *to* local people about carnivores' habitats and behaviour (Parliament's Document Nr. 8:163 S (2010–2011)). The Agreement provides the legal basis and the mandate for the work of the RCCs but has no specific provisions for how to integrate local knowledge in decision-making.

Background for the revision of the CMP

When the RCC in Nordland in 2011 ratified their first management plan under the Carnivore Agreement, it created zones that allowed farmers and herders to continue with grazing their animals in the areas they had traditionally used. This zoning plan was criticized by the government for being too fragmented, by allocating areas too small and narrow for carnivores to thrive (Risvoll et al., 2016).

At the national level, increasing losses of livestock to carnivores and increased levels of conflict due to dissatisfaction with carnivore governance in 2015 led the ministries of Climate and Environment and of Agriculture and Food to request the RCCs to revise their management plans. The Ministers pointed to the need for *clearer zoning*, stating that the management should be more 'robust' and opened up for an evaluation of the 'fragmented zoning' in Nordland.

The national monitoring program for large carnivores estimates carnivore population numbers by *counting reproductive family groups* of each species. This is done through DNA samples and through observations that align with a strict set of rules. Reindeer herders, however, are much more concerned with the *interaction between reindeer and carnivores in the landscape*, and hold that varying numbers of roaming individual carnivores affect their herds. Several herders and sheep farmers challenge the whole concept of 'clear zoning', since they see it as likely that carnivores follow their food, and will eventually move into grazing land where livestock are present. At an RCC meeting in Nordland, the Norwegian Environment Agency (NEA) informed that they have not yet documented carnivores such as wolverines following grazing animals to new areas. This evidence is based on the NEA tracing tracks on snow and collecting faeces samples – seeking to identify reproductive family groups. A prerequisite for this tracing method is continuous snow cover. Hence, tracing the carnivores on bare ground during summer months is not done. The science-based documentation of losses of reindeer to carnivores has similar limitations. Reindeer carcasses are hard to find, as, for example, wolverines usually hide their prey. Often, there are few mortal remains of the dead reindeer, and hence it is difficult to document what caused its death. Hence, there is very limited documentation of losses through established science-based methods. Moreover, during summer months when snow cover is absent, or during winter and spring when the snow is hard with an ice crust, it is difficult for herders to produce documentation of losses to predators that receives official approval. Hence there is limited approved documentation on the predators' movements.

While sheep farmers and Sámi reindeer herders in Nordland are subject to different sets of rules and regulations from the national government, as pastoralists in the region, they feel that they depend on each other for carrying 'the burden' of carnivore pressure. Several reindeer herders point out that with no sheep in an area, the burden of losses to carnivores will be greater for their flocks. Hence, the patterns of interaction between the presence of pastoralism (e.g. prey for carnivores) and the presence of carnivores should be seen within a larger picture, which also takes local topographical features into account. At a carnivore seminar organized in Nordland in 2016, a scientist from the Scandinavian Bear project pointed out that the region (the land area between the sea and the Swedish border) is too narrow to differentiate between bear zones, grazing animals and buffer zones. Everything outside the bear zone becomes a buffer zone for bears (Moen & Støen, 2016). Thus, these interactions, as well as the character of the landscape challenge the effectiveness of 'clear zoning' as a carnivore management instrument.

Sámi reindeer herders have a legal status as indigenous people, with a culture that is upheld through reindeer husbandry, and are protected by international regulations, such as the ILO Convention. The culture and identity of being a herder, and the close connection they feel to the mountains and landscape that they have relied on for years and maybe generations, are all important aspects for understanding the complexity in pastoralists' response to new regulations, which enter into conflict with their attachment to place and the occupation that they value. As we shall see below, in the revision of the CMP for Nordland, the special role of Sámi reindeer herding, though institutionalized in their RCC representation, did not imply that their broad experience-based knowledge on the issue would be taken into account at the central levels of government.

Revision of the CMP – First Act

In 2015, the Nordland RCC and the County Governor in Nordland established a working committee (*Arbeidsutvalg - WC*) to provide advice for the upcoming revision process. The RCC made a mandate for the committee, while the County Governor's office served as secretariat, initially attempting to keep the discussions within this mandate. This led to much frustration amongst the members of the committee, and the secretariat opened up for discussion of issues beyond the framing of the original mandate. The WC itself included representatives from different relevant user groups and interest organizations and started out with a considerable discrepancy in views and commitments. For herders and farmers to agree on tough compromises that disfavoured their livelihoods was extremely challenging. Zoning will necessarily differentiate but also favour certain local areas (the no-carnivore zones, from a livestock perspective). This made it extremely hard for the members in the WC to select certain areas as carnivore zones (e.g. bear zone), and thus 'sacrifice' some areas for the benefit of others.

The WC managed to collaborate in terms of discussion and dialogue, but achieving a concerted advice proved very difficult. It ended up with the different parties having irreconcilable views. The participation from the regional environmental organizations was furthermore marginal. They were invited from the start but few participated. Risvoll et al. (2016) show how the environmental organizations rather pursue their interests in carnivore issues at the national level. In Nordland, the end result was a WC document representing the views of pastoralist associations, and including some text from the local Hunting and Fishing association. The WC did not manage to establish a joint discourse representing the diverse interest groups. To provide a broader basis for the revision of the Management Plan, the County Governor then took the initiative to meet the different interest organizations in their own arenas, and these meetings were generally perceived as constructive in terms of discussing potential solutions.

In late autumn 2016, the County governor presented a suggestion for a revised plan at an RCC meeting. At the same meeting, the WC presented their own separate document. The two suggestions for a revised CMP were clearly diverging. After this meeting followed a regular round of public consultation, and a stunning number – almost 90 'hearing' inputs – were received from various interest groups, including land owners, hunting associations, pastoral industries, and various regional and national interest organizations and municipalities (Saltenposten, 2016).

Elements of unofficial discourses on Sámi 'landscapes in use'

When voicing their concerns, reindeer herders refer to the challenges facing animal husbandry in general; the increased encroachments on pastures, less profit due to high costs and low production in the sector, increased losses from carnivores, increased frequency of icing-thawing events in winter, and how these problems may threaten values, such as cultural landscapes, knowledge, identity and food security. These assets are at the core of the tensions at play in the carnivore–pasture conflict, as pastoralists see their concerns and values not being properly balanced against the protection of carnivores. There is hence a local resistance against external interventions and regulations that promote conservation measures, since these are seen as placing further restrictions on the pastoralists' livelihoods and land use.

The reindeer herders interviewed in Nordland County strongly feel that the knowledge base of carnivore management in Norway is not reflecting the reality they experience on the ground, or considering their ways of viewing and valuing the landscape. All the nuances and complexity that exist locally regarding carnivore populations and carnivores' movements in a particular landscape, as well as the interactions between livestock and carnivores, are to some extent voiced by the Sámi Parliament representatives in the RCC meetings, and in hearing documents that have been part of the revision process. The public administration aims to increase local participation in documenting carnivores by for instance increasing the role of local Hunting and Fishing Associations, and inviting local people to collect faeces, and send them in for testing. Still, the compromises made through zoning leave the complex dynamics existing on the ground invisible.

Topography and climatic conditions play a major role, not only for reindeer mobility but also in carnivore movements according to herders. Concerning the mapping of lynx, one herder said:

> The Nature Inspectorate's tracking and estimates of lynx' movements do often not reflect the real picture in these mountains. They have traced a route for the lynx, and thus estimated the number of reproductive family groups here. But we see that lynx can travel a different track, since we observe this, and we know that they do not necessarily follow the track that has been argued for.[8]

The herder further noted that the Nature Inspectorate's own mobility in the terrain is dependent on weather and topographic challenges. Due to the steep terrain, such field trips usually follow certain paths when looking for carnivore tracks, which – according to the herder –reduce their ability to register the number of carnivores living in an area. Flying a helicopter to track wolverines requires good light and weather conditions, which are often absent in this region. While herders recognize that the people carrying out these tasks are seeking to do a good job, they feel there are not enough resources available for a satisfactory result.

A herder pointed to how difficulties in documenting the real number of reproductive family groups of lynx prevented them from being able to cull those that made damage in their herds:

> Last winter we found thirteen carcasses taken by lynx over ten days. We asked for a culling permit but could not get it. We had a direct line to the directorate and reported two-three times in that period. It felt like they were holding back because each time we called, they wanted to await the situation and see if the lynx wandered out of the area.

The herder continued to say that:

> It was perfect conditions for us to document losses that particular time, because we were in an area high up with our herd, where we had a good overview and there was little wind. But eventually the winds started blowing the tracks away and we were unable to document the requested number of losses for a culling permit – at the same time as we knew we were losing animals.

The herders often point out that the carnivore numbers that exist in formal government documents are not matching the real picture on the ground. This is problematic, according to herders, as these numbers form the basis for zoning and management. During early winter 2017, another herder that just arrived back from the mountains said with a certain desperation:

> The situation is getting so bad in these inland pastures now; we can hardly use them anymore. We are about to shift the herd to the coast. We have found carcasses almost every day lately, and we can see it is from lynx attacking the reindeer calves. On top of this, the ground is becoming too hard [for the reindeer to find food], as it is packed with ice underneath the snow cover. So we see no other way than getting the herd away from here. I feel very frustrated about these mountain pastures. They used to be excellent…these areas that once used to be our winter pastures.

The herders' strategies and actions are based on their experience and knowledge of pasture conditions, animal movement and the landscape. At governance level, this knowledge frequently becomes marginalized, as carnivore management must be based on 'evidence', in the form of available science-based knowledge or officially authorized expert knowledge. A government officer from the County governor noted that this is a question of the ability to test the empirical observations. The official noted:

> The way the system works now, we have methods that can be validated through replication. …The methods are based on carnivore science and carnivore behaviour…additionally, a supplement of voluntary registrations of lynx tracks exists, which is not equally reliable.

Among our interviewees with field experience, we also find some concern with the strict methodological rules governing tracking and the documentation of carcasses. The fieldworkers believe that continued use of these established methods and rules for the reproductive carnivore family group registration also depend on the requirements of making data comparable over time, making them more useful for scientific purposes. Furthermore, the data correspond to how the national and regional 'population goals' have been defined, that is, in terms of reproductive family groups (*ynglinger*). In this way, we also see a mutual confirmation between specific scientific models and one of the key 'rules of formation' (Foucault, 1972; Kaarhus, 1999: 374–376) in official policy discourse on carnivore conservation: 'population goals' should be defined and the success of conservation policies registered through 'reproductive family groups'. Meanwhile, among herders, there is a general feeling of not being able to 'sufficiently' prove what they have experienced and/or found when it comes to the presence of carnivores, making their experience-based knowledge invalid in the context of their own livelihoods.

Several herders experience that their inland pastures, which are subject to high carnivore pressure, are also critical for their production and the sustainability of their livelihoods. One representative pointed out during a RCC meeting:

> We need to be able to alternate between inland and coastal pastures through the different seasons. This is our way of utilizing the different plants, herbs, lichens for fodder, and hence achieve a better meat quality. The best reindeer are those that can utilize the inland mountain pastures.

At this point, we would like to recontextualize the observations made by Sámi reindeer herders in Nordland, as presented above, with a vision of the same environment presented on the webpage of the Rewilding Europe project. Referring to 'Lapland' as a larger area targeted for rewilding, it also covers the Nordland region where our Sámi informants are practicing reindeer herding:

> Lapland – Sápmi – is a unique blend of untamed nature and cultural heritage. Here old-growth forests, mountains, glaciers, free-flowing rivers and extensive wetlands co-exist with the indigenous Sámi community since millennia. There is no other place in continental Europe with such vast, uninhabited, road-less and original landscapes as Lapland. The composition of fauna and flora is still largely intact and the functioning of ecosystems unaltered... However, even under such pristine conditions, there are threats and needs to ensure that the uniqueness of the land remains and that some lost components are brought back.[9]

The 'lost components' referred to here are the primarily larger carnivores that – it is assumed – can be targeted for 'wildlife watching' as a basis for future economic development geared towards tourism, supported by 'more positive attitudes towards controversial species'.[10]

Revision of the CMP – Second Act

After the public consultation round, the first RCC meeting in January 2017 attracted considerable interest from the local media, which was also due to the divergent views on future management that had come up during the 'First Act'. The January meeting should agree on a revised CMP to be submitted to the NEA, which is a directorate under the Ministry of Climate and Environment. During this meeting, the 'discursive field' of official CMP revision was to a certain extent opened up for the local pastoralists' views and perspectives on landscapes in use. The 'alternative discourse' presented did accept a limited presence of large carnivores but referred to their presence as a 'burden' on relatively small stocks of grazing animals. This alternative discourse reflected the locally perceived need for a better balance between the numbers of predators and grazing animals. The principle of 'clear zoning' as a basic management instrument creating conditions for peaceful co-existence between livestock and predators through spatial separation was in part put aside, and 'burden sharing' – in what we can call a 'cultural landscape' – was suggested as an alternative. This proposal for a Revised Management Plan for Region 7 challenged the basic management instrument established in the authoritative discourse on carnivore management, that is, 'clear zoning'.

In late January 2017, a draft management plan was sent from RCC Nordland to the NEA. Only after receiving the Agency's response – and approval – would the RCC be able to formally adopt the plan. However, the NEA did not consider the plan as adequate, and the Nordland RCC soon received a response with clear recommendations for changes in the proposal.

When seeking to comply with these recommendations on the RCCs next meeting, in March 2017, one of the issues that was particularly difficult to decide upon was where to place the prioritized bear zone. Based on available knowledge on bear habitats, the County Governor suggested two areas prioritized for bears. Both are inland areas bordering Sweden, and one of the suggested zones, covers almost a whole reindeer herding district, including its calving land. The same reindeer herding district is also in a zone prioritized for wolverines and lynx.

The NEA further held that the wolverine zone was too small. When the RCC took up this issue for a new discussion, the committee was clearly divided as to how large the zone prioritized for wolverines should be. The representatives from the Sámi Parliament and the party commonly voicing farmers' interests voted for a smaller zone. The other politicians voted for a larger zone, seeking an alternative that they believed was more in line with the government's policy on 'clear zoning' and was also perceived to provide a better match with the wolverines' habitat. Those who voted for the smaller alternative found it difficult to expand the wolverine zone, since they were concerned with the sheep farmers' and reindeer herders' future within this larger area. It was argued that for instance sheep farmers are not able to invest or develop their farms if they are located within a carnivore zone, since no bank will give them loans, the risk being too high.

Finally, the meeting ended with a majority in the RCC deciding to stick to the original revision of the CMP, as submitted in late January. Bringing up the zoning principle itself for discussion, a Sámi Parliament representative had noted during the meeting:

> To talk about zoning, where does it come from? Did someone just make it up? It is something that is impossible to relate to!

Where **did** it come from? Or, how can we explain the emergence of 'clear zoning' as the government's chosen measure to deal with the conflicts associated with carnivore–pastoral coexistence? Let us move on to the third and final act of this process in our quest for a better understanding of the role and functions of the zoning principle.

Revision of the CMP – Act 3

Before the RCC in Nordland held its next meeting, in May 2017, the Committee received the following response to its revised plan in a letter from the NEA:

> The Carnivore Committee has revised the management plan for carnivore region 7 ... The Agency finds that the plan presented is on several points not in agreement with current regulations. The Agency's view is that this draft is unsuited to comply with the national population goals set for the Region... [and it] will most likely boost conflicts... The draft plan is therefore not suitable as an instrument for carnivore management in the Region.

The NEA's highly critical opinion is further explained in the letter. One reason is that 'the carnivores' biology' is not a primary concern in the RCC's plan:

> In the present draft it appears that the primary consideration is the outfield pastures with sheep and Sámi reindeer herding.

The NEA refers to an earlier letter to RCC Region 7 from the Minister of Agriculture and Food and the Minister of Climate and Environment; a letter giving instructions on 'clearer zoning in the carnivore management'. The agency further finds it necessary to remind the Committee that:

> The Carnivore Committee is a public carnivore agency, and must respect current policies and the provisions of the Carnivore Frame Agreement ... The plan should therefore take current regulations as a starting point.

The NEA recognizes that:

> There are inherent challenges in using a geographical differentiation in Nordland. Both the long and narrow shape of the region, as well as the scale of both pastoralism and carnivore populations contribute to this.

Still, the NEA insists that:

> The Carnivore Committee shall in the Management Plan emphasize a long-term geographical differentiation, where...grazing animals and

permanent carnivore populations are separated ... The differentiation shall build on national population goals for each of the carnivore species in the region...

After receiving this letter, at the RCC meeting in May 2017, the leader expressed her concerns about the NEA's strong focus on differentiating zones and felt that the RCC had not been able to get through with the message on the difficulties of zoning in Nordland – due to the complexity of topography, geography, multiple carnivore species and reindeer herding districts without coastal access.

One year later, in May 2018, the NEA was itself present at a meeting in Nordland RCC. The NEA representative called for action from the Nordland RCC to – finally – make the zones on the maps in such a way that the NEA could make use of them. RCC representatives on their part described the difficult situation for pastoral livelihoods and emphasized in particular the cultural and historical significance of Sámi reindeer herding in the region. One RCC member asked the NEA representative:

> What will be the result if we do not make changes in the plan to comply with national government's proposal? Do we place ourselves on the sideline?

The response was that, eventually, the population goals decide. The discussion in the RCC meeting then turned to the difficulties in complying with the defined population goals for the region; while the NEA representative held that the defined population goals is a 'political issue' and outside the mandate of the state bureaucracy.

The outcome was that the RCC – with the leader's double voice – upheld their decision on keeping a smaller wolverine zone, while all agreed on leaving the question of a bear zone open until more knowledge was in place, particularly on the social impacts of a bear zone for local people in the region. Their revised plan was submitted in May 2018, and in July 2018, the Nordland RCC received a letter from the Ministry of Climate and Environment, stating that the Ministry did not find that the changes made by the RCC were adequate to comply with the signals given by the Ministry. The letter continues:

> The Ministry is confident there exists enough knowledge to make the necessary changes regarding zoning for bears in the region...The Ministry sees it as critical to attain a management plan that secures predictability and that is in accordance with current regulations and policy.[11]

The letter to the RCC concluded that the Ministry had, accordingly, decided to take over the management plan revision and would itself make the necessary amendments.

Conclusion: what about complexities across scales and multiple natures?

When the 2011 Carnivore Agreement's provision for an evaluation was carried out in the period 2015–2018, the evaluation focused on revising the regional management plans – with central instructions on following up 'clear zoning' through carnivore zones that sustain carnivore habitats, while the coexistence goal should also be upheld. The revision of the zoning plan in Nordland was thus obliged to relate to the key assumption that separating animals in 'clear zones' is the best way to handle conflicts related to carnivore predators, and that it is primarily a question of drawing the right boundaries and get the zones right. Within this frame, the struggles related to contextual factors such as geography and topography in Nordland are largely overlooked. This is also the case with the experienced-based knowledge of local actors that ask for a more holistic outlook, where interactions between pastoral animals and carnivores are seen in conjunction with the landscape and their surroundings.

Sustainable Development Goal (SDG) 15, *Life on Land,* addresses the need to '*Protect, restore and promote sustainable use of terrestrial ecosystems … and halt biodiversity loss*'[12] When the SDG is concretised into 'targets' and 'indicators' to guide governance and practical action, however, we see that a potentially holistic view of human–nature interactions on land gives way to representations that objectify nature – as separate from humans – such as in a Red List Index. Ensuring that the SDGs will be implemented in ways that do not erode the ability of reindeer herders to continue maintaining ecological and cultural diversity in the outfields –there is a need for improving the knowledge base for land-use change, and a need for knowledge that more accurately represents herders knowledge of human–nature interactions, the role of reindeer presence in specific landscapes and land-use change across time and space. As long as the holistic outlook is lacking, progress towards a locally sustainable development is uncertain, in spite of ambitious SDGs.

We have here described the successive acts in a regional plan revision process, analysed as a 'discursive field' where local actors, such as Sámi reindeer herders, struggle to articulate relevant views on the nature of the problem to be addressed and the rules defining what counts as evidence and valid knowledge. We show how the regional carnivore governance regime during this revision process ends up leaving the local actors, such as reindeer herders, with limited space for addressing and questioning the underlying assumptions concerning the problem and its solutions. Thus, they are also unable to present their knowledge as legitimate and valid.

In Norway, the knowledge-based carnivore management has been based on an established set of methodological rules and specific indicators when registering both 'reproductive family groups' of carnivores and livestock carcasses killed by carnivores. These indicators are part of a science-based system that does not capture needs for more holistic management approaches, where nature's complexity is not only represented through sets of indicators, and governance operates within frames where humans and nature are disconnected. At the same time, conceptions of indigenous pastoral lands as – ideally – untouched and part of wilderness can work to sustain a separation of nature into separate zones. In practice, we have shown how 'clear zoning' generates a struggle between concerns for *production landscapes* and *landscapes for carnivores*, played out as a *conflictive encounter* between national and local levels.

Pastoralists in Nordland are faced with the unpredictable behaviour of carnivores. Based on our analysis of the management plan revision process, one may ask whether coexistence really is the government's goal with regard to the carnivore dilemma? Or is the goal primarily reduced conflicts? We have shown how the national environmental administration insists that the revision discourse adheres strictly to established rules of formation – both regarding 'clear zoning' and 'population goals'. There is no opening for opposing discourses in this field, as shown in the rejection of the RCC's revised plan. We further see how central-level actors in the field resort to the use of a discursive *modality* expressing duty and obligation. They remind local actors of the power relations in the state hierarchy in their efforts to counteract the zoning principle being challenged – as it has been throughout this process of CMP revision.

Notes

1 Other management instruments are licence permits, quota hunting and extraordinary culling, but here we focus specifically on the zoning principles.
2 This mobilisation was part of the Alta controversy; the contested construction of a hydroelectric power plant with a dam that would inundate a Sámi community and affect pastoralist migration routes in Finnmark, northern Norway.
3 Indigenous and Tribal Peoples Convention, ILO Convention No. 169 of 1989.
4 www.rewildingeurope.com/
5 Cf. ILO Convention (C169) §15, which states that: 'The rights of the peoples concerned to the natural resources pertaining to their lands shall be specially safeguarded. These rights include the right of these peoples to participate in the use, management and conservation of these resources'.
6 National population goals for these strictly protected carnivores are: 15 reproducing bear families, 65 reproducing lynx families, 39 reproducing wolverine families; in addition to 3 reproducing wolf families, of which none is located to Region 7, Nordland.
7 www.fylkesmannen.no/Nordland/Miljo-og-klima/Rovvilt/
8 Paragraphs in Italics are authors' own translation of statements in Norwegian by different informants.
9 www.rewildingeurope.com/areas/lapland/ [Accessed March 27, 2017]
10 It may be worth mentioning that several of the 'controversial species, especially lynx and wolverine, are notoriously difficult to spot in the wild.
11 *Authors' translation of letter from the Ministry of Climate & Environment, dated: 02.07.2018.*
12 https://sustainabledevelopment.un.org/sdg15

References

Allard, C. (2015). *Renskötselsrett i nordisk belysning.* Göteborg: Makadam Förlag.

Bartlett, L., & Vavrus, F. (2017). *Rethinking case study research: A comparative approach.* New York: Routledge.

Becker, H.S. (1992) Cases, causes, conjunctures, stories, and imagery. In C.C. Ragin & H.S. Becker (Eds.), *What is a case?: Exploring the foundations of social inquiry,* pp. 205–216. Cambridge: Cambridge University Press.

Benjaminsen, T.A., Hugo, R., Sjaastad, E., & Sara, M.N. (2015). Misreading the Arctic landscape: A political ecology of reindeer, carrying capacities, and overstocking in Finnmark, Norway. *Norsk Geografisk Tidsskrift – Norwegian Journal of Geography.* doi: 10.1080/00291951.2015.1031274

Berg, B.A. (2000). *Mot en korporativ reindrift. Samisk reindrift I det 20. århundre – eksemplifisert gjennom studier av reindriften på Helgeland,* Ph.D Thesis, (March 1999), University of Tromsø. Diedut: 3/2000, Guovdageaidnu/Kautokeino: Sámi Instituhtta.

Bourdieu, P. (1977). *Outline of a theory of practice.* London: Cambridge University Press.

Chapron, G., Kaczensky, P., Linnell, J.D.C., von Arx, M., Huber, D., Andrén, H., ... Boitani, L. (2014). Recovery of large carnivores in Europe's modern human-dominated landscapes. *Science,* 346(6216): 1517–1519.

Díaz, C.L. (2010). The bern convention: 30 years of nature conservation in Europe. *Review of European Community & International Environmental Law,* 19(2): 185–196.

Dressel, S., Sandström, C., & Ericsson, G. (2015). A meta-analysis of studies on attitudes toward bears and wolves across Europe 1976–2012. *Conservation Biology* 29: 565–574.

Dreyfus, H.L., & Rabinow, P. (1983). *Michel Foucault: Beyond structuralism and hermeneutics,* 2nd ed. Chicago: The University of Chicago Press.

Fairclough, N. (2003). *Analysing discourse: Textual analysis for social research.* London & New York: Routledge.

Fairclough, N. (2013). Critical discourse analysis and critical policy studies. *Critical Policy Studies,* 7(2): 177–197.

Fangel, K., & V. Gundersen, V. (2012). Rovviltforvaltningen i et planteoretisk perspektiv. *Utmark- Tidsskrift for utmarksforvaltning,* Nr. 1.

Fischer, F., & Forester, J. eds. (1993). *The argumentative turn in policy analysis and planning.* Durham: Duke University Press.

Foucault, M. (1971). Orders of discourse. *Social Science Information,* 10(2): 7–30.

Foucault, M. (1972). *The archaeology of knowledge.* London: Tavistock Publications.

Hansson-Forman, K., Reimerson, E., Sjölander-Lindqvist, A., & Sandström, C. (2018). Governing large carnivores—Comparative insights from three different countries. *Society & Natural Resources.* doi: 10.1080/08941920.2018.1447179

Huntington, H.P., Gearheard, S., Mahoney, A.R., & Salomon, A.K. (2011). Integrating traditional and scientific knowledge through collaborative natural science field research: Identifying elements for success, *Arctic,* 64(4): 437–445.

Jaren, V., & Løvstad, J.P., eds. (2001). *Delrapport 3 fra forskningsprogrammet bruk og forvaltning av utmark,* 49–60. Oslo: Norges forskningsråd.

Johnsen, K.I., Mathiesen, S.D., & Eira, I.M.G. (2017). Sámi reindeer governance in Norway as competing knowledge systems: A participatory study. *Ecology and Society,* 22(4): 33, doi: 10.5751/ES-09786-220433

Kaarhus, R. (1999). *Conceiving environmental problems: A comparative study of scientific knowledge constructions and policy discourses in Ecuador and Norway*. Oslo: NIBR's Pluss Series, 6–99.

Krange, O., Odden, J., Skogen, K., Linnell, J., Stokland, H.B., Vang, S., & Mattisson, J. (2016). *Evaluering av regional rovviltforvaltning*. Oslo: NINA Rapport 1268.

Krauss, W., & Olwig, K.R. (2018). Special issue on pastoral landscapes caught between abandonment, rewilding and agro-environmental management. Is there an alternative future?. *Landscape Research*. doi: 10.1080/01426397.2018.1503844

Linnell, J., Nilsen, E., Lande, U., Herfindal, I., Odden, J., Skogen, K., & Breitenmoser, U. (2005). Zoning as a means of mitigating conflicts with large carnivores: Principles and reality. In R. Woodroffe, S. Thirgood, & A. Rabinowitz (Eds.), *People and wildlife, conflict or co-existence?, conservation biology*, pp. 162–175. Cambridge: Cambridge University Press. doi: 10.1017/CBO9780511614774.011

Linnell, J. (2015). Dialogue to reduce conflicts (ed.) in *Carnivore Damage Prevention News*, 11, MedWolf Project. [online] Retrieved from: www.medwolf.eu. (Accessed May 20, 2019).

Maxwell, J.A. (2013). *Qualitative research design*. Los Angeles: Sage.

Moen, G.K., & Støen, O.G. (2016). Bjørn I Nordland, Presentation at a Scientific Seminar about Carnivore management, Nordland County Governor, 26.10.2016, Bodø.

Nadasdy, P. (1999). The politics of TEK: Power and the "integration" of knowledge. *Arctic Anthropology*, 36(1–2): 1–18.

Nordland County Governor. 'Fakta om reindrift' (2018). Retrieved from: www.fylkesmannen.no/nb/Nordland/Landbruk-og-mat/Reindrift/Fakta-om-reindrift/

Norwegian Environment Agency. (2014). Norway helps preserve European biodiversity. Retrieved from www.miljodirektoratet.no/en/News1/2015/Norway-helpspreserve-European-biodiversity/

Nustad, K.G. (01 March 2011). Performing natures and land in the iSimangaliso Wetland Park. *South Africa Ethnos*, 76(1): 88–108.

Ragin, C.C. (1992). Introduction: Cases of "what is a case?". In C.C. Ragin & H.S. Becker (Eds.), *What is a case?: Exploring the foundations of social inquiry*, pp. 1–18. Cambridge: Cambridge University Press.

Redpath, S.M., Young, J., Evely, A., Adams., W.M., Sutherland., W.J., Whitehouse, A., ..., & Gutierrez, R.J. (2013). Understanding and managing conservation conflicts. *Trends in Ecology Evolution*, 28: 100–109.

Risvoll, C. (2015). *Adaptive capacity within pastoral communities in the face of environmental and societal change*. PhD Thesis in Sociology, Faculty of Social Sciences, University of Nordland.

Risvoll, C., Fedreheim, G.E., & Galafassi, D. (2016). Trade-offs in pastoral governance in Norway: Challenges for biodiversity and adaption. *Pastoralism*, 6(1). doi: 10.1186/s13570-016-0051-3

Rønningen, K., & Flemsæter, F. (2016). Multifunctionality, rural diversification and the unsettlement of rural land use systems. I: *Routledge International Handbook of Rural Studies*. Routledge ISBN 978-1-138-80437-1. s. 312–322. Retrieved from: http://www.ecologyandsociety.org/issues/article.php/6658

Saltenposten. (2016, December 13). Nesten 90 innspill utsetter møtet i rovviltnemda, *Saltenposten*, Retrieved from: www. Saltenposten.no

Sandberg, A. (1999). *Conditions for community-based governance of biodiversity*. Nordlandsforskning Report No. 11/99. Nordland Research Institute, Bodø, Norway.

Scott, J.C. (1998). *Seeing like a state.* Binghampton: Yale University Press.

Sjölander-Lindqvist, A., Johansson M., & Sandström, C. (2015). Individual and collective responses to large carnivore management: The roles of trust, representation, knowledge spheres, communication and leadership. *Wildlife Biology,* 21: 175–185. doi: 10.2981/wlb.00065

Stortinget 2010–2011 (2010). Parliament's Document Nr. 8:163 S. (2010–2011) *Representantforslag 163 S.* [online] Retrieved from: www.stortinget.no/no/Saker-ogpublikasjoner/Publikasjoner/Representantforslag/

Strand, G.H., et al. (2016). Rovviltbestandenes betydning for landbruk og matproduksjon basert på norske ressurser, Rapport 63/2016, Norsk institutt for bioøkonomi, Ås.

Vatn, A. (1984). *Teknologi og politikk: om framveksten av viktige styringstiltak i norsk jordbruk 1920–1980.* Oslo: Landbruksforlaget.

Veland, S., Lynch, A., Bischoff-Mattson, Z., Joachim, L., & Johnson, N. (2014). All strings attached: Negotiating relationships of geographic information science. *Geographical Research,* 52(3): 296–308. doi: 10.1111/1745-5871.12070

World Commission on Environment and Development's report *Our Common Future* in 1987 (WCED 1987).

11 Through our stories we resist

Decolonial perspectives on south Saami history, indigeneity and rights

Eva Maria Fjellheim

Māori educator and scholar Linda Tuhiwai Smith (2012, p. 1) reminds us that «the term 'research' is inextricably linked to European imperialism and colonialism.» She argues that for centuries, Indigenous Peoples' histories, knowledges, and practices have been written and presented through the eyes and voice of the colonizers. At the same time, she encourages indigenous scholars to be protagonists in research about and for ourselves. According to her, our *counterstories* can constitute powerful forms of resistance and contribute to *decolonize* academia and knowledge construction. Smith's critical analysis of a colonial knowledge hierarchy is ecchoed across the indigenous world, also in *Saepmie*, the traditional territory of the Saami people in Fennoscandia. In this chapter, I critically examine the implications of a colonial narrative of south Saami history, indigeneity, and territorial rights in the Røros area[1] in Norway. Through five generations of struggles and resilience, I have my own counterstory to tell:

In 2009, the Association of forest owners of Røros wrote the following about my family in a written statement to the Norwegian Parliament:

> It is impossible that our counterparts here in Røros, those who are reindeer herders in the Riast/Hylling district, belong to this category of humans. As an example, we want to mention the Fjellheim family, which is the largest reindeer herding family in Riast/Hylling. They are people with a very high intelligence, many of them have university education. (...) We who live in the same community as these people, have off course a hard time accepting that they belong to an indigenous population.
>
> (Skogeierlag, 2009)

The quote is taken from a statement responding to the second Saami Rights Commission's report (SRU II) on Saami rights to land and water south of Finnmark County (2007).[2] Based on two main arguments, the forest owners intend to delegitimize the application of an indigenous rights framework which protects reindeer herding rights in the Røros area. The first argument questions the *indigeneity* of the south Saami, by claiming we are too intelligent, Norwegian-looking, and industrialized to be indigenous. The second argument states that the south Saami immigrated to the area as late as the mid 1700s, and that the agricultural rights are older than reindeer herding rights. In sum, they reject that the south Saami in Røros are entitled to Indigenous Peoples' rights to land, territory, and resources.

The statement from the forest owners expresses racist attitudes and misconceptions about south Saami history, indigeneity, and the right to practice reindeer herding in the Røros area. I argue this is an example of a *colonial narrative* of the kind Smith (2012) encourages us to contest. My aim is not to address the individuals who signed it but rather to understand how the colonial history and legacy of research has shaped and maintained the structures behind such ideas. I argue the two main arguments of the forest owners' statement are informed by two academic contributions with strong affiliation to the colonial project of the Norwegian state. The first is the broader discipline of racial biology rooted in social Darwinist thought from the late 1800 and early 1900s, which legitimated treatment of the Saami as an inferior race (intellectually and culturally). The second is *The advancement theory*, a study carried out by historian and geographer Yngvar Nielsen (1891). Nielsen concluded that the south Saami immigrated to the Røros area after the expansion of the Norwegian sedentary population, a view which legitimated dispossession and marginalization of south Saami territorial rights through political and legal measures. The latter theory has been decisive in several Supreme Court cases settling land disputes in favor of land-owning farmers up until as late as 1997.

Nielsen's theory is no longer actively defended within dominant academia, but the narratives of the historical presence of the south Saami are still disputed. Despite extensive research and documentation work refuting late immigration, South Saami counterstories of historical continuity are still being marginalized. I argue that this uneven power relation is a colonial legacy which can be understood as *epistemic ignorance* (Kuokkanen, 2008). The continued struggle over knowledge and (re)presentation of south Saami history became evident when the extensive book volume "The History of Trøndelag" (Bull, Skevik, Sognnes, & Stugu, 2005) was published, excluding south Saami competence in the process. However, the knowledge hierarchy is constantly being challenged by south Saami scholars and knowledge holders who continue to push for epistemic self-determination and justice. In 2001, the Supreme Court settled a land dispute in favor of reindeer herding based on the principle of *use from time immemorial*. After over 100 years of marginalization of reindeer herding rights, the court took Saami knowledge, research and documentation work, culture and concept of law into consideration for the first time.

Before I continue, it is important to state my methodological approach and positionality, as the references I use are highly personal. My ancestors/relatives were/are active reindeer herders in *Gåebrien Sijte*, the reindeer herding district the forest owners address as Riast/Hylling in Norwegian. They are introduced by south Saami, and translated into the English genealogical denominations. Growing up in a community with a strong sense of identity and strive for justice has provided me with a unique horizon of knowledge about the historical struggles of my people. The analysis is based on literature review and storytelling informed by an emerging indigenous scholarship striving for decolonization and self-determination within education, research and knowledge construction (Porsanger, 2004; Smith, 2012). In particular, Whitinui (2014) proposes *indigenous autoethnography* as a way of repositioning insider ethnography from an indigenous perspective. He encourages a resistance-based research approach, aiming to address social justice and change. Following Whitinui, I part from my own family history, and contest the colonial implications academia has had for the understanding of south Saami history, indigeneity, and rights.

In her groundbreaking book "Decolonizing methodologies," Smith (2012, p. 2) explains this position eloquently:

> Indigenous Peoples across the world have other stories to tell which not only question the assumed nature of those ideals and the practices that they generate, but also serve to tell an alternative story: the history of Western research through the eyes of the colonized.

With Smith's words in mind, I begin telling our story with respect and recognition of the counterstories already told by south Saami scholars and knowledge holders.

Background

The south Saami people is a small minority within the larger Saami society, with a population of approximately 2,000 people in both Norway and Sweden (NOU, 1984, p. 18). In Norway, it is estimated that half still speaks the language (NOU, 2016, p. 18). The assimilation policies carried out by the Norwegian government from the mid-1800s up until the 1980s (Minde, 2003) affected the south Saami particularly hard (Johansen, 2019). In addition to assimilation through the education system, the expansion of agriculture, industries and infrastructure developments encroached on Saami traditional territories. Traditional livelihoods, such as reindeer herding and fishing, were further restricted by new administrative and legal measures. This process has been referred to as *internal colonization* (Lawrence, 2014; Lawrence & Åhrén, 2016), which has had diverse expressions and responses across the national borders of Norway, Sweden, Finland, and Russia, as much as in different localities in Saepmie (Spangen, Salmi, Äikäs, & Lehtola, 2015). For the purpose of this chapter, internal colonization is understood in the specific south Saami context as the state's historical deprivations of territorial, intellectual, and cultural rights.

I acknowledge the complexity of using the term "Western" as opposed to "indigenous/Saami." They are not meant to produce binary and exclusive categories, rather to be used as a conceptual tool to understand the colonial relationship between the dominant Norwegian society and the south Saami. In this context, it is important to clarify that I do not address all Western research as colonial, but rather the scholars and institutions who fail, or ignore to contest colonial narratives with severe implications for the understanding of south Saami history, indigeneity, and rights.

Norway was the first country to sign the ILO-Convention No. 169 on the Rights of Indigenous and Tribal Peoples in 1990.[3] The Norwegian constitution recognizes the right to maintain and strengthen Saami languages, culture, and livelihoods.[4] Reindeer herding has been described as the backbone of south Saami culture and language (Nilssen, 2019), as about half of the population are reindeer owners (Landbruksdirektoratet, 2018) or second- or third-generation descendants of reindeer owners (S. Fjellheim, 1991). This proportion is larger than in other Saami communities, e.g. Finnmark County in the north.

Reindeer herding is characterized by semi-domesticated reindeer and the extensive and cyclical use of seasonal pastures. In the south Saami area, it is to a large degree practiced on private owned outfields.[5] The reindeer herding Act recognizes the State's obligation to safeguard reindeer herding as the material base for Saami culture and allows its practice on private owned outfields within the reindeer herding districts. However, the districts are held collectively liable for any damage reindeer may cause on cultivated farmland,[6] which has led to compensation lawsuits from landowners. The Act does not require fencing to keep the reindeer from entering, in contrast to the legal framework of liability in the case of livestock (Ravna, 2019). As mentioned in the beginning, the forest owners' statement was a response to the second Saami Rights Commission's report, aiming to recognize and secure Saami rights to land and water in the south Saami area.[7] Among other recommendations from the report, the Commission suggested to revise the reindeer herding Act, including the principle of collective liability.

In addition to conflicts around cultivated farmlands, commodification of outfields (Rønningen & Flemsæter, 2016) is putting increased pressure on the already vulnerable south Saami cultural landscape (Nilssen, 2019). Recently, the expansion of the wind power industry as a response to climate change mitigation politics (Normann, 2019; Otte, Rønningen, & Moe, 2018) has been contested as *green colonialism* by Saami politicians and right defenders (Aslaksen & Porsanger, 2017). The racist attitude and clear political motive of the statement from the forest owners needs to be understood in the context of a conflict over resources and rights but not as a natural cause from it. There are also examples of a tolerant coexistence between reindeer herding and farming activity, also within the Røros area. However, as reindeer herding is an exclusive Saami right within the reindeer herding districts in Norway, ethnicity becomes a central component in many land-use conflicts (E. M. Fjellheim, 2013).

The science of racism and its legacy

As quoted in the beginning, the forest owners doubt that the south Saami in Røros are indigenous. My *aehtjie* (father) Sverre Fjellheim came across the statement in official records, and it quickly made it to the front page of local, regional and national newspapers: «Too intelligent to be indigenous» was the headline of an article of the Saami division of the Norwegian National Broadcasting, who interviewed my late *jiekie* (uncle) Anders Fjellheim: «I was laughing well when I read the statement. One should almost believe that it was written 300 years ago, when the Saami were looked upon as inferior,» he says to the newspaper (Larsen, 2009).

In order to understand the racist tone and stereotypical depictions in the statement, we need to revisit history. While I was reading the newspaper coverage, I began to think about a picture from 1922, where five people sit and stand around a wooden table on a grass plain. They are wearing their *gaptah*, the south Saami traditional garments. On the left, stand my 12-year-old *aahka* (grandmother) Paula Margrethe Paulsen (Fjellheim) and her three years younger sister, *aahka* Lisa Antonie Paulsen (Løkken). To the right sits my great-great grandfather's brother, *maadter-maadteraajja* Morten Mortensen, and in the middle of the picture, my *maadteraahka* (great-grandmother) Sara Margrethe Nordlund Paulsen. Maadteraahka Sara looks serious, but her posture is firm and somehow proud. Her hat lies on the table in front of them, and a man stands above her, holding a metal instrument around her head. This man is Jon Alfred Mjøen, one of Norway's most prominent racial scientists in the 1920s and 1930s.

Figure 11.1 The picture was taken at Storelvvollen in 1922, near the family dwelling in Røros municipality. From the left: Paula Margrethe Paulsen (Fjellheim), Lisa Antonie Paulsen (Løkken), Sara Margrethe Nordlund Paulsen, Jon Alfred Mjøen and Morten Mortensen. © Sverre Fjellheim.

Mjøen was part of a school of scientists informed by social Darwinist thought, where racial examinations of both human skeletons and living human beings were conducted. Of the leading physical anthropologists in Norway in the early 1900s, he was by far the most extreme. Although many scholars were strongly influenced by the idea of Eugenics, or racial hygiene, they held different views on its purpose. While prominent scholars such as Kristian and Alette Schreiner were interested in the propagation of healthy individuals, Halfdan Bryn and Mjøen promoted genetic control as a necessary tool to avoid degeneration of the superior Nordic race (Kyllingstad, 2012). During a few decades, the Saami population in Norway and Sweden was photographed, measured, and depicted as primitive, less intelligent and with generally bad genes (Evjen, 1997). Saami families were even portrayed as exotic objects through living exhibitions in Europe and America (Baglo, 2011).

In the 1920s, Mjøen conducted racial examinations on the south Saami population in the Røros area. While physical anthropologists quickly rejected the scientific validity of Eugenics, Mjøen continued to inform the field of study up until the beginning of the second world war. In the book "Racial hygiene" (1938), he describes the phenotypes and abilities of the people(s) he measured, including my ancestors. About the Saami in general he writes:

> In northern Scandinavia there is an element of a rather insignificant number of so-called Saami or Lapps,[8] a mongoloid people. They are short grown, with broad skulls, high cheekbones, dark colors. Their looks and abilities are very different from the Nordic.
>
> (Mjøen, 1938, p. 2)

Just like Mjøen, the statement from the forest owners in Røros is concerned with phenotypes and abilities in their understanding of the indigeneity of the south Saami. In addition to referring to intelligence and education, they suggest that *aehtjie* (my father) and his brothers look like Thor Heyerdahl, the famous Norwegian adventurer and explorer in the 1900s. In this context, the comparison must be understood as some kind of symbol of Norwegianness as opposed to Saaminess in a hierarchy based on a racial distinction. They write: «If we are to find other people to compare with, concerning both intelligence and looks (same human type) – it must be Thor Heyerdahl who is a great celebrity in our country» (Skogeierlag, 2009).

Finally, they underline that «these 'indigenous' people are practicing industrialized reindeer herding» and that «DNA-tests should be provided» (Skogeierlag, 2009). The criteria they adhere to indigeneity is to be less intelligent and unindustrialized, and genetics is required as proof for Saaminess. These assumptions have strong parallels to the racial theories presented by Mjøen and other racial scientists of the time. The idea of the Saami as a race claiming rights based on DNA is problematic, as it is far from how the ILO convention No. 169 defines the peoples entitled to indigenous rights.

Still, it is not rare to find racial and genealogical references in public debates concerning Saami territorial rights. As an example, the documentary "Brennpunkt – The first right" from 2011 insinuates that the Saami claim territorial rights based on their DNA, and not their ethnic origin and practices (E. M. Fjellheim, 2013). The notion of indigeneity as pure and static is an illustrative example of what Jeffrey Sissons (2005) names "oppressive authenticity." Such misconceptions of Saaminess are also dominant in contemporary Norwegian textbooks which portray the Saami as stereotypical or exotic (Gjerpe, 2020).

While writing this chapter, I was reminded that racist argumentation and misconception of indigeneity in public debate around Saami territorial rights is an ongoing structural problem. In June 2019, a controversial meeting between landowners was held in the municipality of Selbu, 130 kilometers north of Røros. As was the case of the statement from the forest owners in 2009, the meeting was a response to a political process concerning reindeer herding and Indigenous Peoples' rights. To be specific, it concerned the proposition for a consultation law and revision process of the existing reindeer herding Act. One of the main speakers of the event, Jarl Hellesvik, chairs the controversial organization Ethnic Democratic Equality (EDL) and is known to argue against the recognition of the indigenous status of the Saami and to encourage racist and hateful attitudes in public debates (Berg-Nordlie & Olsen, 2019). At the meeting, he gave a speech with the title «Are the Saami entitled to be protected by ILO 169?» This was clearly an anti-Saami rights meeting and was met with fury from the Saami community who claimed it was an attempt to spread "fake news" about Saami indigeneity and territorial rights (Balto, 2019; Bransfjell & Magga, 2019). As a response to the critique, Hellesvik sums up EDLs main argument, which follows the same understanding of indigeneity and Saaminess as the forest owners' statement put forward ten years earlier:

> At the meeting in Selbu, I asked the public the following question: Is there anything suggesting that ILO was concerned to adopt a convention aiming to protect well-educated, well-integrated, urban and resourceful humans, as the Saami in Norway today? (…) a convention meant to apply to secluded and marginalized peoples.
>
> (Hellesvik, 2019)

In addition to promoting anti-Saami content in a meeting where approximately 100 persons attended, the organizers attempted to prohibit a Saami landowner, and leader of one of the reindeer herding districts in the area, from attending (Tretnes Hansen, Balto, Aslaksen, & Paulsen, 2019). The meeting in Selbu was a reminder that the forest owners' statement was not a single and exclusive event. It shows how racialization is repeatedly used through organized structures to influence public perceptions of indigeneity and policies concerning indigenous and Saami territorial rights.

The advancement theory and its consequences

The second argument from the forest owners claim late south Saami immigration to the Røros area. In the statement they write: «We want to refer to the fact that there were no permanent living Saami in our area as late as 1742. There were no Saami place names, graves, offering sites nor a living Saami tradition at that time» (Skogeierlag, 2009).

While most would agree that a racial understanding of indigeneity has little to do with legal claims to territorial rights, the question of whose right came first, has been central in land disputes the Røros area. The expansion of a sedentary agricultural population is related to the establishment of a copper mine in 1644, and the increased necessity of local food sufficiency to support the workers and their families. When the mine was established, only 15 people were registered as sedentary dwellers in the area which today constitutes Røros. In about 100 years, the population grew to become one of the largest industrial societies in Norway, numbering 3231 inhabitants (S. Fjellheim, 2020). In order to get recognition of private agricultural rights over collective reindeer herding rights, the forest owners had to reinforce the narrative of late south Saami immigration.

The immigration narrative of the south Saami is based on historian and geographer Yngvar Nielsen's *advancement theory* published in the yearbook of "The Norwegian Geographical Society" in 1891. In 1889, Nielsen was granted a scholarship to study the old dwelling sites of the south Saami population between Namdalen in the north and Femunden in the south and to explore the relationship between the sedentary farmers and the nomadic Saami. According to himself, he made a «scientific contribution to the practical question» (Nielsen, 1891), referring to the conflict arising when farmers expanded further up into the mountains where the Saami kept their reindeer and dwellings (S. Fjellheim, 2012). After a weeklong fieldwork, he concluded that the south Saami population in the Røros area had migrated to the south from Namdalen as late as 1742. Among the "scientific" evidence supporting this theory was the absence of south Saami place names or pre-Christian graves or offering sites, exactly the same arguments used in the forest owners' statement.

Nielsen's advancement theory quickly became the leading narrative of south Saami origin in the Røros area and had severe implications for reindeer herding rights. My great-great-grandparents and other reindeer herders were violently chased away or convicted in court to pay high compensation due to alleged damage on the farmers' crops. The consequences were severe: From 10 to 12 families having reindeer herding as their main livelihood in the beginning of the 1800s, only one family remained in 1889 (S. Fjellheim, 2012). This was maadter-maadteraajja (great-great grandfather) Paul Johnsen and his family.

The legal grounds to hold the south Saami reindeer herders liable for damage caused by their reindeer was the Common Lapp Act from 1883, whose intention was to strengthen the property rights of the farmers in relation to the reindeer herders. In the new Act, reindeer herders were made collectively liable for any damage caused by reindeer on cultivated land, despite being strongly criticized by two Supreme Court judges in Sweden (Ravna, 2007). In 1889, the Lapp Commission decided within which areas, now named reindeer herding districts, reindeer herding should be permitted. Nielsen's theory legitimated the new Act,[9] the work of the Commission and the first Supreme Court case concerning collective liability in 1892 (S. Fjellheim, 2020). The verdict (in S. Fjellheim, 2020) shows that Nielsen's scientific contribution was decisive in the court's decision:

> Paul Johnsen claims that the Lapps are the indigenous inhabitants, whereas the Norwegians need to depart from the area. However, it is the other way around. According to a dissertation by professor Yngvar Nielsen about the expansion of the Lapps towards the south in the dioceses of Trondheim and Hedmark it appears that the Lapps in their expansion towards the south of Norway had not reached here until the year 1742. The agriculture of these mountains is of course much older.

My *maadter-maadteraajja* Paul lost against the ten farmers who sued him during the years of 1875–1877. He had to pay compensation for alleged damages on their private properties, without any proof put forward in court. Only five years later, in 1897, he lost another case in the Supreme Court. In this verdict, reference was made to "scientific research" proving that the rights of the sedentary farmers were older than the Saami's. In addition to paying the compensation, the reindeer herders lost the entire right to pasture near the Aursunden lake (S. Fjellheim, 2020; Ravna, 2019).

Smith (2012) argues that the systematic exclusion from writing history went hand in hand with fragmentation of lands and forced evictions through legislation. Saami scholar Jelena Porsanger (2004, p. 107) claims «research has been used as a tool of the colonization of Indigenous Peoples and their territories.» This is fair to argue for the south Saami case, where Nielsen's advancement theory legitimated colonial control over south Saami territory.

The struggle over history, knowledge and rights continues

As mentioned in the beginning, Smith's book "Decolonizing methodologies" (2012), first published in 1999, has become a classic inspiration for indigenous scholars with a critical perspective on the colonial entanglements of academia and knowledge construction. Her work has especially been echoed in the English-speaking world, by indigenous scholars from settler colonies, who propose alternative research agendas (e.g. Kovach, 2010; Nakata, 2007; Wilson, 2008). In *Abya Yala*, the indigenous Latin-America, decolonial epistemological perspectives have an equally strong presence, providing literature in Spanish, e.g. among critical Mapuche historians in Chile

(Antileo Baeza, Cárcamo-Huechante, Calfío Montalva, & Huinca-Piutrin, 2015; Nahuelpan, 2018) and Mayan intellectuals challenging epistemic racism in Guatemala (E.g. Cumes, 2018).

In the early 1980s and 1990s, critical thoughts about research were also emerging in the south Saami area. *Aehtjie (my father)* is an important knowledge holder and community historian who has published various articles and books about south Saami history in the Røros area. At that time, he was the first director of the newly established south Saami cultural institution *Saemien Sijte*. Based on the experience of the institution's work on the documentation of south Saami cultural heritage sites, he proposed a "process model" as a response to the "object model" of research on Saami issues. In the former model, he emphasizes the need for a continuous relationship between the institution and the Saami community, and to integrate Saami knowledge in the process. He argues for the importance of knowledge transfer between generations and says the participants valued it as an identity strengthening process. According to him, the problem with the "object model" is that knowledge is "extracted" and analyzed by the so-called external experts who easily can misinterpret their findings (S. Fjellheim, 1991).

The Saami process model of research and documentation work has been particularly important in areas where the invisibility and rejection of south Saami history has been strong. From 1985 to 1989, my father led a large cultural heritage project encompassing ten regions in the entire south Saami territory in Norway. Through this work, the concepts of *cultural competence* and *territorial affiliation* were introduced as crucial criteria for the participants. Most of the cultural heritage sites in the south Saami area are somehow related to nomadic reindeer herding and the life around it. Thus, the ability to locate and recognize them requires cultural knowledge about how reindeer herding in the specific area has been practiced. In order to secure this competence, 32 south Saami community members were selected by their respective regions to speak with elders and to use their knowledge to document and map cultural heritage sites. The group registered a variety of sites, such as dwellings, milk and food storages, spring water sources, hunting pits and fences, and offering sites (S. Fjellheim, 1991).

From the 1970s and onwards, a range of scholars from different disciplines have refuted Nielsen's *advancement theory* and supported the south Saami counterstories of ancient origin. The first who challenged Nielsen's theory was professor of linguistics, Knut Bergsland (1970, 1992) who identified several south Saami place names which cannot be explained by modern Saami language. As an example, *gåebrie* is the south Saami name of the reindeer herding district *Gåebrien Sijte* addressed in the forest owners' statement. Following Bergsland, archeologists documented south Saami burial sites and dwellings from as early as the iron age (Bergstøl, 2008; Gerde, 2016; Skjølsvold, 1980; Stenvik, 1983; Zachrisson, Alexandersen, Gollwitzer, & Iregren, 1997). A thorough systematization of Nielsen's critics can be read in S. Fjellheim (2020).

Figure 11.2 The map is drawn by Saami artist Hans Ragnar Mathisen and shows the most southern part of the Saami territory in Norway and Sweden. It contains south Saami place names from the area around Røros and is adorned with traditional ornaments, symbols, and historical illustrations. Hans Ragnar Mathisen: KM 21: ÅARJELSAEMIEH MAADTOE-DAJVE made in Sálašvággi 1998–2011–2017 © Hans Ragnar Mathisen / BONO, Oslo 2019.

Despite of extensive critique of Nielsen's methods and conclusions, two historians at the Norwegian University of Technology and Science, Jørn Sandnes (1973) and Kjell Haarstad (1992), kept the narrative of late south Saami migration alive until the late 1990s. The latter acted as expert witness defending land-owning farmers in several Supreme Court cases (S. Fjellheim, 2020; Sem, 2019). In 1997, exactly 100 years after my ancestors lost the Aursunden case, their decedents lost another case in the same area. Professor of law Kirsti Strøm-Bull (2005) reflects on the relation between history and law in Norwegian Supreme Court verdicts concerning south Saami territorial rights and questions the political motivation of Nielsen's theory, in the past and present. She says:

> It is tempting to critically question the rapid acceptance of the theory as it supported the majority population in the conflict with the Saami. And one can wonder if it is due to the same reason that the theory has survived despite new research presenting another story.

The unequal power relationship in the struggle over knowledge and south Saami history in the Røros area is evident but constantly being challenged. In 2001, a Supreme Court verdict marked an important shift when it took Saami knowledge, documentation and research, culture, and concept of law into consideration for the first time. The claims from the 201 land-owning plaintiffs in Selbu were rejected by the ruling court. The two reindeer herding districts *Gåebrien Sijte* and *Saanti Sijte* finally experienced that the same knowledge and arguments our ancestors presented a 100 years ago were taken seriously in the courtroom. For the first time, Saami reindeer herding rights were considered legitimate in relation to the legal principle of *use from time immemorial* (Eriksen, 2004; Ravna, 2019). The extensive south Saami documentation work and research carried out in the 1980s and onwards must be seen as a decisive contribution for the court to shift course. It is also important to mention that the question of "who came first" has become less significant, as the legal status of Saami is safeguarded by Norway's ratification of the ILO-Convention No. 169. The convention does not define Indigenous Peoples as exclusively the peoples who first inhabited an area (Ravna, 2011).

The Supreme Court verdict from 2001 was an important victory after centuries of political and legal marginalization of reindeer herding in relation to agricultural practices. Not only in the Røros area, as the verdict set precedence in Norway as a whole. In 2018, a similar case was raised by land-owners in Tufsingdalen against Gåebrien Sijte and Saanti Sijte, who have their common winter pastures in *Femund Sijte*. The reindeer herding districts appealed the decision on compensation from the Court of Appeal and requested the Supreme Court to address the provision on collective liability as discriminatory according to the Norwegian Constitution and human rights principles. The Supreme Court verdict did not give reason to the entire appeal but revoked the decision regarding compensation payment and expressed it was unfortunate that the Saami Rights Commission's rec-ommendation to revise the provision on collective liability is unresolved (Ravna, 2019). The case was sent back to the Court of Appeal and resolved through settlement (Rensberg, 2019).

Even though there have been some positive legal precedence resolving land-use conflicts between reindeer herders and farmers, the right to use the territories lost in previous Supreme Court cases has not been restored. In addition, new opportunities through the commodification of outfields have intensified the conflicts (Rønningen & Flemsæter, 2016) and the disputes over legal interpretations remain. Recently, Gåebrien Sijte and Saanti Sijte resisted a wind power project to be built in the mountain of Stokkfjellet, in Selbu municipality. They feared negative impacts on their calving land and pastures would have substantial negative effects for future reindeer herding in the area. In the public hearing process concerning the development plan, the municipality and land-owners in favor of the project argued that the Selbu verdict from 2001 limits grazing rights outside established boarders of the reindeer herding district. However, the Ministry of Oil and Energy, the authority for energy licenses in Norway, confirmed the actual use of the area for reindeer herding would lay the grounds for their decision, not the district limits (OED, 2017). Yet, the final licence for construccion was approved, without the consent from the reindeer herding districts.

Back to academia, the struggles over south Saami history and knowledge continues. About the same time as Nielsen's theory was "defeated" in the Supreme Court, a major book volume about the "History of Trøndelag"[10] was commissioned by County officials. Due to the fear of a revival of the advancement theory, central south Saami institutions demanded to affiliate a person with Saami history and cultural competence to the project, but the editors refused and claimed they had sufficient competence on the matter (Sem, 2019). The book consists of three volumes and was published in 2005 without any participation of Saami scholars or knowledge holders. *Aehtjie* was central to this critique and called it «a history supporting lies, myths and prejudices which the south Saami cannot recognize» in an opinion in the newspaper Adressa (S. Fjellheim, 2005). Other scholars criticized the organization of the project, use of sources, and methodological foundation on which the historical part of the volume is based (Bergstøl, 2008; Her-manstrand, 2009; Sem, 2017, 2019). Leiv Sem (2017, 2019) presents the most thorough evaluation, where he claims editors have structurally excluded Saami representation and integration into the story. He also states that the editors avoid to settle the controversies around Nielsen's advancement theory:

> The thesis of Saami advancement may be said to have been somewhat modified, but it is equally true that this controversial theory that has laid the grounds for Saami losing rights to land in favor of farmers, is rendered without challenge in *Trøndelags Historie*.
>
> (Sem, 2019, p. 167)

Sem's critique is essential for understanding the power of history writing, and the consequences of the choices scholars and institutions make. Kuokkanen (2008) suggests that academia and its institutions need to address what she calls epistemic ignorance, meaning the lack of inclusion and visibility of indigenous epistemes in academia:

> Epistemic ignorance occurs at both the institutional and individual levels and is manifested by exclusion and effacement of indigenous issues and materials in curricula, by denial of indigenous contributions and influences and the lack of interest and understanding of indigenous epistemes or issues in general by students, faculty and staff alike.
> (Kuokkanen, 2008, p. 64)

According to her, *ignorance* is not only about passive lack of understanding but also an active avoidance of other knowledges and ways of knowing. She urges universities to address the "academic practices and discourses that enable the continued exclusion of other than dominant Western epistemic and intellectual traditions" (Kuokkanen, 2008, p. 60). The editors of the volume the "History of Trøndelag" included south Saami content, but it was presented from a colonial perspective. They could have made an active choice to critically address the colonial history in the region and include south Saami competence and perspectives in the process. A critical position of academia is particularly crucial in a context where the legal and political debate over territorial rights continues to be influenced by colonial narratives of south Saami history, indigeneity, and rights.

With this in mind, it is timely to ask why south Saami counterstories and knowledge contributions continue to be excluded, and why their impact is so slow. The answer is probably not one sided. Interpreted at best, it is a matter of epistemic *blindness*, understood as a more passive omission of other ways of knowing and a reflection of the lack of knowledge about Saami issues in society in general. Interpreted at worst, it can be viewed as epistemic *arrogance* when Western scholars and institutions place themselves at the top of a knowledge hierarchy. I think it can be a matter of both. Accordingly, there is a need for an active south Saami scholarship on one hand and self-critical decolonial initiatives from dominant academia on the other.

Final reflections

Through the knowledge and experience of five generations, this chapter provides decolonial perspectives on south Saami history, indigeneity, and territorial rights in the Røros area in Norway. Based on our counterstories, I have argued that the struggle over history and knowledge in the south Saami area is closely intertwined with the struggle over territorial rights. I have critically discussed two academic contributions which have shaped a dominant colonial narrative of the kind Smith (2012) encourages us to contest. By addressing the controversial role of racial biology and Yngvar

Nielsen's "advancement theory," I have shown how they have had severe implications for the understanding of south Saami history, indigeneity, and rights up until today.

The racial stereotypes expressed in the forest owners' statement undoubtedly have their roots in social Darwinist thought and racial science conducted in the early 1900s. My point here is not to say that racist expressions today are the same as they were 100 years ago, but rather that racialization is common to find in the public debate about Saami territorial rights today. Racial biology was rather quickly rejected as a legitimate scientific tradition. However, Yngvar Nielsen's advancement theory strongly informed the narrative historians used to discuss south Saami origin in the Røros area up until the late 1990s. It has not only influenced public opinion but also had severe implications for the current legal status of reindeer herding in the area. The lack of repatriation of lost territories and revisions of the reindeer herding Act must be seen as an unresolved colonial legacy.

In this context, academia has a critical role. Even though the advancement theory is no longer actively defended within academia, south Saami knowledge contributions and counterstories continue to be marginalized. I argue that the knowledge hierarchy in academia is upheld in the book volume about the "History of Trøndelag" as an expression of epistemic ignorance. It is timely to call for a greater responsibility of academic institutions and scholars to strive for epistemic justice.

The unequal power relationship between colonial narratives and south Saami counterstories persist but is constantly being challenged. A 100 years ago, my ancestors were made objects of research, with no control over, nor influence on how this research was conducted or used. Now, south Saami scholars and knowledge holders are (re)writing our history and providing research rooted in our own horizon of knowledge. These counterstories are, as Smith (2012) suggests, powerful forms of resistance and can be a tool for self-determination and justice. The Supreme Court settling the Selbu case in 2001 is a clear example, as it ruled in favor of historical rights for reindeer herding in the area after 100 years of marginalization.

The statement from the forest owners in 2009 and the anti-Saami rights meeting in Selbu in 2019 indicates that we are facing severe structural challenges beyond the academia and the courtrooms. It feels like a cold shiver from the past when racist ideas and language are used to question south Saaminess and the right to practice reindeer herding in the 21st century. Some might ask why these events should be given more attention than the public shaming they received in the news. To be honest, I have asked myself the same question. However, the statement was signed by an association with an influential role in the community and lacked public rejection by the majority population in Røros. Ten years later, the landowner meeting in the neighboring municipality of Selbu reminds us that we are not talking about individual and exclusive events but rather long-lived colonial narratives embedded in organized structures. I sustain we need to ask ourselves where these attitudes and arguments come from, rather than reducing their significance. It is important to critically address them, because they continue to influence our well-being, how we are perceived as a people, and how our right to continue practicing our culture, knowledge and livelihood in the Saami cultural landscape is recognized.

Through our stories we resist.

Acknowledgements

Thank you to my colleagues at the Centre for Saami Studies at UiT The Arctic University of Norway, and my supervisors; Else Grete Broderstad, Hans Christian Hernes and Mariel Aguilar Støen. Thank you also Sverre Fjellheim, Nanni Mari Westerfjeld, Susanne Normann, and the editors of the book for valuable comments. The study was funded by the Norwegian Research Council through the project TriArc – The Arctic Governance Triangle: Government, Indigenous Peoples, and industry in change.

Notes

1 The area around Røros where reindeer herding is practiced, including the municipalities of Holtålen, Selbu and Tydal.
2 The second Saami Rights Commission was established the 1st of June 2001, and the report was published by the Justice- and Police department the 3rd of December 2007.
3 Norway ratified the convention the 20th of June 1990: /www.regjeringen.no/no/tema/urfolk-og-minoriteter/samepolitikk/midtspalte/ilokonvensjon-nr-169-om-urbefolkninger-o/id451312/ (Retrieved 15.10.2019).
4 The Norwegian Constitution: https://lovdata.no/dokument/NL/lov/1814-05-17/KAPITTEL_6 (Retrieved 15.10.2019).
5 95% of Finnmark was previously owned by the State, but as a result of the first Saami Rights Comission – SRU I, the Finnmark Law was approved to create a new legal entity, the Finnmark Property. The Finnmark Comission was also established to identify user- and owner rights due to use from time immemorial.
6 The reindeer herding Act, revised in 2007: https://lovdata.no/dokument/NL/lov/2007-06-15-40
7 Saami rights to land and water have only been formalized in the northernmost County in Norway, through the Finnmark Act. The Finnmark Act was approved in 2005 and was a result of the first Saami Rights Commission's recommendation (SRU I).
8 Historically, the Saami population has been named Lapps, a derogatory term used by the majority population in historical sources.
9 The Common Lapp Act applied to the reindeer herding districts south of Finnmark. Reindeer herding in Finnmark was included in the revised reindeer herding act in 1933 (Ravna, 2019).
10 The Røros area belongs to Trøndelag County.

Literature

Antileo Baeza, E., Cárcamo-Huechante, L., Calfío Montalva, M., & Huinca-Piutrin, H. (2015). *Awükan Ka Kuxankan Zugu Wajmapu Mew – Violencias coloniales en Wajmapu*. Temuco: Ediciones Comunidad de Historia Mapuche Centro de Estudios e Investigaciones Mapuche.

Aslaksen, E. F., & Porsanger, N. J. (2017). Påtroppende sametingspresident om vindpark: – Grønn kolonisering. *NRK Sápmi*. Retrieved from https://www.nrk.no/sapmi/kaller-vindparkplaner-for-gronn-kolonisering-1.13701272

Baglo, C. (2011). *På ville veger? Levende utstillinger av samer i Europa og Amerika.* (Ph.D). Tromsø: University of Tromsø.

Balto, R. M. (2019, 14th of June). Regjeringen bør imøtegå «fake news» om samene. *Nordlys*. Retrieved from https://nordnorskdebatt.no/article/regjeringen-bor-imotega-fake

Bemerkning på vedtak "TrønderEnergi Vind AS – godkjenning av detaljeplan og miljø-, transport og anleggsplan for Stokkfjellet vindkraftverk" datert 08.05.2019, (2019).

Berg-Nordlie, M., & Olsen, T. (2019). Derfor gikk det veldig galt i Selbu. *Adressa*. Retrieved from https://www.adressa.no/meninger/2019/06/14/Derfor-gikk-det-veldig-galt-i-Selbu-19252260.ece?fbclid=IwAR0-9fsc-HCpkYOmWKNsjiS_5sOx7GYx8l-Ym1VxCxEy11nXcqSG7q04VvQ

Bergsland, K. (1970). Om middelalderens finnmarker *Historisk tidsskrift, 4*, 365–409.

Bergsland, K. (1992). *Bidrag til sydsamenes historie* (Vol. Nr. 1). Tromsø: Senter for Samiske Studier.

Bergstøl, J. (2008). Samer på Dovrefjell i vikingtiden–et bidrag til debatten omkring samenes sørgrense i forhistorisk tid. *Historisk tidsskrift, 87*(01), 9–27.

Bransfjell, S., & Magga, H. (2019). Hva var rasistisk ved Selbu Utmarksråd sitt møte? *Trønder-Avisa*. Retrieved from https://www.t-a.no/meninger/2019/06/09/Hva-var-rasistisk-ved-Selbu-Utmarksråd-sitt-møte-19223700.ece

Bull, I., Skevik, O., Sognnes, K., & Stugu, O. S. (2005). *Trøndelags historie Bd. 1–3.* Trondheim: Tapir Akademisk Forlag.

Cumes, A. (2018). La presencia subalterna en la investigación social: reflexiones a partir de una experiencia de trabajo. In X. Leyva, J. Alonso, A. d. Hernández, A. Escobar, A. Köhler, & A. Cumes (Eds.), *Prácticas otras de conocimiento(s). Entre crisis, entre guerras (Tomos I)* (pp. 135–158). Mexico: Cooperativa Editorial RETOS, Taller Editorial La Casa del Mago, CLACSO.

Eriksen, G. (2004). Samiske sedvaner og bruk av naturressurser før og etter Selbu-og Svartskogdommene fra 2001. *Kritisk juss, 55*(03), 289–304.

Evjen, B. (1997). Measuring heads: Physical anthropological research in North Norway. *Acta Borealia, 14*(2), 3–30.

Fjellheim, E. M. (2013). Utmarkskonflikt i sørsamisk område: Etnisitet, identitet og rettigheter. *Plan tidsskrift for samfunnsplanlegging byplan og regional utvikling, 45*(03), 28–31.

Fjellheim, S. (1991). *Kulturell kompetanse og områdetilhørighet: metoder, prinsipper og prosesser i samisk kulturminnevernarbeid.* Snåsa: Saemien sijte.

Fjellheim, S. (2005). *Trøndelag og samenes historie.*

Fjellheim, S. (2012). *Gåebrien sijte-en sameby i Rørostraktene.* Røros: Sverre Fjellheim.

Fjellheim, S. (2020). Når en professors teori blir en samisk tragedie. In L. C. Ruud & G. B. Ween (Eds.), *"En trængslernes historie". En antologi om Yngvar Nielsen.* Orkana Forlag.

Gerde, H. S. (2016). *Sørsamisk eller førsamisk. Arkeologi og sørsamisk forhistorie i Sør-Norge-en kildekritisk analyse.* Oslo: Universitetet i Oslo.

Gjerpe, K. K. (2020). The articulation of "Textbook Sápmi" – An analysis of Saami content. In T. Koivurova, D. Dorough, F. Stammler, E. G. Broderstad, & D. Cambou (Eds.), *Handbook on Arctic Indigenous Peoples.* Routledge, forthcoming.

Haarstad, K. (1992). *Sørsamisk historie: ekspansjon og konflikter i Rørostraktene, 1630–1900.* Trondheim: Tapir.

Hellesvik, J. (2019). Hva mener EDL? *Trønder-Avisa.* Retrieved from https://www. t-a.no/meninger/2019/06/09/Hellesvik-svarer-på-Trønder-Avisas-leder-1922 2072.ece?fbclid=IwAR0cBkfdK6rdz7mN9urBTt-zUz5m3X1zA4FM_NGL dgj3ykbWIjthVPo75uQ

Hermanstrand, H. (2009). Sørsamisk historie. *Historisk tidsskrift, 88*(03), 485–491.

Johansen, I. (2019). But they call us the language police! speaker and ethnic identifying profiles in the process of revitalizing the south Saami language, culture and ethnic identity. In H. Hermanstrand, A. Kolberg, T. R. Nilssen, & L. Sem (Eds.), *The Indigenous identity of the outh Saami* (pp. 29–46). Cham, Switzerland: Springer.

Kovach, M. (2010). *Indigenous methodologies: Characteristics, conversations, and contexts.* Toronto: University of Toronto Press.

Kuokkanen, R. (2008). What is hospitality in the academy? Epistemic ignorance and the (im) possible gift. *The Review of Education, Pedagogy, and Cultural Studies, 30*(1), 60–82.

Kyllingstad, J. R. (2012). Norwegian physical anthropology and the idea of a Nordic master race. *Current Anthropology, 53*(S5), S46–S56.

Landbruksdirektoratet. (2019). *Ressursregnskap for reindriftsnæringen 2018–2019.* Retrieved from https://www.landbruksdirektoratet.no/no/reindriften/for-siidaandeler/ publikasjoner/ressursregnskap-for-reindriftsnæringen-2018-2019.

Larsen, D. R. (2009, 06.03.2009.). Vil genteste sørsamene *NRK Sápmi.*

Lawrence, R. (2014). Internal colonisation and Indigenous resource sovereignty: Wind power developments on traditional Saami lands. *Environment and Planning D: Society and Space, 32*(6), 1036–1053. doi:10.1068/d9012

Lawrence, R., & Åhrén, M. (2016). Mining as colonisation: The need for restorative justice and restitution of traditional Saami lands. In L. Head, K. Saltzman, G. Setten, & M. Stenseke (Eds.), *Nature, temporality and environmental management* (pp. 149–166). London; New York: Routledge.

Minde, H. (2003). Assimilation of the Saami – Implementation and consequences. *Acta Borealia, 20*(2), 121–146.

Mjøen, J. A. H. (1938). *Rasehygiene.* Oslo: Jacob Dybwad.

Nahuelpan, H. (2018). Los desafíos de un diálogo epistémico intercultural: pueblo mapuche, conocimientos y universidad. In X. Leyva, J. Alonso, A. d. Hernández, A. Escobar, A. Köhler, A. Cumes, et al. (Eds.), *Prácticas otras de conocimiento(s). Entre crisis, entre guerras.* Mexico: Cooperativa Editorial RETOS, Taller Editorial La Casa del Mago, CLACSO.

Nakata, M. N. (2007). *Disciplining the savages, savaging the disciplines.* Canberra, Australia: Aboriginal Studies Press.

Nielsen, Y. (1891). Lappernes fremrykning mod syd i Trondhjems stift og Hedemarkens amt. *Det norske Geografisk Selskabs Årbog,* Kristiania, *1*(1889–1890), 18–52.

Nilssen, T. R. (2019). South Saami cultural landscape under pressure. In H. Hermanstrand, A. Kolberg, T. R. Nilssen, & L. Sem (Eds.), *The indigenous identity of the South Saami (pp. 171–186).* Cham, Switzerland: Springer Open.

Normann, S. (2019). Constructing dialogues and solidarity through "Radio-Cinema" in the Saami-Norwegian colonial context. *Community Psychology in Global Perspective, 5*(2), 1–18.

NOU. (1984:18). *NOU 1984:18 Om samenes rettsstilling.* Retrieved from https://www.regjeringen.no/no/tema/urfolk-og-minoriteter/samepolitikk/midtspalte/nou-198418-om-samenes-rettsstilling/id622185/.

NOU. (2016:18). *NOU 2016:18 Hjertespråket — Forslag til lovverk, tiltak og ordninger for samiske språk.* Retrieved from https://www.regjeringen.no/contentassets/ad82d773c3094582a2660908b48886d3/no/pdfs/nou201620160018000dddpdfs.pdf.

OED. (2017). *Trønder Energi Kraft AS – Stokkfjellet vindkraftverk – klage og innsigelse.* Retrieved from http://webfileservice.nve.no/API/PublishedFiles/Download/201106956/2173480

Otte, P. P., Rønningen, K., & Moe, E. (2018). Contested wind energy: Discourses on energy impacts and their significance for energy justice in Fosen In A. Szolucha (Ed.), *Energy, resource extraction and society. Impacts and contested futures* (pp. 140–158). London: Routledge.

Porsanger, J. (2004). An essay about indigenous methodology. *Nordlit, 8*(1), 105–120.

Ravna, Ø. (2007). Gjerdehold til støtte for reineiers driveplikt etter reindriftsloven § 26 tredje ledd. *Reindriftsnytt Nr. 2,* 40–43.

Ravna, Ø. (2011). Samenes rett til land og vann, sett i lys av vekslende oppfatninger om samisk kultur i retts-og historievitenskapene. *Historisk tidsskrift, 90*(02), 189–212.

Ravna, Ø. (2019). *Same- og reindriftsrett* (Vol. 1). Oslo: Gyldendal.

Rensberg, V. (2019). Løste årelang konflikt ved å gi en pengegave til kirka. *NRK Sápmi.* Retrieved from https://www.nrk.no/sapmi/loste-arelang-konflikt-ved-a-gi-en-pengegave-til-kirka-1.14561471

Rønningen, K., & Flemsæter, F. (2016). Multifunctionality, rural diversification and the unsettlement of rural land use systems. In M. Shucksmith, David L. Brown (Eds.), *Routledge international handbook of rural studies* (pp. 312–322). London: Routledge.

Samerettsutvalget. (2007). NOU:2007:13 Den nye sameretten. Retrieved from https://www.regjeringen.no/no/dokumenter/nou-2007-13/id491883/.

Sandnes, J. (1973). Om samenes utbredelse mot sør i eldre tid. *Historisk Tidsskrift, 52*(1973), 113–137.

Sem, L. (2017). Om framstillinga av sørsamar i Trøndelags historie. *Heimen, 54*(02), 130–144.

Sem, L. (2019). Out of print. A historiography of the south Saami in regional and national works of history. In H. Hermanstrand, A. Kolberg, T. Risto Nilssen, L. Sem (Eds.), *The indigenous identity of the south Saami* (pp. 153–169). Cham, Switzerland: Springer.

Sissons, J. (Ed.) (2005). *First peoples. Indigenous cultures and their futures.* London: Reaktion Books.

Skjølsvold, A. (1980). Refleksjoner omkring jernaldergravene i sydnorske fjellstrøk. *Viking, 43,* 140–160. Oslo.

Skogeierlag, R. (2009). *Høringsuttalelse vedr. Samerettsutvalgets instilling.* 08.02.2019.

Smith, L. T. (2012). *Decolonizing methodologies: Research and Indigenous Peoples.* London: Zed Books Ltd.

Spangen, M., Salmi, A. K., Äikäs, T., & Lehtola, V. P. (2015). Saami histories, colonialism, and Finland. *Arctic Anthropology, 52,* 22–36.

Stenvik, L. (1983). *En sørsamisk offerplass ved Forolsjøen, mellom Hedmark og Sør-Trøndelag* (Vol. 83). Snåsa: Saemien Sijte.

Strøm-Bull, K. (2005). Yngvar Nielsen med prejudikatvirkninger. *Institutt for offentlig retts skriftserie, ISSN 0803–2106*, 137–149.

Tretnes Hansen, T. S., Balto, P., Aslaksen, E. A., & Paulsen, S. P. (2019). Lars Aage ble stoppet i døra: – Det var etnisk sortering. *NRK Sápmi*. Retrieved from https://www.nrk.no/sapmi/selbu-motet_-_-det-var-etnisk-sortering-i-dora-1.14583649?fbclid=IwAR0qFijY6Z9_jqLcaSICkX-LtcwpTTnj-goHf7EV_SqUwPhivHsJaH9TDro

Whitinui, P. (2014). *Indigenous Autoethnography: Exploring, Engaging, and Experiencing "Self" as a Native Method of Inquiry*. Journal of Contemporary Ethnography *43*(3), 456–487.

Wilson, S. (2008). *Research is ceremony: Indigenous research methods*. Canada: Halifax, N.S: Fernwood Publications.

Zachrisson, I., Alexandersen, V., Gollwitzer, M., & Iregren, E. (1997). *Möten i gränsland*. Stockholm: Statens museum. (Nahuelpan, 2018)

Index

Note: **Bold** page numbers refer to tables; *italic* page numbers refer to figures and page numbers followed by "n" denote endnotes.